Laugh?
I could
have cried

Also by Joe Bennett

Just Walking the Dogs (Hazard Press)
Sleeping Dogs and Other Lies (Hazard Press)
Fun Run and Other Oxymorons (Scribner UK)
So Help me Dog (Hazard Press)
Sit (Hazard Press)
Bedside Lovers (and Other Goats) (Scribner UK)
Doggone (Hazard Press)
Barking (Hazard Press)
A Land of Two Halves (Simon & Schuster UK)
Unmuzzled (Hazard Press)
Dogmatic (Hazard Press)
Mustn't Grumble (Simon & Schuster UK)
Down Boy (Hazard Press)
Eyes Right (and They's Wrong) (HarperCollins)
Life, Death, Washing Up, Etc (Simon & Schuster UK)
Where Underpants Come From (Simon & Schuster UK)
Alive and Kicking (HarperCollins)

Laugh?
I could have cried

JOE BENNETT

HarperCollins*Publishers*

The columns that make up this collection
first appeared in *The Press*, *The Dominion Post*,
the *Otago Daily Times*, *The Southland Times*,
the *Waikato Times*, *The New Zealand Herald*,
Hawke's Bay Today, *The Northern Advocate*
and *New Zealand Gardener*.

National Library of New Zealand Cataloguing-in-Publication Data
Bennett, Joe, 1957-
Laugh? : I could have cried / Joe Bennett.
ISBN 978-1-86950-745-9
1. New Zealand wit and humor—21st century.
828.202—dc 22

First published 2008
HarperCollins*Publishers (New Zealand) Limited*
P.O. Box 1, Auckland

Copyright © Joe Bennett 2008

Joe Bennett asserts the moral right to be identified as the author of this work.

All rights reserved. No part of this publication may be reproduced,
stored in a retrieval system or transmitted in any form or by any means,
electronic, mechanical, photocopying, recording or otherwise,
without the prior written permission of the publishers.

ISBN: 978 1 86950 745 9

Cover photography by Photosouth Photographers
Cover design by Matt Stanton
Typesetting by Janine Brougham

Printed by Griffin Press, Australia

70gsm Classic used by HarperCollins*Publishers* is a natural, recyclable product
made from wood grown in sustainable forests. The manufacturing processes
conform to the environmental regulations in the country of origin, Finland.

Contents

Introduction *11*

Dogs and other Beasts

The anagrams of God *14*
Communing with shags *15*
Lying doggo *18*
She smuggled a tortoise *20*
Messing *22*
They don't own nothing *24*
He was a pretty good dog *26*
For our convenience *28*
Easter rising *30*
How to be happy *32*
Dogtape *34*
Necks, please *36*
Mister Muster *38*
Felix means lucky *40*

Games

The Boys from Brazil *44*
Testosterone and tonic *45*
The end of the road *47*
The long slide to paradise *49*
The cricket, exclamation mark *51*
Toast him *53*
Big cherub *55*
Not quite death in the afternoon *57*
Balloooooon *59*
Passion on the sofa *61*
Rod and gut *64*

Language

- Principal principles *67*
- Creep into thy narrow bed *69*
- In the bad lands *71*
- Or else say nothing *73*
- Natch *75*
- Murder your darlings *77*
- Grammar with teeth *79*
- SOBS *81*
- Talking lousy *83*
- Good as a rich monk *86*
- Lucy mon *88*
- Five and a half intimates *90*
- Mean *92*
- Do you care? *94*
- Fifty thousand an hour, money-makingly *96*

Teaching

- The tongue-thing *101*
- Prizing advice *103*
- A call to arms *105*
- Cosh the teacher *108*
- He was my English teacher *110*
- The values of Minscum *112*
- More tosh *114*
- A lot like us *117*
- Kneeing Zucchini *119*

Domestic and personal stuff

- Be the boss *123*
- Cars and frying pans *125*
- Baking nuts *127*

Twenty Yak   *129*
Love for lunch   *131*
Small stuff   *133*
Einstein's bus   *135*
Lie lie lie   *137*
Hope and pile-cream   *139*
A tale of two mice   *141*
White rectangular domestic things   *143*
Lotsadeadredindians   *145*
Land you can play with   *147*
Dreams on wheels   *149*
At two drunks swimming   *151*
A cup of Eros   *154*
When your turangawaewae crumbles   *156*
Between us and dust   *158*
Hello, heat   *160*
Where do you go to?   *162*
Nannies and billies   *164*
Nesting recruits   *166*
See me saw   *168*
The threshold of the ginge   *170*
Up Apophthegm Mountain   *172*
Ah, winter   *174*
Hello again   *176*

Travel

From here to prostate   *180*
Moose-hunting by supermarket trolley   *182*
Aleppo   *184*
Cuchulain's children   *186*
Ooooh la bloody la   *188*
Wrong room   *191*

The things people do

The ods roll over   *195*
Eating with experts   *197*
I believe in pigs   *199*
Of chopping and sticking   *201*
Would you care to?   *202*
The squeals of children   *205*
Hobbes at the trough   *207*
Mad as accountants   *209*
The big question   *211*
How far away is the lizard?   *213*
You too   *215*
I shall   *217*
Hope is dead   *219*
At the Dickens   *221*
Warm, wet and threatless   *224*
Hapsburg staplers   *226*
Let's make with the jam   *228*
Train me, please   *230*

The things people believe

Standing for nothing   *234*
Deep in the dogs   *236*
The thyroid of Unks   *238*
Girlie sox   *240*
Oi Popey-boy   *242*
Lies to spare   *244*
Glossy lala   *246*
Destiny's children   *249*
Hi ho   *251*
Dear College of Cardinals   *253*
Not if, but when   *256*

Funny and true *258*
Reverend reasoning *261*
Little Miss Moss *263*
In the deep midsummer *266*
Circumbloodychristmas *268*

Political and social stuff

P.C. Sturrock *272*
Ringing the world *274*
The man was a pornographist *276*
Because he is a man *278*
Jules *280*
Food, fun and a tickle behind the ear *283*
Is there anybody there? *285*
De mortuis nihil nisi Latin *287*
I, speechwriter *289*
For we are young and free *292*
White brain, black body *295*
Dung time *297*
Gotcha *299*
Can't hear you *302*
All you need to know *304*
Sprawled and gurgling *306*
Brand life *308*
You can say things like *311*
Catabingo *313*

Introduction

When I submitted my first newspaper article in 1997, a sub-editor rang up and asked if I'd got any more. 'Lots,' I said, and sat down to write some. I've now written over a thousand. In 1998 they stopped being articles and became columns, and I stopped being a teacher and became a columnist.

I like being a columnist. It makes me think. It has taught me that readers like what they agree with and dislike what they don't; that they often read what they want you to have written rather than what you wrote; that reason is defenceless against emotion; that stories outmuscle ideas; that the tracks on which our minds run are laid down young; that civilisation is a frail thing; that we are far more similar than we are different; that most things have happened before; that I'd be a better bloke if I'd suffered; and that nothing I write changes anything.

I like to imagine that I'm maturing with age. I'm not. The columns prove it. As I read through ten years of them to make the selection for this book, I was surprised by how little I was surprised. What I thought ten years ago is what I more or less think now. All that varied was the quality of the prose. I tried to choose the clearest and simplest columns. Clarity and simplicity don't make a column true, but they please me.

Similar subjects kept recurring, so I organised the book by topic. And I began with dogs, because I like them so much.

Dogs and other beasts

I wrote a book when I was seven. It consisted of a dozen or so pages in pencil. The book was about dogs and its title was 'Dogs'.

I wrote my first column when I was 40. It too was about dogs, but its title was 'The anagrams of God'. Thirty-three years had simply made me more pretentious.

I was brought up with a mongrel called Rebel. I loved him more than I loved my brothers and sister. But he fought. He fought only bigger dogs and he lost. Once he took on two boxers in a stream. They pinned him under water with their teeth in his skull and I thought he would die. But I was too scared to intervene. When the boxers released him, bleeding and gasping, he charged back for more. The memory still makes me shudder.

For 15 itinerant years of adulthood I was dogless, apart from one night in Spain when a mutt adopted me and we toured the bars together. I lost him in the small hours. I remember running through the silent streets of Zaragoza wailing for him. In 1994, aged 37, I was offered a resident housemastership at a school. I didn't want to be a housemaster but I did want to live in school because it meant I could have a dog and not leave it behind when I went to work. I got Abel the day I moved in. He looked like Rebel. In 1995 I acquired Jessie, in 2004 Baz. All three are now dead. Now I have a mongrel pup called Blue. I will have dogs till I die.

That the cosseted West gets more frightened of dogs every year shows how far we have lost sight of our own natures and the nature of the world. When I see people haul their children away from my pup, I feel grateful that more than half my life is over.

The anagrams of God

I, too, am a victim. The dog was asleep when my tennis ball stopped beside it. The dog woke to find me apparently making a grab for its testicles. It bit my wrist. I was seven years old, and so, as it happens, was the dog.

The dog's owners drove me to hospital in their admirable open-topped MG and bought me a Heart ice-cream which I'd never had before because they cost a shilling. I presume I had a tetanus jab but don't remember it. But I do remember spending the rest of my childhood rolling tennis balls hopefully towards sleeping dogs.

Last week a dog killed a man. The anti-dog lobby has gone rabid. With just the sort of cool, detached reasoning that did so much for Yugoslavia, they are slavering at the bar of public opinion and calling for fierce new laws to quell the canine menace.

In search of the true scale of the problem I studied a recent issue of the local newspaper. It contained thirty-seven accounts of human misery. These I divided into four sections: misery caused by people; misery caused by God; misery caused by dogs; and misery caused by goats. People beat God 34–2. The dogs failed to score. The goats notched a single spectacular goal.

My dog Jessie loves everyone. Jessie even loves golfers. In the urge to serve the merry golfers of Hagley Park, Jessie will leap into the rough to retrieve their muffed drives. The merry golfers roar like stags and wave their graphite shafts. And well they might, because the golfers of Hagley Park know that golf matters; some of them indeed have handicaps comfortably under thirty. Not for them the cheerful self-deprecating laugh. One of them once took to Jessie with a four-iron.

You see, the dog-haters and the Tiger Woodses of Hagley have something in common: they've got the world sussed. They know what's what. They are civilised and they have got it right. The rest of creation has got it wrong. Dogs merely sleep and eat and love their owners. Dogs play games but they don't fill out their scorecards properly and they forget who won. They show enthusiasm and they shit without embarrassment. They own nothing and like sex and never hold grudges and love to serve and are grateful for all affection and don't judge. No wonder the four-irons scythe the air. No wonder people hate dogs.

The irrefutable statistical truth is that if something kills your child, that something will be a person or God. Not a dog. The one case brought against a dingo was thrown out of court.

Admittedly goats do get the odd child but not enough to be statistically significant.

Mankind invented virtue. We have built pulpits from which to preach forgiveness, loyalty, honesty and love. Yet if we anatomise man our scalpel discovers vanity, acquisitiveness, deceit and golf.

I have not met a vain dog, nor an acquisitive one, nor yet a deceitful one, and only a few who play golf. Dogs forgive. They are loyal. They are honest. They love. And for the very few who are bad there are already perfectly adequate laws to control them.

I would point out to the dog-haters and the hackers of Hagley that there are five anagrams of God and surely it is no coincidence that one of them is ogd. There's also dgo, gdo and odg. I have never owned any of these.

But I have owned dogs. My dogs know nothing. Unlike me they don't imagine they know anything. My dogs are happier, better and wiser than I shall ever be.

Communing with shags

I've never had any time for the sceptics of this world who don't believe in telepathy. Life, you see, is contact with people, any sort of contact. 'Only connect,' said E.M. Forster. And if you think that's hooey, try playing the hermit for a fortnight and then get back to me. Or rather don't.

But if life is all about contact, what do you do when your telepathy is picking up only static, the e-mail has crashed, the letter-box is empty, everyone you ring is out or dead or both and there's a knock at the door from Sister Solitude and her pale and silent daughter Loneliness? I don't know about you, but I go and look at shags. There is solace in shags.

'Come on, dogs,' I say and we bound to the door, our tails walloping the crockery.

Round Lyttelton the shags roost in a couple of clifftop conifers, and very decorative they look, too, with their plump white breasts, one to a bird, and their necks like those bits of plumbing under the sink.

But it is not for their looks that I visit the shags, nor for the way they gurgle like outboard motors, nor indeed for the comfort of their brute insensibility. I go to laugh at them for being called shags.

They bring to mind a boy I went to school with called Tinker, which may not be the best of surnames, but there are worse, several of which end in bottom. Tinker, however, was christened Simon. There are worse names than Simon too, but few worse than S. Tinker.

Then there was the little Egyptian boy whom I taught and who was called Fallik. He was only seven, the poor dear. And so very cheerful. It made one weep.

Anyway, off to the shags we go for a giggle, and it's a wild night. Clouds scud, trees thrash, and King Lear would have felt at home. The dogs disappear into the bush in yelping pursuit of imaginary prey, the night swallows them, and I am alone among the thrashing trees and the scudding clouds and the eerie dark.

I've always been a gutsy bloke, especially when alone in the bush on stormy nights, so even though I can hear the footsteps of an axe-murderer on the path behind me I just chuckle a nonchalant chuckle and carry on shagwards with my pulse comfortably under 200. And there I am, humming a catchy little Leonard Cohen number about suicide and the sea is crashing at the foot of the cliff and I'm thinking thoughts when whoompha, SOMETHING comes flying out of the darkness, headbutts my thigh and disappears over the cliff to certain death.

I react calmly. It is the work of only a few moments to locate my heart under a pittosporum, dust it off and slip it back in. Then I gather my wits. A couple of the more timid wits are gibbering behind boulders, but when all are safely gathered I set about seeking a rational explanation of the assault on my thigh, and of course there is a rational explanation; viz, I have just been attacked by an alien.

Well, good to have sorted that one out. The walk ends without further drama. Naturally, however, my mind chews over this encounter with a thigh-butting kamikaze Venusian.

And I recall a story I heard the other night from a learned gentleman in a hotel on the Lyttelton waterfront. It is a story of Russian science. (Be patient now; this will all come together.)

What the clever Russians did was to take half a dozen baby rabbits on a cruise to the bottom of the Baltic Sea in a submarine. Then they killed them.

Meanwhile, and here's the cunning part, up on dry land, other Russians sank electrodes into the mother rabbit's brain to measure the synaptic polarity of her ganglions. And sure enough, as each of her little brood was garrotted fifty fathoms below decks, there was a measurable discharge of protons. And if that doesn't prove the truth of telepathy and I don't know what else, but probably homeopathy, I'll eat a sceptic's hat.

Now, as you know, Lyttelton is currently home to a sad gang of Russian sailors stranded here through no fault of their own. And I have no doubt that in their sadness they often take a stroll along the cliffs to cheer themselves up with a treeful of shags.

One thing I have noticed about Russians is that they look remarkably like human beings. So, from about 10am most days, do I. The point of all this is that down by the cliffs on a stormy night, what with the clouds scudding, trees thrashing, etc., it would be easy to mistake me for a Russian. And that, of course, is exactly what happened.

The thing that assaulted my thigh was no Venusian. It was a rabbit. A rabbit, furthermore, which was telepathically aware of the cruelties its fellow rabbits had suffered on the other side of the world and which was bent on revenge against the race that had done it to them.

Although the rabbit failed in its mission, and may well have perished, I think it all rather moving. Here was a rabbit that connected. Here was a rabbit that felt itself to be a part of the greater scheme of things. Here was a rabbit that laid down its life for its friends. Which of us can lay his hand on his heart and say he does not envy that rabbit its fate?

Life is contact.

Lying doggo

My dog ran down the drive after a cat and hit a car. The impact bowled him twenty metres down the road. His thigh bone was smashed to pieces.

When twenty years ago I broke my leg, there may have been a couple of Mongolian peasants who didn't hear about it but I think I let everyone else know. My screams split the sky and, in the days that followed, the fading echo of those screams was replaced by the gentle sloshing sound of a young man wallowing in self-pity.

Not so the dog. He whimpered, more it seemed from bewilderment than pain. When I reassured him he fell silent and merely trembled.

The vet doped him so strongly that the dog didn't even notice when I left him lying on a synthetic sheepskin on a floor that smelt of disinfectant. On the operating table the following morning the vet reassembled the pieces of bone and held them together with a system of metal rods and clamps, most of them sitting outside the leg. I saw the X-rays. I thought the reconstituted leg looked haphazard, too jumbled to knit into strong new bone, but I didn't say so.

The X-ray was easier to look at than the leg itself. It was shaved, angry, bloody, taut and hugely swollen. It looked like what it was, a piece of damaged meat, a condemned leg of lamb, a vast and putrid ham, a dead thing.

The dog was too weak and drugged to stand but he moaned when I left him. I drank sedatives myself that evening but slept fitfully. My mind conjured images of suffering.

I picked him up the next day. When I arrived his tail thumped the linoleum. He struggled onto three legs, leaning against a plastic cage and panting. When I went to the till to pay he whimpered and hobbled after me.

In the car park he smelt out my car. I had a towel to wrap under his belly to lift him onto the back seat but he needed no help. Back in a familiar place he whined gently with what seemed both pleasure and pain. I wound the window down. He stuck his face into the rush of passing air in the ancient manner of dogs and fell silent.

I dreaded having to help him up the steep and sharp-edged concrete steps to my house but I need not have worried. His lust for home drove him up them in a supercanine effort, dragging his useless leg like a sack of offal. My other dog nuzzled and licked the wound. The cat cautiously toured him.

He checked the familiar details of the house and he saw that it was good and he drank a bowl of water and I swear that he sighed with relief. Then he lay down to get better.

It is now five days since I brought him home. In that time he has uttered no complaint except when the cat batted a ping-pong ball around him. Even when he tried to climb onto the sofa and crumpled backwards onto the floor he merely yelped a single involuntary yelp.

The leg remains useless. Thin, bloody fluids have leaked from it and he has licked them away. He has cleaned every wound a hundred times. The plum-coloured anger has drained a little from the outside of the leg but the inside of the haunch remains as bruised as a tropical sunset. On the shaved skin a grizzle of hair has sprouted, like the first awakenings of a spring crop.

I am confident he will recover.

Far more significantly, so is he. In the last half hour I have battled to pin down in words what it is that I find so touching and admirable in my dog's manner. It is something to do with acceptance and faith, with trust and modesty. Patience seems to be the key word, derived from *patior* which means to suffer. I have sought the exact words but I have not found them.

And then a woman rang from Ashburton and we nattered of this and that and dogs and literature and for some reason a passage of Whitman came into my mind and it says all I want to say.

> I think I could turn and live with animals,
>   they're so placid and self-contained,
> I stand and look at them long and long.
> They do not sweat and whine about their condition,
> They do not lie awake in the dark
>   and weep for their sins,
> They do not make me sick discussing their duty to God,

Not one is dissatisfied, not one is demented
    with the mania of owning things,
Not one kneels to another, nor to his kind
    that lived thousands of years ago,
Not one is respectable or unhappy over the whole earth.

She smuggled a tortoise

'World,' wrote Louis MacNeice, 'is crazier and more of it than we think.' I have known these words for years and have indeed bored class after class of children with them. The children have yawned, I suspect, because to them the idea is obvious. But in middle age I find I lose sight of the truth of MacNeice's words. The world seems weary, stale, flat and unprofitable. But then something happens to remind me that it is sweetly crazy. This week, for example, I met a tortoise-smuggler.

The woman has smuggled only one tortoise, but that is one tortoise more than I have smuggled or am likely to smuggle.

Smuggler and tortoise met in Corfu, an island where the tortoise is apparently indigenous. This particular specimen, a small one, appeared by her bed one morning in the villa that she was renting. She took momentary fright, but the tortoise made no threatening move so she scooped it with a tray and bore it to the garden where she laid it gently down and watched it unfurl its neck and legs, nibble a snatch of something green for sustenance then head once more for the house. She raced it back and shut the door.

That evening the tortoise was at the step, whining silently to be let in. She left the door open. In the morning the tortoise was beside her bed. She let it stay, feeding it scraps of vegetable matter and sometimes a little pasta. It seemed contented and stayed for the remainder of her holiday. Once or twice she trod on it, but it did not take offence. She grew fond of it, she said.

I did not know that tortoises could show enough character to arouse affection. But this one had been, if nothing else, persistent and she said she liked its undemanding manner and also the curious way it drank.

At the end of the holiday she was loath to leave the tortoise. She did not flatter herself that the tortoise had attached itself specifically to her, but neither did she trust the next occupants of the villa to treat it with due kindness. She resolved to take it home to London with her.

She made enquiries of the authorities which deal with such things, and learned that it was illegal to import tortoises to Great Britain without a permit. Rabies was the problem. Corfu has rabies and Great Britain doesn't. Now the woman in question is a responsible citizen. She insures her car and rarely drops litter and does not bury garden rubbish in her council bin bags. But when she weighed the issue she resolved that Great Britain had little to fear from a single tiny tortoise, even if it were later to foam at the mouth and go on rabid rampage.

So when she left she sat the tortoise in the bottom of her carry-on luggage along with an apple core and a carrot to keep it amused on the journey. As she passed through customs at Heathrow she felt the gaze of a dull-booted officer. She caught his eye, looked too swiftly away and was summoned. The officer rummaged unsmilingly through her suitcase, turning over her underwear and nightdresses and shaking a doll in native costume which she had bought for a niece. Then he indicated her shoulder bag. With tremulous fingers she emptied the contents onto his table, feeling no doubt as the frightfully rich American must have felt when the sniffer dog barked at his bag, although he, of course, was rightly let off on the grounds that if he had come to watch the America's Cup yachting then he needed every drug he could get.

The customs officer fingered her cosmetics, her tube of disposable contact lenses and then the tiny tortoise. It had, understandably, retracted its wrinkled head and feet. She said it was a brooch. The customs officer impounded the carrot and the apple core and let her go.

When she reached home she found the tortoise had eaten her lipstick and it was dead.

It is a little story and a sad one, but it filled me and thrilled me, in MacNeice's words, with 'the drunkenness of things being various'.

Messing

It is all very well to mess with ourselves, but when we mess with nature we get problems.

For example, my mate Pat's got a radioactive cat. The beast developed a growth in its thyroid so the vet injected it with a substance that makes it glow in the dark. I should feel sympathy for the mog but, as with most misfortune, I find it funny, and besides it's one of those cats that expresses affection by biting.

The vet isolated the thrumming cat for a few days in a lead-lined cage but now that it's back home it has to be locked out at night so that it doesn't sneak onto Pat's pillow and make him grow a second head. So instead it wanders luminously over the neighbour's roof, warping the corrugated iron and alarming the passing drunks.

Each morning Pat scans the yellowing vegetation of his garden with a Geiger counter, finds the beast and lets it into the house. But if he falls asleep on the sofa and wakes with the thing on his lap he has to take a two-hour shower and check his sperm count. One million and one, one million and two . . .

Now luminosity hinders hunting, so I doubt if Pat's cat at present is much good at catching birds, but I expect it gives them a fright. My own cat, however, which to my knowledge has never been radioactive, is in mid-season hunting form. Only this afternoon I found it torturing a sparrow with the sort of glee that I find it hard to like. Had there been any point in doing so I would have rescued the sparrow but I was already too late by a matter of several organs. The sparrow still tried to flutter away but aerodynamically it was a gone possum.

Five minutes later the cat brought me the tubular remains and rubbed against me in search of praise which I refused to give. Indeed, right now if my cat developed a dicky thyroid I don't think I'd fork out for the plutonium.

On the day I acquired my three chickens the cat stalked them. Ten metres from the coop it slunk down into that low-bellied crawl which it learned from David Attenborough, and then spent the best part of an hour sneaking up on the unwitting chooks across the lawn. On my lawn that's no great feat. In a recent gale my dustbin blew away

— not much to my regret because its lid had always stuck and now I had the excuse to buy a green deluxe model from The Warehouse — but as soon as I'd replaced it I stumbled on the old bin which had been hiding in the depths of the lawn.

So the cat in the lawn was like a pedestrian in Manhattan, but still it stole towards the chickens with extraordinary caution, moving each limb separately with a rapt and sinuous malice. Eventually it parted the grass at the edge of the coop, beheld the chooks clearly for the first time, saw that each bird was twice its size, stared at them in a wild surmise then promptly lost interest.

Since then two chickens have gone broody, which means that they spend their days trying to hatch the eggs they haven't got. If the one active chook lays an egg the broodies fight over it until I take it away. Broody chooks don't lay, so I was keen to snap them from their broodiness. Pat of the luminous cat told me that one way to do it was to toss the chickens into the air.

So every day for the last two weeks I've tossed my chickens. As I reach into the nesting boxes the broodies swell like puffer fish, cluck weakly in protest and peck at my hands, but once they've been tossed and have fluttered back to earth and stood for a while to reorder brains the size of paper-clips, they suddenly remember that they are chickens and peck madly at grain and grass and swig beaksful of water. Then they go back to their brooding till it's tossing time again.

Confronted with the failure of the tossing gambit I consulted the Internet. In ten minutes I had found a website called Fowlnews where I joined the hugely popular 'Poultry Information Exchange' and posted my problem on its virtual bulletin board. I expect you saw it.

Anyway, within the hour I had received several bits of virtual advice. Among them came an e-mail from a chicken-fancier known as Buzz from Wisconsin. Buzz told me that it is sometimes possible to snap chickens out of broodiness by scaring them. I'm going to borrow Pat's cat.

PS. I thank the correspondent who asked whether my phrase 'black women's shoes' in a recent column was the result of illiteracy or racism. I would love to plead illiteracy but I must admit to racism.

I should of course have written 'Afro-American women's shoes'. I apologise to all whom I offended.

 They don't own nothing

I like to spend money on my dogs but I can't find much to buy for them. A new collar every couple of years, perhaps, sometimes a lead. They don't thank me for the lead. They don't like leads. They like freedom. They like the world and they like novelty. I admire that.

I buy them food and it pleases them but there is no point in buying them fancy food. They like crude bones with gobbets of meat and fat and ligament buried in the crevices. They can work at these gobbets, applying extraordinary force to the task by pinning the bones with their paws, gripping with their precise and deadlocked teeth and hauling with the massive muscles of their necks. I like to watch them. They do not care if I watch them or not.

The dogs' lives depend on me. They would find it hard to survive in the wild because game is rare and if they attacked farm animals they would be shot. Each night when the dogs sleep they do not know what will happen tomorrow. They curl up owning nothing. As far as they know there is nothing for breakfast. Every tomorrow is an adventure that starts afresh.

They sleep in my bedroom but if I slept in the garden they would sleep there too. On cold nights they curl in on themselves and generate prodigious warmth. They sleep in the same fur on hot nights and cold nights and they smell only of dog. They drink only water.

In the morning they do not know whether I will take them out. When I do they rejoice. The hills always thrill them.

When nothing is happening they sleep. They sleep lightly and wake on the instant. D.J. Enright wrote a poem called 'The Poor Wake Up Quickly'. It isn't much of a poem but I've always thought well of the title. It's pure dog. And when the dogs wake they stretch, luxuriating in the strength and lissomeness of their flesh and guarding it wisely. They tend to their bodies with their tongues and teeth but they never clean the house. If they are sick they sometimes eat it back up.

If I went away and did not return they would pine briefly, but they would not cling to my memory. They would attach their affections to whoever fed them. If their new owners treated them worse than I did they would not make comparisons. They would hope for nothing and accept the good bits with relish.

When they are ill or damaged they make no complaint. They curl and lick and wait to get better. They do not imagine what will happen if they do not get better. They do not dread.

Theirs is the state of most creatures on the planet. It is a state of unknowing. It is a state of acceptance. It is not humanity. They are not vain and they do not accrete possessions. They do not consider themselves better or worse than others. They will fight if they have to for their territory or their food, but they prefer to warn enemies off. They pay no attention to tomorrow.

Though people often personify them, dogs do not lose their dogness. They are incorruptible.

My dogs and I spring from the same process of evolution. In them I can see a lot of where I came from and a lot of what I retain. And I can see what I have lost by being human. I can see the bad bits of the bargain. I can see the crippling effects of self-consciousness. My dogs are my touchstone, my rock of comparison.

Many of the qualities we love to see in people — loyalty, modesty, zest — are exhibited full time in dogs. Many of the things that we do not like to see in people — duplicity, greed, malice — dogs are innocent of.

That is why I cherish my dogs. And because they are beautiful. And because they appear to love me. One of them has just come to nuzzle my elbow. I read him these words and he wagged his tail. But had it been a story of abuse that I had read him, he would also have wagged his tail.

He has a bad leg. Some years ago the front bumper of a car smashed it. The vet put it back together and it served, but now it has gone bad again. He carries it off the ground. I have taken him for treatment but the likelihood is that at some time in the next year or two I shall have to decide whether to have his leg cut off or have him killed. Whenever I think of having to make that decision I start crying.

He was a pretty good dog

Around midnight last night I went up the hill with my dogs, one of them walking beside me unusually subdued, the other one in a bag over my shoulder, dead. I carried a spade. I knew the spot where I wanted to bury him. Nothing special about it, but some distance from the path so that the grave would not be disturbed.

The hill is steep. The dogs and I have climbed it perhaps a thousand times. I usually stop at a couple of places to pant, and three-legged Abel would always stop beside me, panting too.

He was a big dog, 30 kilos or so, more than half a hundredweight. The straps of the bag bit into my right shoulder and I walked in a slewed hunch, climbing perhaps 20 yards at a time and then pausing for breath. But I didn't unsling him from my shoulder. It would have seemed disloyal.

When I came home at 9 o'clock last night he was waiting for me. He whined with pleasure as I got out of the car. I could hear his tail thumping the deck. But when I opened the gate he didn't come to me. I went to him and he was on his haunches. He tried to get up but his one back leg buckled and he sat down again. I put my hand to the leg and he nuzzled at the hand to keep it away from the point of pain.

I went inside. As I knew he would, he dragged himself to the space under my desk that was his den. For obvious ancestral reasons dogs take comfort from a den. My other dog joined him and I lay on the floor and stroked the pair of them together and whispered to them. Then I rang the vet.

On the phone the vet said he thought it would be a problem with a disc that he could fix with cortisone. I doubted it but I didn't say so. I lay with the dogs until the vet arrived.

When Abel heard the car he sat up and barked. The vet examined the leg and tapped the knee with a little rubber hammer and then drove back to his surgery to fetch the drugs that kill. While we waited Abel licked my face a lot.

I rang a friend who looks after the dogs when I'm away and told her what was happening. She arrived before the vet returned and from the floor Abel greeted her with glee.

The vet sedated him with an injection in the scruff of the neck. A quarter of an hour later when the dog's head had sunk onto his paws and his eyelids drooped, the vet tied a tourniquet around the knee of the right front leg, shaved a little fur from the shin, found a vein and inserted the needle. The dog looked at the needle with drowsy curiosity. I said I would like to take over from there.

There was a little blood in the barrel of the syringe, swirling slowly in the bright blue barbiturates. I pressed the plunger and my dog slumped immediately onto his side. I stroked his ears and the top of his head and his flanks and the band of darker fur that ran from his muzzle and up between his eyes. I asked if he was dead and the vet checked the eyes and gums. The pupils had dilated and the gums turned purple.

It took half an hour or so to lug him up the hill. January 31st was a warm night, with a butter-yellow almost full moon, and by the time I started digging, my shirt was soaked with sweat. At the place I had chosen to bury him the topsoil was only 6 inches deep. My spade rang against rock. I tried a few yards to either side but it was the same.

I picked him up again, still in the bag with his head lolling lifelike from the opening, and I went over the ridge and dug again. At the third attempt I found deep enough soil and I dug for a long time down into the clay.

His tongue was sticking out so I opened his jaws and eased the tongue back. Then I lifted him from the bag and kissed him and laid him as gently as I could in the hole, folding his legs so that he looked all right. His eyes were open. I closed them and they opened again. I sprinkled earth over his body and then over his face, and then because I didn't like to use the spade I scooped the rest of the earth in with my hands. I trod the grave down softly, then sat and looked out over the harbour and the dark hills and smoked a cigarette. The sweat cooling on my shirt made me shiver. Then I went down the hill with one dog.

For our convenience

Dr Killjoy and Sister Grumbles are at it again. They want all the dogs of Christchurch to be tethered to their owners when in public.

Of course my first reaction was disbelief. Could they be serious that no dogs should run free? I read the piece again. They could. They were. And the Christchurch City Council, bless their pretty little chains of office, has listened to them.

Disbelief gave way to outrage and with outrage came malediction. I cursed Dr Killjoy. I cursed Sister Grumbles. I cursed them high and I cursed them wide. May their Dowson's footwear, I cursed, land unerringly in poop. May they subscribe to Sky. May their houses get termites and their children worms. May their soft furnishings fade and their oven doors explode and may they watch *Fair Go* until their brains turn to soup. May they have invested in Enron.

I resolved to flee. I would tuck my dog in one pocket and a sandwich in the other and we would head for saner pastures, for the wide beaches of freedom in the country of Elsewhere.

But even as I planned my flight, my spine stiffened. Because here at last was a cause. I have never had a cause. The greats of yesterday stole all the causes. Those greats were scourged or flayed or toasted for their causes but they died with grins as wide as letter boxes. For they knew that they'd find immortality in the display case of history.

Now I would join them. On the day the by-law was enacted I would stride into the council chamber and let slip the dog of war. Her name is Jessie. And as she bounded towards the mayoral throne in the hope of a pat I would stand strong against the agents of tyranny. Let the jacks-in-office flip the tops of their flip-top notebooks. Let them lick their pencils. Let them record the details of my crime. They would only be carving my name in granite and gold. Their dinky uniforms and hats would bed down to compost before my name would fade. Defensor Canis, I would be, a virtuous outlaw, a Robin Hood, a man whose spine would not buckle under injustice.

But then above the swelling bass-note of rebellion I heard a different note. It was the piping treble of pity. Pity for Dr Killjoy.

Pity for Sister Grumbles. Because the Zeitgeist has poisoned their souls. Theirs is the way of the world to come. A sour, thin way, the future's dismal cul-de-sac.

For this proposal goes far beyond dogs. It springs from two emotions that are increasingly influential. One is arrogance. The other is fear. Both are base.

Have the doc and his bloodless woman no sense of a dog's need to run? They have not. Do they not care that their proposal would be cruel? They do not. Because in their arrogance they believe that only the human species has any right to draw joy from the world.

When dogs exult in freedom in the park, when dogs play games for the fun that is in them, when dogs cavort in the present tense, they grant a glimpse of something we've lost. They simply revel in being alive. They don't fret for their share portfolios. They don't hunch over pornography. They run with the wind and they pant with zest. It does my dog good to run. It does me good to run with her. Dr K and Sister G would excise that good.

They want to take us all one step further down the path to a sanitised world. A shopping-mall world. A world of endless consumption of tat until we peg out. A world as sterile as a hospital ward. A horrid pointless bloodless colourless world, a world ruled by Starbucks and the six o'clock news and OSH. A world of plastics and disc jockeys and car grooming.

Why should they want this? Because they are afraid.

Children get it right. Last week I took my dog to a primary school. Two hundred children rushed to stroke her. She took it on the chin. And on the ears and the tail and the neck.

But if Dr K and Sister G win the day the children will be taught to fear. They will learn that my dog is dirty, and that the planet owes them a living. They will be taught that society is hostile, and then they will be surprised when it becomes hostile. They will be disabled by fear. Their blood will be watered to transparency. And we shall have arrived at the future. It will look like Disneyland. Disneyland where people are fat and the thrills synthetic. Disneyland where the lawns are rectilinear and death is banned. Disneyland where the only animals are stuffed monstrosities with floppy ears and imbecilic grins, apart of course from those animals whose tongues and guts and nostrils have been ground into hamburger patties and smeared with mustard the colour of pus. For our convenience.

Easter rising

Easter Sunday, Hitler's birthday, mine too, as it happens, and this morning saw the resurrection of Grandma Chook, which is as good a birthday present as I've had since the pair of handcuffs. To be frank, Grandma Chook wasn't actually dead, but I thought she was, which if you think about it, and I did, is worse. I mean, if you're not dead but people think you are, and they're rootling in the cupboard for something to wear to your funeral and a few words to say about you that aren't actively malicious, it's no time to pop back up saying, 'Yoohoo, it's me, yes, that's right, I was just foxing, God what a horrible suit.' No, you're better off out of it.

Which is what I thought Grandma Chook was, only I couldn't find the corpse. She disappeared on whatever they call the day before Good Friday — Okay Thursday, perhaps — and no hint of her since.

She was a callous old matriarch, much given to bullying the other chooks, all of whom are her daughters or granddaughters. Having ruled the roost for half a decade she had grown monstrously fat, far too fat to even think of flying, too fat indeed to hop up a 1-foot retaining wall that I built and which is still, remarkably, retaining. So fat was Grandma Chook that whenever I appeared at the back door and she came barrelling down the slope with her greed and fluffy underskirts to ensure she was first to bury her beak in the trough, gravity regularly took her a couple of yards past the target and dumped her in a feathery heap against the fence with her multiple offspring trying hard not to giggle.

But then, suddenly, on Okay Thursday, there she was, gone. I checked her usual roosting sites, I checked the nesting box where she retires twice a year to brood, I fossicked through the undergrowth like a police search party of one, but zilch, zip, nothing, only a hole where she'd been. And to my surprise I missed her. I missed her bossy clucking selfish vigour, and it didn't make for a very Good Friday. Nor, for that matter, a Super Saturday, especially when added to the antics of the Post Office.

Did you get one of those billets doux from New Zealand Post? Dear Householder and Victim, it said, we've decided to give our coochy-coo postie-wosties an extra day off on Super Saturday so they can have a really jolly time at Easter with their kiddiwinkies and you can have virtually a whole week without mail. Please use this card to tell us whether you think this is a good idea, even though we're going to do it anyway, or whether you think we should keep our postie-wosties working every hour that God gives until they are skeletal husks fit only for paupers' graves.

Naturally I wrote back. Whip 'em to death, I wrote, in red ink and capital letters, but it won't make any difference. Not that it matters, I suppose, since no one writes letters any more and all the postie ever brings me is illiteracies from real estatists, and supermarket fliers telling me how cheaply I can buy a dead chook, which, frankly, was not what I needed right then.

What I needed right then on Super Saturday, with a pall of gloom, loss and solitude descending, was available at the Lava Bar for four dollars a pint. Down the evening hill I toddled with the slightly less than full moon squatting above the plantation ridge like a giant egg. Never — and when I say never, I mean not all that often — have I seen the moon looking more egglike, which, as I said straight off to the barman, was singularly apt for Easter. That, inevitably, led to a grand discussion on the etymology of the word Easter, which I said went back to some pagan festival called Oestre that the church hijacked, as is its habit, and the barman said was it related to oestrogen, that being something to do with eggs and fertility, to which I said with resonant conviction that I hadn't got a clue. I went on to lament the fate of Grandma Chook and everyone said how sad they were, which was about as convincing as a party political broadcast, and then the evening ended in the not so small hours in a bizarre escapade with someone else's dog which was jolly while it lasted.

So ten seconds or so after waking on Easter Sunday I realised I was unwell and forty-six for the first time in my life. I stumbled out to feed the chooks and from under the house there came a huffing and a clucking and a flapping of elderly wings and out waddled Grandma Chook. She was famished. I watched her eat a bushel or two of grain and then followed her back under the house where somehow she had amassed a clutch of twenty eggs, all of them infertile, which she was spending her Easter holidays trying to hatch. And as I reached under her to remove the eggs — because if I didn't she would sit on them till Easter next — she pecked my hand with what I can only describe as undisguised and entirely typical malice. Welcome back from the dead, I said, and I meant it.

How to be happy

Take your dog with you on holiday. Dogs love holidays and are good at them. They also love you and hate kennels. Furthermore, if you do take your dog with you, you will add to the sum of happiness in the world. And if those aren't reasons enough to convince you, then you are sick.

You don't have to wait for a dog to pack. A dog is always packed. It's got its collar on and it won't sulk if you forget the lead.

Dogs rarely throw up in the car. And if they do, they eat it back up. Nor do dogs squabble in the car. They just stick their heads out of the window and are happy. They like ice creams, but they don't whine for them. And they never ask if you're nearly there yet. Dogs think you're already there, because, for a dog, there is here, and here is the best possible place to be. In five minutes' time the best possible place to be will be where you are in five minutes' time. But dogs don't know that until they get there, because they have no command of the future tense.

Dogs don't mind if you go to the same place every year. Nor do they hanker for abroad in the belief that abroad is better. They don't imagine that if they go abroad they will somehow become more adventurous. A dog knows that wherever it goes it will just be the same old dog, and it is happy with that.

A dog doesn't ask if its bum looks big in this. A dog hasn't got a this for its bum to look big in. Nor has it got a big bum.

Dogs admire the way you barbecue. They will watch you barbecue for hours. If you burn all the meat you can hide it inside the dog. After the barbecue you can lay the cooled griddle on the ground. It will be clean in the morning.

Having a dog on holiday will excuse you from guided tours, craft galleries, souvenir shops and other places where you would spend money on stuff you don't want. Dogs don't want you to buy stuff you don't want. Dogs want you to play. Playing is better for you than buying stuff.

Because you have spent the year watching sport on television you will have forgotten how to play beach cricket. The dog will remind you. When you are trying very hard to win, the dog will pick up the ball and run into the sea. You will swear at the dog and chase it and then you will give up, stand still, look at the sky and laugh. Then you will say 'Thank you, dog, for reminding me how to play beach cricket.'

Dogs will help you meet people. Some people will say 'What a nice dog' and 'How old is your nice dog?' and 'What's your nice dog called?' These people are good people. If you are single you may have sex with some of these people. If you are not single, you can imagine having sex with all of these people. If you imagine having sex with them, the dog won't know. If you do have sex with them, the dog won't mind. Though it will want to join in.

You will also meet people who bunch their eyebrows and swear and say 'That dog should be on a lead.' These are sad people. They have become infected by fear and by the media and they have forgotten how to find happiness, and in particular how to find happiness in the happiness of others. Have nothing to do with these killjoys until after midnight. After midnight, go out and let their tents down. Take the dog with you.

When the killjoys are writhing and squealing under the canvas, the dog will think it's a game. Encourage the dog to join the game, then go back to your tent. The dog will come home eventually. The killjoys will go home in the morning. You can then move your tent to the killjoys' camping site because it is better than yours. The dog will be as happy in the new camping site as it was in the old camping site as it is in any camping site.

In sum, then, the best way to enjoy a holiday is to imitate your dog. Wear as little as possible. Presume people are nice until you find out otherwise. When something is going on, join in. When nothing is going on, sleep.

But it is hard to imitate a dog that isn't there. Take the dog with you. Everyone will be happy.

Dogtape

081/22561361 is not a promising name for a dog.

A dog's name needs to be simple and unremarkable, because there will be times when you need to summon the dog from embarrassing situations such as a picnic on the beach. There is a lot to be said for a dog eating a picnic on the beach, but rather less to be said for it when the picnic is someone else's. So you need a name that attracts the dog's attention but does not attract attention to the dog. In such circumstances a name like 'Ferlinghetti' is unhelpful. So is 'Fire'. And 081/22561361 is not a lot better.

But that is how I first knew this dog. The dog was a gift. A friend acquired the dog for me in Australia without asking, and posted it over. I got a telephone call from a nice man in Auckland telling me how to collect 081/22561361 from Christchurch airport. He said that the paperwork might take a while so I would be wise to do it on the day before 081/22561361 flew into Christchurch. The man was right.

When I described the dog as a gift I was using the word in a technical sense. Gift in this sense means something that costs the receiver a lot of money. For the cash that I laid out at Christchurch airport I could have bought just over 100 Dalmations and taken them all to the cinema. Twice. With lollies at half-time. (Assuming that there is still half-time and that there are still lollies available. I no longer go to the cinema because I can't smoke, take a dog or understand why I have paid money to listen to people eating in the dark.)

At the cargo depot a nice man filled out an abundance of forms and then gave me a map of the airport. I had to go next to customs which he marked with an X, and then to MAF which he marked with an X, and then back to the cargo depot which he marked with an X even though I'd already found it.

Call me cantankerous but I asked why I had to return to the cargo depot. Because, said the man, he had to sell me a little sticker to affix to the MAF clearance papers. I asked why he couldn't give me the sticker now and then I could stick it on the MAF forms myself. He said the sticker cost $22 and he didn't want me to lose it. I said I was willing to take the risk and paid him $22.

There was another nice man in customs with wrapover hair and a shirt under pressure. The stretches between the shirt buttons gaped like vertical eyes. He told me that I had to pay GST on the value of the dog. I said the dog was a gift in the traditional sense and that the man in Auckland had told me that, because I didn't plan to breed from the dog or to sell it but merely to eat other people's beach picnics with it, I wouldn't have to pay GST on it. Mr Wrapover told me with a highly amused snort that distorted the eyes on his shirt, that they didn't know much in Auckland. I paid GST on the dog.

Or rather I paid GST on the market value of the dog. I use the term 'market value' in the technical sense, which means a sum arrived at by taking the number of staplers on the customs desk and multiplying by the square of the date.

And then Mr Wrapover, towards whom I was feeling increasingly warm, told me I had to pay GST on the freight.

'I'm sorry?' I said, though I wasn't. I was uncomprehending. But Mr Wrapover explained.

'You've got to pay GST on the freight,' he said.

'Oh,' I said, 'I understand now. I have to pay a tax levied on New Zealand goods and services on a sum of money already paid in Australian dollars, in Australia, by an Australian, to an Australian airline, a sum, furthermore, on which the Australian government has already levied its own GST.'

'You've got it,' said Mr Wrapover, evidently pleased with his explanatory prowess.

Call me cantankerous but I said that I thought this was theft.

'Do you want the dog?' said Mr Wrapover. Levering myself off the barrel over which I found myself, I paid GST on the freight.

After customs, MAF was frankly a disappointment. Their requirements cost me five minutes, no arguments and a mere $28. And they gave me a piece of paper on which to stick my $22 sticker which, remarkably, I hadn't lost.

So now all that was left for me to do was to hire a wheelbarrow to ferry the documentation home, go to bed, fail to sleep for the excitement, return to the airport the next day, show them the wheelbarrow, go round the back, find a crate wrapped in red tape, take the shears to the tape and open the door.

Scattering tape as he came and exuding gales of un-uniformed, unofficial, un-carbon-copy-in-triplicate exuberance, 081/22561361 leapt out of the crate and into my heart.

Necks, please

I've got an inexplicable bad neck. Went to sleep last night with a neck so pliant I had ostriches asking me my secret, but awoke this Sunday morning with a neck like a crankshaft — not that I quite know what a crankshaft is, but if it's as inflexible and knobbly as I imagine it to be, then it's bang right. Perhaps I should ring an osteopath — not that I quite know what an osteopath is either.

And anyway I expect osteopaths play golf on Sunday, swinging their spine-straight clubs with such smug rubberiness that they drum up custom even on the Sabbath — not that I'm quite sure what the Sabbath is, since Jews, I believe, think it's Saturday, Gentiles Sunday, and teenagers the name of a rock group. I could look it up, I suppose, along with crankshaft and osteopath, but the dictionary's down there to my right and I'm up here at my desk nursing my neck, and the fear of pain beats the thirst for knowledge. Injury does that. The world shrinks to the point of pain and nothing else matters.

But swivelling my eyes, which is the only form of exercise I feel up to, I can see birds with irritatingly good necks. Greenfinches are clinging to the seed bell I thoughtfully hang for them, and jabbing at it with necks all lissome and enviable. They keep their balance by fluttering one wing. I didn't realise birds could move their wings independently, although if you think about it, which I'm doing for the first time, it makes sense. I mean, if you wave your right arm, the left one doesn't flap in sympathy. It would make carpentry tricky.

Anyway I can't remember ever seeing a bird with a crook neck, though I've seen plenty with crooked necks, most notable among which are shags, herons and bitterns. Shags fold their necks into an 'S' when roosting, but straighten them in flight. Herons do the opposite. Bitterns, meanwhile, whose necks are habitually as crooked as snakes, stick them vertically into the air whenever they sense danger. The idea, apparently, is that they then resemble reeds. At which point the prowling predator says 'Well, bugger me. Could have sworn there was a bittern round here but no, nothing but reeds. Guess I'll just go off to the beach and get myself a shag.'

Bitterns are rare birds and, to be frank, I'm not surprised. The reed-imitation gambit doesn't seem like a winner to me. Though I suppose it is just possible that bitterns are actually the most abundant birds in the world and what you and I imagine to be reed beds are in fact enormous flocks of bitterns. In which case, I suppose, bitterns may have been used over the years to thatch cottages, which is a picturesque notion so long as the bitterns didn't suddenly and collectively decide to migrate — not that I actually know whether bitterns migrate. I could look it up, of course, but the bird book's next to the dictionary.

Anyway I wouldn't make a very good bittern this morning. While mooching through the reed bed in search of a frog to spear for Sunday lunch, I'd sense the presence of a predator, a polecat, say — not that I'm quite sure what a polecat is — and I'd switch into reed mode. The polecat would catch the creaking of vertebrae, spot the reed with a wince on its face and a suspiciously feathered stem, and suddenly, well, once bitten no bittern, and one less bit of thatching for your cottage. Which perhaps explains why I've never seen any sort of bird with a crook neck. Though a bloke I met yesterday told me he saw a duck pretending to be crippled. It was limping around begging bread from sympathetic children. But when the bread ran out, it straightened up and walked off a well duck. Good on it, I say, in this dog eat dog world, not, as it happens, that I've ever seen a dog eat a dog.

But I have seen chickens eat chicken. I used sometimes to collect a bucket of leftovers from the Volcano and bring it back for my chooks. They'd dive into the swill with gusto, flinging fish and peas and anchovies over their shoulders as they frantically rummaged for any morsel of their own kind. Not liking to think I had a backyard of clucking cannibals, I've stopped bringing them leftovers, but I've since discovered that chooks aren't choosy carnivores.

Only this week my dog threw up after chewing her morning cow bone. Dogs are supposed to return to their own vomit but Jessie never got a chance. Before you could say nausea, the gutsiest of my chooks had strutted up and was picking through . . . well, you don't need the details.

Which reminds me that I haven't got any food in the fridge which means that I'm going to have to go to the shops which means that I'm going to have to reverse out of the drive. And since my chances of twisting my neck to look over my shoulder when reversing are about as high as a bittern's chances of being mistaken for a reed, perhaps I should just sit in my front garden looking woebegone and hope that some sympathetic children pass by on their way to the duck pond, not that we've actually got a duck pond round here. Or many sympathetic children. It's all, to be frank, a pain in the neck.

Mister Muster

Failure is better than success. Failure is funny and it teaches you stuff. It also inoculates you against hubris, the pride that the gods enjoy pumping into your heart before they introduce the banana skin.

In general, then, I am a fan of failure. But today I have to report a success, a success that has pumped me as full as a blimp with hubris. The event was the summer muster.

The summer muster is a staple of televisual farming. It appears on *Country Calendar* and on Speight's ads, which are more or less the same thing. Farmers prepare for the muster by donning Drizabones, applying make-up for that seriously weathered look, mounting horses, surrounding themselves with dogs, and riding slowly up the winding track towards the snowline, saddle-bags crammed with tins of beans and the air thick with guitar music. Then the director shouts cut, the music stops, the farmers dismount, the horses go back to the props department and everyone gets into a Toyota Hilux.

My muster involved neither horses nor Hiluxes. It involved two sheep, two goats, one small paddock and one large labrador. What made it a triumph was that they said it couldn't be done.

By they I mean he. He was a Banks Peninsula farmer with whom I played cricket last week. Actually he was watching the cricket rather than playing, because he had been temporarily disabled. A calf had kicked him in the knee for reasons that the farmer did not elaborate.

I explained my mustering plans to him in the hope of receiving tips. I received discouragement. After ten minutes of discouragement I was tempted to drive to Banks Peninsula and buy the calf a beer.

It was the labrador that provoked the farmer's particular scorn. Labs were, he said, the very worst dogs with sheep. He told me cheerfully how many labs he had had to shoot. They totalled one, but one was ample to alarm me.

I readily admit that Baz is not a sheep dog. He would like to be a sheep dog, I suspect, but only in the manner that a lion would like to be a wildebeest dog.

'Forget it, Joe,' said the farmer in summary. 'Get a proper dog and someone who knows what they're doing.'

I told him that I had got someone who knew what she was doing, a warm-hearted woman who keeps a few sheep, and shears them herself. She is approaching seventy years of age but I didn't tell the farmer that.

Averil arrived at my station on Tuesday morning with two sets of shearing blades and an infectious confidence that I would have liked to be infected by. We climbed to my steep little paddock. Averil admired the pen in the corner, and pretended to admire the race that I had constructed out of waratahs and chicken wire. Baz the lab and I had tested the race that morning by trying to herd the chooks down it. Baz enjoyed the procedure enormously but didn't quite cotton onto its purpose. The chooks cottoned onto it immediately. I consoled myself with the thought that sheep can't fly.

The sheep and goats had taken refuge in a distant corner of the paddock. Averil waited by the race while Baz and I went up the hill to muster. We took with us, respectively, a vigorously wagging tail and a vigorously beating heart.

The sheep stared at the dog. The goats stared at the dog. The dog stared back. 'No,' I said, and he didn't. 'Stay,' I said, and he did. I approached the stock. They skittered down the hill. The dog did not move. 'Good dog,' I said in a tone of voice that I hoped did not betray my astonishment.

'Come,' I said, and he came. 'Sit,' I said, and he sat. The stock skittered further down the hill. I skittered after them. Every few yards I summoned Baz and repositioned him. It was like repeatedly shifting a roadblock with teeth. That the stock moved away from the roadblock did not surprise me. That the roadblock did not move towards the stock, did.

We crept ever closer to the chicken-wire race. The stock made a bid for liberty up the hill. 'Stay,' I said and the roadblock stayed. So did the stock. I held my breath. The stock moved towards the pen. Man, woman and dog closed in. And the goats and the sheep went meekly into the pen. 'Well, bugger me,' I said. The hills were ringing with the gods' applause.

Five minutes later I was learning how to shear and Baz was fast asleep under a pine tree.

Shearing proved a breeze. We whistled through it. When the dog woke up an hour later we were already onto the second sheep.

Another forty minutes and Baz didn't even bother to stand as the goats and the shorn sheep raced past him and out of the pen. The fleeces were as rich and sweet and dense as pride. I carried them down the hill like booty, my labrador sheep dog happy at my heels, my heart as fat as a cauliflower, my mind already riffling through the phone book in search of a Banks Peninsula number, and my eyes scanning the horizon for the banana skin to come.

Felix means lucky

I've had this garden for 18 months, and I've just planted something in it for the first time. It won't grow. It was a cat. My cat. Her name was Felix. I buried her last night.

There are few things as tedious as other people's pet stories, so you should turn the page now. But I have to write the page. Otherwise my cat goes unrecorded except by a plot of turned soil and a cairn of stones that I started to build this morning.

I'm not a cat man. The cat was a gift. A dozen years ago I co-wrote a show called *Dear Felix*. It wasn't about cats. It was about a shonky fortune teller. After the show was over the cast gave me a voucher to get a kitten from the SPCA. I thought it was a joke. I had two young dogs whose main joy in life was cat-chasing. It wasn't a joke. The cast expected me to get a cat. I got Felix.

She was black and silky and small. I brought her home in a cage and the dogs were delighted. I stashed her in a bedroom with a litter tray and food and water. Several times a day I took the dogs in to see her. They were keen. I had to hold on to their collars. After a week their keenness had not abated. I decided to let the cat take her chances and I left the bedroom door open. Half an hour later the cat appeared silently at the door of my study. The dogs woke, took a second to grasp the fact of her presence, then charged. She fled into the back garden and out of my life. Ah well, I thought. I'm not a cat man.

That evening she crept back in, leapt out of reach onto furniture and stayed there. She moved from table to chair back. Whenever a dog passed beneath she swiped at it with a paw as fast as thought. A few days of this and the dogs became as twitchy as Vietnam vets. Then one morning she came slowly down off the furniture and offered a truce. The dogs accepted, grudgingly.

She grew to love the dogs, saw them perhaps as giant kittens. The dogs only ever tolerated her. She would sleep with her head resting on the head of my dog Abel. Abel's jaws were big enough to take her whole. She slept and purred. He sighed and put up with it.

For most of her life she slept. In her few hours awake she caught plenty of mice and a few birds and tortured them as cats do. Her last kill was three weeks ago. It was a rat. By then she'd been sick for a month, eating little and often vomiting. I'd taken her twice to the vet. He'd palpated her and found nothing wrong, then injected her with cortisone, which helped a little.

She didn't seem to be suffering. She still slept on my bed and purred. Her coat still shimmered. But she lost weight. I could feel the knuckles of her spine. She didn't touch her food. Yesterday morning I made an appointment at the vet's but couldn't find her and had to cancel. In the evening she walked in. I stroked her and put her in a cage and drove her to the vet. She squawked as I drove, short single squawks every 30 seconds or so.

The vet found a lump on her liver. Her gut was likely to be affected as well. He outlined several courses of treatment, all of which offered only postponement and suffering.

'Put her down,' I said, and I held her and stroked her and listened to her purr while he prepared the needle.

When the vet tried to shave her leg Felix fought and won. The vet had to sedate her with a jab in the loose fur at the back of her neck. A quarter of an hour later she was effectively dead. She lay limp on a blue towel on the stainless steel table. The vet found a vein and injected barbiturates. There was no change in her. She just lay. He put a stethoscope to her chest. 'The heart has stopped,' he said. 'I'll leave you alone with her.'

'I'll be all right,' I said and scooped up the body and laid it in the cage I'd brought her in and arranged it so that she looked as though she were sleeping. I shook the vet's hand and drove home with the cage on the passenger seat.

My dogs come everywhere with me, but when I carried Felix up the slope behind my house they didn't follow. I don't know why. In the darkening dusk I dug a couple of feet down into the clay and laid her softly on the crumbled soil and filled the hole. And I came back down to a house with a gap in it. The gap was the size of a cat.

I took the dogs for a long run in the dark, then went to the pub and drank too much alone. I stripped the labels from my beer bottles and tore them into thousands of tiny pieces. She was a cat. My cat. Her name was Felix. She didn't know her name. She's in the garden now. It doesn't matter.

Games

As plenty of people have observed, sport is warfare by proxy. Watching sport is warfare by proxy by proxy. Its roots are tribal and dumb. And in the supposedly civilised West, it's never been more popular. It is a huge commercial absurdity.

A couple of thousand years ago Juvenal observed that the two things required to keep the mob from revolting were bread and circuses. Professional sport is today's circus. And like most people, I enjoy a circus.

The Boys from Brazil

There's a town in Spain called San Sebastian where the Basque Separatists used to murder a lot of policemen. It's a beautiful place built around a bay called La Concha. At low tide the sea empties from La Concha, and on Saturdays all the men and all the boys of San Sebastian stop murdering policemen and run out onto the beach to scratch lines in the sand and put up goals and play a soccer tournament. Teams win, teams lose, legs snap, nets bulge, players hug and players weep, and then the sea returns and the players pick up their goals and go home. The sea erases the lines and irons the sand and until next Saturday La Concha belongs to the fishes.

This weekly tournament at San Sebastian is exactly like the World Cup. It differs only in scale. Like the World Cup it seems to matter hugely at the time, but it proves ephemeral. When Brazil have won the World Cup and all the hugging and weeping have died away, the tide of oblivion will sweep back in, leaving only litter on the terraces and a few Englishmen too drunk to know it's over.

Soccer is the greatest of games because it is the simplest. It is the game one instinctively plays with toddlers on the living room carpet. Add an off-side rule, a few billion spectators and an official snack bar and you've got the World Cup.

All you need to play soccer is a ball, and because the ball is round chance plays little part. What emerges is character. To play good soccer you need youth and skill. To play sublime soccer you need to be born within shooting range of the equator. Your skin must be the colour of milk chocolate or olives. You must also have only one name and it must end in 'o'. Ronaldo, for example. Or Pele.

In soccer it does not help to be white. I have just watched Holland play Brazil and none of the white Dutch players had names ending in 'o'. Their names all ended in 'donk' — apart, that is, from the chap whose entire name was Jonk. Jonk and the donks — now there's a name for a band — never had a hope. They played fine football but you could see that they were trying. What they sweated was sweat. What the Brazilians sweated was *eau de framboise au chocolat*.

The Dutch played as a team. They brought the ball upfield in beautiful neat triangles. They did what they'd been taught; but the

Brazilians did what they felt. It was science against art, industry against genius, life insurance against love, beer against wine, Landrover against Maserati, Protestant against Catholic, northern cloud against southern sun. And the sun won.

Not that the Dutch didn't have their moment. Two minutes from time their svelte black centre forward, donkless of course, rose like a cobra and headed home as sumptuous a goal as you could wish to see. But only because the Brazilians let him. They were enjoying themselves. They wanted extra time.

In the end, of course, it came down to penalties. I went to make coffee because penalties are taken by individuals. As individuals the Brazilians could not lose. I heard the cheers from the kitchen.

Brazil will win the final 2–0 but that doesn't matter. For the ninety minutes that the game lasts they will create an ephemeral beauty that will make the world gasp. After that someone will take the goalposts away and in will come the tide and the little pecking fishes.

Erratum

Due to typesetting difficulties the word 'France' was repeatedly misspelt as 'Brazil'. My apologies.

Testosterone and tonic

Roll up, roll up. In the tent to your left, the bearded lady, to your right the rubber man, and dead ahead, sir, the fattest woman in the world. Roll up, roll up.

Those were the days. I would have rolled up to every freak show going. But nowadays the circus tents are empty. The freaks have stolen away to an even bigger circus. The freaks are playing sport.

I do not understand sumo wrestling, but I just love the wrestlers. From their dinky pony-tails to their dinky bare feet, they were made for staring at. I love those breasts like hammocks of squid, those barrel bellies, that shire-horse collar round the midriff with its worrying dangle of spikes, the audacity of those bared buttocks like the rinds of vast cheeses, those ridiculous legs, puckered monsters of cellulite atop ballet dancer ankles.

Sumos live, I gather, on sumo battery farms tended by little monks who groom them and grease them and above all feed them. I love reading lists of what the sumos eat: six bushels of rice, a hundred eggs, a cow.

But the most fertile sporting field for freaks is the USA. Not so long ago a gridiron team featured a character called The Fridge. He was considerably wider than he was tall and he ran like a garage. The Fridge was cool.

Basketball's good, too, except they're all so tall you forget how tall they are. If I was in charge of basketball I would make it a law that every team had to field one short chap to remind us how tall the tall chaps are. The best basketball team ever was the Chinese Olympic team of a few years ago. Four of their five players were minuscule, but somewhere in the forests of Szechuan the authorities had found a freak. He could barely run but he dwarfed buildings. So the tactics of this wonderful team were for one player to dribble the ball around in buzzy little circles while the rest of the squad helped the arthritic colossus up the court. Once they'd stationed him beside the basket, buzzy little dribbler lobbed the ball towards the ceiling. The vast one lazily plucked the ball from the air and dropped it through the hoop.

Now, it is obvious that so long as the rules of any sport favour freaks, then that sport will be beset by drugs because drugs can aid freakishness. It is equally obvious that the war against drugs cannot be won. The drug-makers are driven by wealth and glory. The poor old drug-detectors are driven only by a sense of fair play. Wealth and glory will win every time.

So why not let them win? Let them create the freakiest freaks you ever did see by shaking up every narcotic cocktail they wish. Steroid stingers, barbiturate bombers, testosterone and tonic, let them go to it. Let the giant pharmaceuticals compete to sponsor the pharmaceutical giants.

The result will be a glorious parade of freaks for me to ogle at. It will be like the Olympics of the seventies when the East German chemists cleaned up every strength event going, apart from the women's shot-put. The latter was invariably won by the Russian chemists who had created two magnificently hairy sisters called

Press. When the Presses won they wept. A thimbleful of their tears could defoliate a Siberian beech-forest.

We are constantly told that international sport these days is a global circus. Let it be a circus, then. And for those of us who do not want to pervert our bodies for a little ephemeral glory, we can continue to play beach-cricket badly for the fun of the children and not care who wins.

The end of the road

I don't know how it happened. I did not see it coming. Life has snuck up behind me and stuck me between the ribs. I see little point in going on.

As a rule I expect the worst. If a friend is late for a meeting I immediately imagine that he or she is bleeding to death in a ditch. If one of my dogs doesn't emerge from the bush to my whistle I know instantly that it has been shot.

The truth, of course, turns out to be mundane. The friend arrives, the dog lollops out of the bush and life resumes its placid course.

But although I imagine the worst for other people I do not imagine the worst for myself, for the obvious reason that the worst cannot happen to me.

The Greeks had a word for this. That word was hubris. It is defined as the pride that the gods will punish. For someone stuffed with hubris, one moment all is fine and dandy, the dogs are lolloping, the sun is shining, God's in his heaven, all's right with the world, then wallop. Down comes the thunderbolt and all is sorrow. Just like that. Unpredicted and unpredictable. The nightmare that was so bad that you couldn't even dream it, becomes horrendous reality. And that is just what has happened to me. I have taken up golf.

I know, I know, you think I lie. Golf. It defies belief. Golf. Even its name sounds like a Scottish skin disease. Celtic dandruff as sport. There is nothing to be said for it. Mark Twain called it a good walk spoiled. He didn't know the half of it.

Nothing in life so confirms my fear that I have reached middle age. I had always felt somehow that I was young, that I stood, as it were, on the first tee of life, shielding my eyes against the low sun of dawn and gazing over the glistening fairways of a world made fresh with promise. But now I know that the shadows are lengthening and I am only a chip and a putt from life's eighteenth hole and the eternal clubhouse. I cannot explain how it happened. One moment of inattention and it was all over, a life in ruins.

All sport is absurd, but golf is monstrously absurd. The ball is so tiny, the course so vast and the purpose so ridiculous. God must giggle. Now he is giggling at me.

Everything about golf is wrong. President Clinton plays it. The language is wrong. I am expected to talk of birdies and bogeys without throwing up over my golf shoes with their dinky little tassels. The scoring system is wrong. A six-inch putt is worth the same as a 250-yard drive. Putting is wrong. I can't putt. I regularly putt into bunkers. I don't care. I don't want to be able to putt. Putting is for people who know their cholesterol levels.

And, oh, the unspeakableness of golfers. Men with fake Fair Isle sweaters, fake Rolex watches and genuine prostate problems, their bodies ruined by the excesses of what they like to think of as success, towing several thousand dollars' worth of titanium clubbery around in a little invalid's trolley, waddling, wobbling their buttocks and grunting, hating every minute of it but persevering because golf is the thing to do, don't you know, so suitable for someone who has made his way in the world, hacking, cursing, cheating, wheezing, then scuttling into their spiritual home the oh-so-wittily-named nineteenth where they settle round a fat glass of gin and cut deals and tell lies and burst a few more nasal capillaries. And I am now of their number. No, it's unthinkable.

Worse still are the weasel golfers, scrawny descendants of the thieving Picts who invented the game. The weasels have eyes like razor blades, they know the rules and they always win. Down the middle of the fairway they play their conservative little shots, every club producing an identical risk-free Presbyterian hippety-hop a hundred yards down the dead dull middle of the fairway. Not for them the expansive swing, the royal drive that roars and soars and takes the world at a venture. Oh no, moderation in all things, caution is the key, know your limits, play it safe and sink the putt.

Golfers are wrong. Golf's wrong. I'm wrong. Everything's wrong. But yesterday, on the third at Charteris Bay, I swung a four-iron. It was my twenty-fifth shot of the day. But this time I did not hook and neither did I slice. No turf flew. No curses flew. The ball soared like a lark, a thing of beauty and joy for ever, and straight as destiny it flew across a duck-egg sky and with my heart swelling like a football I watched it come to earth as gently as a kiss two paces from the hole. And, heaven help me, I was happy. There is no hope. Shoot me.

The long slide to paradise

Like most good things, skiing costs a lot and serves no purpose. If you believe in evolution then skiing suggests it's come to an end. Man no longer has to fight to survive. At the weekend he can afford time off from hunting and child-rearing to don hundreds of dollars' worth of clothes, rent thousands of dollars' worth of equipment, and ride millions of dollars' worth of ski-lift up the side of a mountain in order to slide down it.

But if you don't believe in evolution, if you believe that God made man in his image, then one glance at the skifield and you get doubts. If these people dressed in puffer-fish jackets and wigwam hats are baby godlings then it suggests nasty things about the manufacturer of the universe, suggests indeed that earth is probably a cosmic joke, which of course it is. And skiing is part of the fun.

When I was a kid at school we made ice-slides by pouring water on the playground. Once they had frozen we ran at the ice, hit it at speed and slid with feet a shoulder's width apart and arms spread like wings, whooping and squealing all the way to the end of the ice. Then we fell over. But the five-second slide was a wonder. It was cheating the natural order of things; it was movement without effort. We felt like gods, like free-wheeling kings of locomotion, the albatrosses of solid earth, untameable lords of creation. Ice-sliding was the childhood equivalent of gin.

The other joys of ice-slides was that they were illegal. Teachers with gloves and moustaches banned them. Ice-sliding, said the teachers, was dangerous. We could break bones. What the teachers meant was that if they tried it, they would break bones. Their osteoporotic hips would shatter like chalk. We never broke bones. We skinned knees and banged heads and funny-boned elbows into numb agony but we were fine. We were the flexible gods. We had rubber bones, the bones of young chickens. The teachers banned the ice-slides for the same reason adults ban all children's activities — envy.

Adults like all children's games. Adults at parties drink gin, talk politics and think sex, but they would rather play sardines. In their hearts adults prefer *Hairy Maclary* to *Anna Karenina*. They prefer *The Simpsons* to the news. But guilt makes them want to attain some mythical status called adulthood. Adulthood equals seriousness. It probably stems from having money.

Skiing, then, is the perfect adult pastime. It reverts to childhood but it appears serious because it costs a lot. The expense validates the exercise. It also validates the Pajero. One annual trip up the ski-road justifies the rest of the year puttering from home to mall to school in a vehicle built of testosterone.

Because skiing is just ice-sliding made expensive, it is best done by children. Infants use skis as a dolphin uses flippers. Toss a newborn child onto a ski slope and it will start doing parallel turns. Toss a fully fledged adult onto a ski slope and it turns into a child who can't stand up. Adults use skis as a dolphin uses a can-opener.

Just as ski slopes come in degrees of difficulty, so skiers come in levels of incompetence. The level not to be at is adult-beginner level. Adults cherish dignity which they achieve by relinquishing all activities that look undignified. Dancing is one such activity. So is sex. So, in excelsis, is learning to ski.

For the adult beginner, putting one ski on is a breeze. Putting the second on is a farce. Like any farce it involves a lot of falling over. Unlike a farce it involves falling over in full view of thousands of brightly coloured children who ski past at a speed that resembles a noise.

To learn to stand up and slide, adults hire an instructor who doesn't speak English. Instructors who do speak English are working in Austria. This is part of the global plan to make ski lessons incomprehensible. The longer you remain at the toddler stage the more lessons you have to pay for.

Nevertheless the beginner eventually masters the snowplough. This means grinding down the bottom bit of the learner slope at a speed that resembles reverse. The correct physical posture for this exercise is that of a man squatting over a foreign lavatory. The correct facial expression is terror.

But once the terror leaves, the pleasure comes. The pleasure of sliding down slopes which the grooming machine has turned into alpine streets. The pleasure of speed, of innocent danger, of whooping to the frosted air, of trailing clouds of glory, of falling down and laughing and getting up and going again, of letting go of adulthood to snatch at the tantalising tail of freedom, fun and folly. Like life itself it is pointless, expensive, downhill and glorious. Could you ask for more?

The cricket, exclamation mark

'Sorry, but no,' I said into the receiver. 'It's kind of you and I'd really like to go. I just love Bulgarian films, especially from the 50s, those gritty black and white tonal values, that daring absence of plot, but it's just . . .'

'You want to watch the cricket,' she said.

'The cricket,' I said with vehemence, 'the cricket, exclamation mark. Yes I do.'

'Cricket,' she said in the manner of a public health official diagnosing threadwarts, 'is 20 boys who somehow got through puberty but didn't let it change a thing, wasting five days of what they like to think of as their lives playing a game devised in the 19th century to keep schoolboys from masturbating and the British Empire from revolting, a game that, if it ever had any virtue, has now surrendered it entirely to commercial interests.'

'Twenty-two boys,' I said.

'Haven't you noticed,' she swept on, 'that the team from this country is sponsored by an offshore telecommunications company and that the team from the other country is sponsored by another offshore telecommunications company and that the whole shebang is televised by a third offshore telecommunications company whose only purpose is to keep drongos like you rooted to the sofa, beer in hand and brain in neutral, cramming pepperoni pizzas into your mouth for 50 years until you die? You're a dupe, a stooge, a dummy, a victim of commercial manipulation, a life-form in suspension, a passive receptacle for trash, a donkey at the water wheel drawn ever forward by the synthetic allure of the business of sport. It's manhood by proxy, war by proxy, nationalism by proxy.' She paused for breath.

'I wish,' I said, 'you wouldn't say offshore. What's wrong with foreign? Or,' I added conciliatorily, 'even overseas', but she was in no mood for conciliation.

'The saddest thing of all,' she said, and the word 'said' comes nowhere near accommodating the rising swell of her passion, 'are the people known as commentators, aged fools who once upon a time were young and played the game until their bodies betrayed them and who were then so deeply terrified of having to grow up that they scuttled like so many shell-less hermit crabs into the commentary box where they could bathe forever in the perpetual infancy of reminiscence and mendacity.'

'I see,' I said.

'Is that all,' she snorted, 'all you've got to say to defend the way you choose to spend a day of your life?'

'It ought to be,' I said, 'but since you ask, it isn't. Cricket's beautiful.'

Her gasp was gratifying.

'Truly beautiful,' I said. 'Like you,' I almost added, before wisdom stilled my tongue. 'Have you not,' I asked, 'seen Shane Warne? A man whose manner I find utterly repellent, a man who has the aura of a moral vacuum, a man whom I would cross the road to miss, but a man who bowls a cricket ball as Leonardo wielded paint. To watch him shuffle with his surfboy hair a few short strides towards the stumps, his wrist furled up, his fingers wrapped like tentacles around the ball and then to toss a leg break up in such a way that it will dip and curve and land and bite and spit and leave a batsman baffled, that, my dear, is beauty. Forget the artist — Leonardo, after all, had pimples and breath like Agent Orange — but love the art.

'And have you not,' I added, 'seen Stephen Fleming bat? He gropes and looks ungainly and then from furnaces where art is forged he leans onto a bent front knee and puts the ball past extra cover so sweetly that confectioners swoon. The right elbow may not be elevated as the coaching books would wish but that's the imperfection that makes beauty. There are moments when he conjures up a hint of David Gower, and praise can go no higher. Gower batted like the Holy Ghost in whites.

'I could go on,' I said. 'I could tell you of a dumpy little Englishman called Philip Sharpe who caught the ball at slip with such deft ease I swear that, had he wished, he could have plucked a swallow from the summer air.

'And even,' I continued, 'in these grim commercial times of sponsorship and chewing gum, the sport can still produce a game like the one that has just been, a game that over five long days swung one way then the other, a game embracing luck and misery along the way, and heroism, courage, subtlety and thought, a game of such intensity it drained the colour from my hair. And in the end it was a draw. Beat that for irony,' I said. 'Beat that for simulation of the way we are. Beat that.'

She couldn't. She'd gone.

Toast him

If you were planning to do great things, things that would rock the earth's foundations and make you *Time* magazine's person of the year, forget it. Postpone your plans till 2003 because 2002 is spoken for. I have no doubt that the front cover of the December issue of *Time* has already been put to bed. Come Christmas we'll be raising our glasses to big Brian Savill.

Actually he may not be big. From the newspaper story I have read I know only that Brian Savill is 47 years old. He may, for all I know, be weedy, bald and paunchy, with spectacles, erectile problems and an unreliable Ford Escort, but none of that matters a jot. Just as Snell had his mile, Hillary his Everest, and Newton and Adam their apples, so in 2002 Brian Savill has had his moment of apotheosis.

The setting for this apotheosis was as mundane as they come: a sodden soccer pitch in Eastern England and a game of no account. The wind swept off the gaunt North Sea. Of the spectators, one left early because he was frozen to the bone and the other stayed only to bark at seagulls.

The game was not a close one. With ten minutes left the score stood at Earls Colne 18, Wimple 1. The teeth of the Earls Colne goalkeeper were chattering like a typewriter. Even the Earls Colne strikers had tired of the massacre. Only one of their number, a shaven-headed weasel, kept them at it, urging them to score an unprecedented 20 goals.

Then a miracle occurred. Somehow the ball found its way to the Earls Colne end. It bounced off a fullback's knee, bypassed the hypothermic keeper and lodged in the mud in front of an open goal. And it was at that moment that Brian Savill stepped up and casually booted it into the net: 18–2. For a moment all was silence. Both teams stood like statues. Even the wind abated as Brian Savill, with spectacular nonchalance, raised his hand to his mouth and blew his whistle. 'Goal,' he said. For Brian Savill was the referee.

The shaven-headed one ran straight at Brian. He put his face an inch or two from Brian's and he said words. Brian Savill turned away. The goal stood.

Brian Savill's been a referee for eighteen years. He likes his sport. But in that fraction of a second when the ball appeared in front of him he heard a voice. It rose from a great depth, a depth that normally is plugged and silent. It rose from a deep seam of mischief. It rose from a sense of the ridiculous. It rose like a giggle and Mr Savill, bless his little referee's shorts, gave in to it.

What Mr Savill committed was an act of comedy. Comedy's anarchic. It's founded in surprise, surprise that pulls the rug from under the feet of the serious and sends them toppling. And that's exactly what the shaven-headed weasel couldn't stand.

Inevitably someone ratted on Brian Savill. And so last week the Essex County Football Association Disciplinary Committee summoned him to appear before them and with the power vested in them by the national football association they sentenced him to a seven-week suspension.

In the same week as Scottish fans threw sharpened coins, invaded a pitch and fought, the good committee men of Essex found Mr Savill guilty of bringing the game into disrepute. In the same week as an American was found guilty of beating his son's hockey coach to death, they condemned Mr Savill for inappropriate behaviour on a sporting field. In the same week as I heard a man on talkback radio boast that he had taught his cricketing son never to walk when he knew he was out and to take every chance to sledge the opposition, they judged Mr Savill to be a bad sport.

Of course Mr Savill was guilty, but not as charged. The crime the mandarins could not forgive was that Mr Savill had said sport is sport and in the end it doesn't matter as much as all that. He'd done something funny.

Comedy is serious. It cocks a snook. Mr Savill cocked a snook at all the shaven-headed weasels of this world. He cocked a snook at dull committee men, at self-importance, at the talkback ranters and the sledgers and the Yours Disgusteds. He showed, quite simply, a sense of proportion.

Angels can fly, said Chesterton, because they take themselves lightly. For one brief moment Brian Savill, my man of the year 2002, flew with them.

Big cherub

Sometimes I think of Michael Catt.

I wonder how he is and what he's up to. Whether he's selling real estate or training to be a plumber. Or whether, and this seems to be more likely, he's retired to a cottage in the mountains in some obscure and unvisited country, Lithuania, say, to read books of an escapist nature behind walls topped with razor wire.

Because Michael Catt was the English rugby player who half a dozen years ago was erased by Jonah Lomu. Even if you live in Lapland and smoke fish, even if you're a director of feminist studies, or even if your mind is wandering in a rest home that smells of disinfectant, you will have seen the tape.

The giant Lomu, puffing his cheeks like one of those cherubs in the corners of old maps, bore down on the English try line. He shrugged off tacklers as if they were so many cobwebs. One stood square in his way but succeeded in impeding the giant's momentum to about the same extent as a garden wall impedes a bulldozer. Lomu simply lowered his shoulder, braced his body and then proceeded over the rubble.

And finally in front of him stood Michael Catt, alone on a thin white line. Michael Catt adopted the position, the position they had taught him at school, the crouching position from which you launch a tackle on an oncoming opponent, driving with your legs and placing your head to the side of the body and . . . Lomu simply went both through and over Michael Catt. He chose to inhabit the space that Michael Catt had thought was his, and with the commentator memorably forsaking speech in favour of a series of gasps that shortened and quickened and overtook each other as if he, the commentator, were approaching sexual climax, Lomu scored the try. And in doing so he wrote Michael Catt into the catalogue of memorable images, images that are the common property of the world: Armstrong on the moon, the slumping Kennedy, the man and the tank in Tiananmen Square.

Life today cannot be easy for Michael Catt. In the Lithuanian corner shop the women in headscarves will pause in their perusal of the rollmop herrings and nudge and point and ask each other whether that isn't the poor chap who . . . For Michael Catt exists in the public mind as the frontispiece in Jonah's book of fame. Though an international rugby player in his own right he is known to millions only as the man who fell that another should rise.

Jonah's fans are not primarily rugby players. They are children who like Superman. And at heart we are all children who like Superman. In a decade of rugby Lomu has given us half a dozen glimpses of the human body taken to a new dimension. He's as near as reality has come to the *Übermensch*, six-gun Arnie, the Hydra-slaying Hercules, the muscled superhero of the comic strips and a thousand identical video games. Hence the clamouring excited mobs, the mobs in London, the mobs in Paris, the mobs everywhere he goes. He is a myth made flesh. His pneumatic thighs are objects of reverence.

A poor child, from an immigrant underclass, he found success through physique. And now men from the overclass, men in ties, come flocking to hear him speak and to laugh with propitiatory willingness at his jokes. But in truth the men don't come to hear him. They come only to be near him, to be in his presence.

I've never met the man but he seems to be good. So far he has stayed loyal to New Zealand, resisting blandishments no doubt from every country in the world where rugby is played and where there is money. He is rich but he could have been many times richer.

And yet he retains something of his mean-streets heritage. He drives the sort of car I can neither understand nor condone, a low-slung throatmobile, with a boombox in the back that can shatter paving slabs. And he wears a tuft on his shaven head that on anyone else would look silly. On a superhero it looks apt.

There is also something endearing about him. I saw him interviewed some years ago about his clandestine wedding. The interviewer asked him questions in the tone one would use to a child lost in a shopping mall. It was nauseating, intrusive, wrong — and faultless tabloid television. The big man wept. The ad break was delayed as the camera zoomed in on the ratings.

I have heard Lomu called a genius. He is not a genius. Despite ten years of coaching by the best in the land he still passes, catches, kicks and tackles with little more skill than the average club player and he seems to have learnt no new tricks. But when he runs at people, the crowd rise to their feet as one and roar without knowing that they're roaring. They're roaring at a myth on the move. They're roaring for the man in front of him to crumple. They're roaring for another flattened Catt.

Not quite death in the afternoon

I gave up rugby in 1997. The decisive moment arrived when I realised not only that I didn't want to tackle anyone but also that I didn't want the ball. I left the field in a blaze of self-awareness. And if I'd auctioned my boots right then I would now be able to move my shoulder.

The damage was done last Friday in Lyttelton Supervalue. One moment I was sunk in gastronomic reverie amid the tins of haricots au jus de tomates and pain blanc au sac plastique, the next I was backed up against a refrigerated display of certified genuine olde Englishe sausages and being subjected to a stream of flattery so transparent that I took a few pieces home to repair the greenhouse.

The upshot of this encounter was that on Saturday afternoon I found myself on a suburban park in an autumnal breeze and my ancient rugby boots. The opposition stood in the distance quietly grazing. They comprised seven big men and eight huge men, bedecked in fetching blue jerseys that matched my funk.

My teeth were shrouded in a plastic mouthguard that had lain untouched for six years and for the contents of which I had turned down several substantial bids from an eminent mycologist.

I was there partly out of pity. My interlocutor in the supermarket had spiked the long drink of flattery with a sharp cry of woe. 'We need you, Joe,' he said, 'not just because you're the most talented ex-loose forward to enter this aisle of the supermarket in the last thirty seconds, but also because we're short.'

He wasn't wrong. None of my comrades in arms stood more than 5 foot 10, which in metric terms is two furlongs shy of a line-out jumper. But what they lacked in height they made up for in age. Indeed I recognised most of them from my retirement function when they tearfully farewelled me from the club with the traditional salute of two raised fingers. Even the grizzled old captain was there, still suffering from the rare medical condition that renders him unable to run without shouting. In the waistband of his shorts a pension book flapped.

But there were also a few younger things, several of whom were sons of team mates, children whose rattles I had tossed back into the pram. And the number eight was a youth who had shown such promise that he had once been entrusted into my care in that breeding ground of stars, the Christ's College Under 14 Cs.

A substantial crowd had gathered, reminiscent of the mob who used to roll up for those bottom-of-the-table clashes featuring the Colosseum Christians.

As every top sportsman will tell you, there is a moment just before the start of a contest when the senses are tuned to an altogether higher pitch. Thus I was able to detect at one and the same time the fragrant drip of my armpits, the ruminant belches of the opposition, and the wail of a circling ambulance.

The game began well with the ball being kicked to the far side of the field. Timing my jog to perfection I arrived in time to assist several of my team mates to their feet, reset their limbs and point them in the direction of a tackle that urgently needed making.

Trotting around the park at a discreet distance from the ball proved a tolerable way of spending the afternoon, until I sought a moment or two of repose on top of a comfortable-looking ruck. There I met a forearm whose progress I chose to impede with the bridge of my nose.

The blood bin consisted of a patch of mud and a moustached Florence Nightingale, who urged me to shove a wodge of vaseline up each nostril and get back out there. Dizzied I may have been by the sight of my own blood, a fluid of which I am fond but whose existence I am happy in civilian life to take on trust, but I am prepared to swear that he added the word 'nancy'.

Stung by the slur, I returned to the field with such reckless impetuosity that I found myself stationed between the try line and a ball-carrying opponent. The gentleman in question had had his neck surgically removed in order to allow him to pass through doorways with only a little stooping. The surgeon had also taken the opportunity to sew a hogshead into the man's stomach.

Pausing only to ring my lawyer about an ambiguous codicil, I drove my shoulder into the hogshead. When I sat up several yards from the point of impact it was to the sight of Goliath celebrating. 'Great try,' I said. He looked at me. 'Sir,' I added.

The rest of the game passed in a blur of self-preservation that was not entirely successful. At the final whistle the damage inventory consisted of a road kill nose, a finger like an olde Englishe sausage and a shoulder whose rotator cuff will rotate barely sufficiently to lift a gavel. But lift a gavel it will.

What am I bid for one pair of boots?

Balloooooooon

I flew to Rotorua to speak at a breakfast function. I arrived the afternoon before. My hosts met me at the airport and said come this way. I thought I would get drinks. I got Christmas decorations. We had to titivate the breakfast room. I was put in charge of blowing up balloons.

It must be ten years since I blew and tied a balloon, and thirty since I did so with any frequency. But like knotting a tie or skiing it proved to be a skill you never lose. As I gripped the little rubber nozzle between finger and thumb and sealed my lips around the little rubber rim, I was flung back through time as if down one of those corny swirling tunnels in a bad science fiction film. Everything was familiar, from the taste and smell and texture of the rubber, to the sense of imminent gaiety.

The only hard breath is the first breath. Sausage balloons in particular can be obstinate, remaining the size of peapods while your cheeks turn the colour of bruises and your eyeballs bulge. But these were round balloons, and round balloons are easy.

The balloon stiffens, momentarily resists, then suddenly, gratifyingly swells before your nose like an out-of-focus vegetable. And with it comes a noise, a sort of one-way roar like a distant engine. That noise says fun to come.

As the rubber stretches, its colour thins from rich to pale, from ruby to pink, from National Party blue to thin spring sky.

You pinch the nozzle to trap the air and you hold the half-inflated balloon in front of you. It's a breast, rounded by the laws of physics and tipped with a nipple, a protuberance of still-dense colour. The flesh yields easily to the touch, moulding, not taut.

A few more breaths and the breast is a pregnancy, hugely swollen, tautly burstable, belly-buttoned and exciting. As the thing grows to block your vision it is tempting to bail out early. You must not bail out early. You must blow that critical extra breath, the one that makes the pregnancy grow a stem, turning a sphere into a pear. It's the peak of inflation and like all peaks it's the moment of greatest danger. You have to judge the exact point between not enough and too much. Not enough and the thing is never a true balloon. It is too small, too dense, a fraction too heavy. Too much and suddenly there's no balloon, only shocked nerves and laughter and a scattering of damp rubber. It's the thrilling razor-edge of harmless peril.

Get it right, get the pear when it's ripe, and a balloon's a rich fat thing. You take it from your mouth and grip it lightly between your thighs. It squeaks like a shoe-sole on linoleum. As you loop the nozzle round and through itself to seal it, sometimes it slips from the fingers and, hey presto, a flying fart. The fart does momentary random loop-the-loops, belching hilarity, and then it's down, floored, scuppered, limp and silent.

You laugh and pick it up again. It's warm. You reinflate it, more easily now that the rubber is stretched and dimpled. You clutch it a tad more tightly between the thighs, tie the knot, pull it tight and then just let it go. What you've made is a wonder. It almost floats. It doesn't fall. It drifts. It's captive happiness. It's impossible to resist batting it.

When you bat it it goes ping, a unique noise, a noise of childhood. It goes away when batted, but slowly and not far. It wants to play.

It begs for a game. It stirs the infant self.

Gravity has hauled at your flesh for years, has slowed you down, withered and bent you, made you ugly. But gravity only grazes a balloon. It's crockery you can drop without consequences. It's a world made soft and pointless, a cartoon world.

A balloon's an equaliser. Everyone's a superstar soccer player, one who can keep the ball aloft with head and shoulder and chest and heel for minutes on end. The cruel rules are in suspension. You're close to the weightless moon of playtime.

Be gentle, says the balloon, wait, I shall come down. And if, as it sinks in its own good gentle time, you swing a real-time foot with real-time venom and volley the balloon with all your muscle-swung might, it scoffs. It goes perhaps a yard at speed, then slows and drifts again, ridiculously soon. It's held and fragile, as temporary as happiness and as good.

Balloons either burst or seep. The held air scatters or leaks. Balloons aren't built to last. They aren't possessable. They exist in the present tense, for fun now, while you can.

The organisers of the breakfast were all as old as I or older, with warts and worries and doctor's appointments. But as the balloons were blown and tied we waded through them laughing at their rulelessness and playing pointless games and being children, now.

The breakfast was okay. But the balloons were better.

Passion on the sofa

What were you doing at four o'clock on Monday morning? I was on a sofa doing love. And sweat. And dread. I was watching cricket.

England needed 130 runs to beat Australia. I could no more go to bed than I could vote for New Zealand First or eat broccoli.

Yes, yes, I know, cricket's only a game. I've heard the headmasters. I've met the sourpusses and the blue stockings and the pontificators in polo-neck sweaters. I've seen them tut and shake their clever heads and I've heard them mutter about bread and circuses. And I don't care. They're wrong. As wrong as spiritualists, as low-fat diets, as wrong as tourism.

This cricket mattered. It mattered viscerally. It mattered to the thousands who'd crammed into the tiny Trent Bridge ground to whoop and groan and lunch on their fingernails. And it mattered to me. As the bellbirds in the wattle announced the dawn's approach, and as the evil Warne went whittling through the English batting, his wrist curled like a cobra's neck, I was pinned to that sofa by the two most potent forces in the world. Nurture had me by the heart, nature by the crotch.

Nurture had me because I was dunked in cricket at the font. I have played a thousand games of cricket. I am intimate with its intricacies. Everything about it pleases me as only something can that you have known all your life. It has the reassurance of continuity. It is an old lover.

But nurture also had me because I'm English. Though I have lived abroad for almost all my adult life, and though I have taken out New Zealand citizenship, I have no choice. I am umbilically linked to England as Romanians are to Romania, Kiwis to these green and pleasant rocks and Eskimos to ice. It is not a question of liking or disliking one's place of birth. That place is mother. You have only one mother.

And I loved the England cricketers, if that is what is meant by fearing for their survival, praying for their triumph. It was easy to see national types in each of them: Marcus Trescothick as a cider-cheeked village policeman, heavy and rustic, slow on his feet but giving the ball a mighty simple thwack; Michael Vaughan as the colonel who doesn't know funk, who keeps himself in check with the imperturbable suavity of the ruling class; shag-haired Hoggard as a rural oik; and Flintoff as the giant and pasty-faced football hooligan who's crossed to the side of the angels and on whose behalf he now employs the clubbing thuggery he learned on the terraces.

All nonsense, of course. If any one of them were Australian he would seem typically Australian. Hoggard would be a Bondi-boy, Flintoff a crude colonial, Vaughan a remorseless chisel-chinned Ocker. But I don't and didn't care. My nurture made me love them for being English. And nature made me love the match.

That match unleased a flood of feelings: the heart-grip of dread, the feeble candle-flame of hope, the rending passion of suspense, and great whooping yelps of joy, none of which I feel with such intensity in daily life. For what our peaceable and prosperous society has done is to bulldoze the alps of emotion. In making life safe it's flattened the peaks of delight and triumph, backfilled the chasms of terror.

We may imagine that safety's what we want, but we deceive ourselves. We crave trauma. We are hard-wired to crave it. Why else should people bungy jump or ski or run before the mad Pamplona bulls? We need the fork of lightning, the epic event, the momentary wrestle between death and glory. We have glands that exist solely to respond to fear and thrill and war. You can't argue with glands. There they squat, all fleshy and instinct-driven, ready to secrete adrenalin, testosterone and I don't know what other ungood chemicals that fire us up and make us feel.

And how well cricket caters to them. Cricket is life and death. The bowler is fate, the force of circumstance. He comes again and again, biffing missiles that threaten extinction, or juicy baited loops that tempt. And the batsman is us. The batsman must fail. In the end his stumps will fall. For every second of his innings he is one mistake from the grave, from the long trudge back to the necropolis of the pavilion, suddenly deprived of all the stuff that being alive brings with it. But before he fails, in the interlude before the stumps lie shattered, how brightly he can live. What scope he has for heroism, standing with his back to the abyss, defying fate by giving it a smack.

And England triumphed. My tribe won the war. When lumbering Farmer Giles gave fate and Warne a final cuff about the chops and hit the runs that won, I stood and spread my arms and filled my chest and bellowed like a beast. The dogs came running from the bedroom. They thought I was in pain or hurting. Poor simple creatures.

Rod and gut

I told her I had been away fishing with friends. She snorted.

'That's so . . .' she said, then paused and I saw the muscles at the top of her cheeks tense and bulge as she sought the best word to express her distaste. She found the word. 'It's so primitive,' she said. 'Fishing is just primitive.'

'Mmm,' I said and sipped at my fancy foreign lager. She was drinking the same fancy foreign lager, but had put it aside on the bar so she could reinforce words with gestures. The gestures were not loving gestures, not peaceable gestures.

'There you are, a bunch of sad blokes finding yourselves washed up on the infertile beach of middle age and feeling castrated by a changed world, by the rise of women, by us having seen through you and being no longer obliged to suck up to you and warm your slippers and tolerate your smugness, so off you toddle into the bush in pursuit of fish that you don't need, solely so that you can beat your chests and play King Kong in the theatre of your own mind. It's primitive, regressive, wrong.'

She paused. She wanted a reaction. She wanted me to toss another log on the fire of her disdain.

'Mmm,' I said.

'Is that it?' she said.

'It's the word primitive that puzzles me,' I said. 'If, by primitive, you mean wading into the wide flat of a river early on an autumn evening and standing thigh-deep in the water waiting for the light to fade amid bush, bush that's grown and died and fallen and rotted without purpose for thousands of years, for hundreds of thousands of years, and as the sun's last rays quit the tips of the trees and the night seeps in and a weka screams and a morepork calls from deep in the bush and is answered from somewhere deeper, the mirrored surface of the river flat starts to dimple with the hatching of the caddis flies and those flies infest the air and cling to the brim of your hat and alight on your lips and cheeks and wriggle down the neck of your shirt and the back of your shirt so that you writhe and swat, and what may be an eel knocks against your leg, but then you hear the first splash of a trout rising to those hatching flies and all thoughts of discomfort melt on the instant and you become taut, intent, aware only of fish and water, and the rises become more frequent and are visible in the dark as concentric glinting swirls of steely water and you peel the line from your reel and cast with all the delicacy you can muster and your fly lands invisibly on the black water and in the area where it ought to be you hear a splash and you strike and either the water erupts into hooked fish or it doesn't, if that's what you mean by primitive, then yes, fishing is primitive.'

I took a sip of lager. So did she. Her eyebrows told me to go on, to dig my grave a little deeper. I picked up the spade.

'Or if, by primitive, you mean arriving one morning at the flood plain of a big river, and you stand on the stop bank to scan the water for the dark torpedoes of trout and to assess where it will be possible to cross and where it will be best to fish and what direction the wind is coming from, and the morning is bright with the promise of fishjoy, and you slither down the bank and step into the cold fringe of the river's vastness and feel the sheer weight of the water against your legs, the huge unstoppable tonnage of water pouring off the mountains, hundreds of thousands of tons of it on the constant move, and you are there to raid it, to try to pluck fish from its hugeness, and all that you have to raid it with are your wits, a 10-foot rod, a line that tapers to a nylon point too fine to see, and at its tip a barbed nymph the size of a maggot, so that your venture seems not so much an act of hunting as an act of bravado against monstrous odds, an impertinence, an audacity, and yet against these odds you cast your puny line into a likely flow and the line tip veers to one side and you strike and feel the thrilling chunk of a fish that plunges faster than thought towards deeper water, and your reel screams and your rod bends and you whoop whoop whoop for the fierce joy that has hold of you, if that is what you mean by primitive then you and I look on that word in different ways. You think it bad. I don't.'

And we both sipped at our lager.

Language

Language is imprecise. It perverts the complex actuality of things. It can deceive and manipulate and kill. But it's all we've got to handle the world with. And it can be beautiful. To read a truth captured pithily in words gives me a sense of yes.

I like language pared to the bones. The bones are verbs and nouns. Any flesh packed onto those must have good reason to be there. For me the art of writing is the art of rewriting, and rewriting means shortening and simplifying. It is never finished. I have always understood the character in a novel by Camus who constantly rewrites the opening sentence of a novel that he never gets any further with.

I could write every week about bad language. I could berate the obfuscations of bureaucracies, the evasions of politicians, the reach-me-down clichés of television. It would make no difference.

The best language is a window pane. But it is always, inevitably, however much you strive for clarity, stained glass.

Principal principles

In the bad old days it took two people to run a school, the principal and the deputy principal. They were the yin and yang of education. Principals were dreamers. They saw their schools as ideal states. Deputy principals, on the other hand, were realists. They saw schools as battle zones. Old-fashioned deputy principals frightened children into obedience. If this failed they hit the children with implements.

In the old days the position of deputy principal was advertised thus: 'Wanted: Deputy Principal. Must have gimlet eyes, small moustache and private armoury. The position is open to both men and women. Send photograph of armoury.'

But the bad old days are over. I have in front of me an advertisement for a deputy principal for a school in Christchurch. The school has employed a 'consulting group' to write the ad for them and I would like to thank the school for doing so, since it has produced a spectacular piece of consultant-speak.

The ad starts quietly by stating that the deputy principal will be 'a key member of the management team'. Even though this phrase appears to say something, an alert nostril will sniff the approach of piffle. The phrase suggests that the deputy principal will help to run the school. Such information will hardly come as a surprise to applicants. Notice also the magnificent use of the word 'key'. It means nothing.

The author then revs up. '. . . the appointee will facilitate the ongoing development of the school's future positioning, strategic, quality management and planning processes . . .' Every budding consultant should study this extract. Its only fault is that it contains the concrete noun 'school'. This should be replaced with 'educational environment'. Otherwise it's perfect. In addition to the vacuous nouns, the author has made use of 'ongoing', an adjective so empty it can, and should, be slotted in anywhere.

'Facilitate' is in vogue. According to the dictionary, it means to make easy, but from my experience of 'facilitators' it means the opposite. Such ambiguity brings joy to a consultant's heart.

In the old days when the art teacher arrived at school late, dishevelled and smelling like a goat, it was the deputy principal who took him aside and barked at him. The modern d.p., however, will do nothing so drastic. Instead he or she 'will manage the effective operation of the performance management and development systems'. I suspect performance management still means barking at smelly art teachers, but one has to admire the verbal mush. I particularly like the idea of managing the operation of management. A word to note here is 'effective' which can be used in the same way as ongoing. The only difference is that effective does mean something. It means ineffective.

It takes an exceptional person to manage the operation of management, and the ad spells out just how exceptional. 'The position requires proven leadership and management skills, complemented by sound administrative and interpersonal capabilities.'

As a rule, any writing that uses the word 'skills' is claptrap, but here we see claptrap *in excelsis*. The phrase 'interpersonal capabilities' is the work of a maestro.

Nevertheless, the author has yet to climax. Cop this one. 'Central to this role is the customer service interface, both internal and external.' Years ago and in a foreign country I knew a divinity teacher who was fond of internal customer service interfacing. Then one of the customers told his mum.

I have attacked consultant-speak before. When I did so, one consultant wrote to tell me that I was unfair. Not all consultants wrote rubbish, he told me, and I hope he is right. Nevertheless, lots of them do write rubbish and I am mocking their language again because it needs to be mocked. Bad language is dangerous.

We live in a world of things and deeds. Language names those things and deeds and enables us to consider them, to order them and to understand them. It is our best tool for thinking. In short, language civilises us.

If we use language badly we think less clearly and we become less civilised. The advertisement for the deputy principal is a wicked thing because it is most likely to attract applicants who use similar language. Since applicants must apply in the first instance to the consulting group rather than to the school, I fear for the chances of any aspiring deputy principal who writes a blunt and honest application.

To become a deputy principal is to set foot on the ladder of educational promotion. On higher rungs stand principals and school inspectors (who are now called something else) and higher still stand policy makers. If blather can get you onto the ladder, then it can also push you up it. If you do not believe me, read anything that emerges from the Ministry of Education or the NZQA.

Language is what distinguishes us from the beasts of the field and the fowls of the air. The advertisement I have quoted from makes as much sense as the quacking of ducks. I am fond of ducks, but I do not want them in charge of education.

Creep into thy narrow bed

Do you fret about apostrophes? When the menu says 'curry with vegetable's' do you froth?

Well, it is time to give up. Stop frothing. We've lost. The illiterates have won and it just doesn't matter. They have swarmed down from the hills with horns on their helmets and oaths on their breath, and they have ransacked the citadel, burned the library, ravaged the virgins, broken the necks of the vintage bottles and killed the little apostrophe. And they don't care. They care for their cellphones and their foreign bottled lager but they do not care for the apostrophe, and because they are so many and so heathen you might as well stop resisting.

> Let the long contention cease!
> Geese are swans, and swans are geese.
> Let them have it how they will!
> Thou art tired; best be still.

By their signs shall we know them and their signs are everywhere: Egg's for sale; Hot Chip's; Womens Toilets'.

Using the apostrophe to indicate ownership is a modern convention. To be sure, Shakespeare used the apostrophe, but only to indicate a missing letter, just as it is used in other languages. When Shakespeare wrote St James's Street he inserted an apostrophe only because he had omitted an e. The possessive use of the apostrophe was unheard of before 1725 and much derided thereafter. But you and I know in our bones that when the possessive apostrophe dies, the civilisation will wither, and we will be left atop a heap of rubble and we will be left lamenting.

How fiercely we once fought for it. I smile when I recall how we mocked the shops that sold sausage's, and how we wrote ferocious letters to newspapers, and how we who laboured in the classroom expended gallons of red ink circling childrens and childrens' in children's essays and did not count the cost. But it has got us nowhere. And now it is time to give up. We have lost.

> Creep into thy narrow bed,
> Creep, and let no more be said!

The illiterates will tell you that we don't need the possessive apostrophe. They will say, if they can be bothered to say anything, that putting an apostrophe after an s to indicate a possessive plural makes no sense because no letter is omitted. They speak true. And they will say that we do not need the apostrophe to make our meaning clear because we get by perfectly well with the spoken language, despite the apostrophe being inaudible. And again they speak true, but there are greater causes than truth and the apostrophe is one of those.

Nevertheless the war is over and it is lost. Illiteracy has won the day. All you can do is to hold up your head in the knowledge that you fought the good fight and that your wounds are in the front.

> They out-talk'd thee, hiss'd thee, tore thee?
> Better men fared thus before thee.

But, in the end, what greater thing can a man do than stand and fight for punctuation? Though the apostrophe may be irrational, irrelevant, confusing, pointless, modern and wrong, a man can love it more dearly than he loves life itself. Do you, as you read these words, feel something that swells in the chest and stirs in the loins like a lizard quickened by the sun, something that goes beyond reason, something that says with quiet strength, 'I am and I believe'? You do?

Charge once more, then, and be dumb!
Let the victors, when they come,
When the forts of folly fall,
Find thy body by the wall!

In the bad lands

It rose in front of us, sheer, gaunt and majestic. I gasped. Pete gulped. Side by side we stood to gasp and gulp in wonder. Much had we travelled in the realms of cliché but never had we seen so steep a learning curve.

In comparison with this awesome steepness, every other peak that Pete and I had climbed seemed little more than a level playing field.

We knew immediately that we had no choice. Before us stood the ultimate challenge, our new mission statement. We would tackle this learning curve head on. We would put our noses to the grindstone till they bled. Nothing would stand in the way of our ascent.

'Enjoy,' said Pete with a wry grim smile.

'Enjoy what?' I asked, but he was already away.

Up we plodded, step after laborious step, pausing occasionally to look around us. We knew what we were looking for. We sought a window of opportunity, just a small one that would grant a view of the knowledge economy from the top of the learning curve. But windows of opportunity are few and far between and the going was tough. Obstacles abounded. We waded through income streams and held each other back from cunningly concealed poverty traps.

After twenty-four hours we were on the point of calling it a day when Pete clasped my shoulder.

'Look,' he said.

I looked. On the slope ahead of us, miraculously it seemed, stood a small city square, immaculate with cafés and bars and colonnades. We sank gratefully down at a café table, ordered refreshments from the waitperson and applied ourselves to the problems that faced us. But hard though we thought, no ideas came. Then silently Pete rose and went to stand beyond the furthest building, his chin cupped in his hand. Almost immediately he yelped with delight.

I ran to join him.

'I've got it,' he exclaimed.

'Ah,' I said as the truth dawned on me, 'of course, thinking outside the square. Why didn't I think of that?'

'Never mind that,' said Pete. 'Look!'

I looked and beheld a sight I shall never forget as long as I remember it. There stood the window that we sought and oh what light through yonder window broke. It was the light of opportunity. Without another word Pete and I ran to it, fumbled frantically with the catch, threw open the window and beheld spread out before us ... but the story is almost too sad to tell. Our hopes were dashed. They lay in tatters round our ankles. There seemed no point in hauling them back up.

For where we had expected to see the verdant fields of a knowledge economy, or at least the pleasant pastures of a win-win situation, we beheld nothing more and nothing less than the smoking rubble of a worst-case scenario. It was almost too much to bear.

I looked at Pete. Pete looked at me. It would not be stretching a point to say we looked at each other. Despair was etched on our faces. Horror was tattooed on our chests. Hopelessness was scribbled on our thighs. There was nothing for it. We had only one card left to play and we played it.

Pete reinvented the wheel. Instantly I put my shoulder to it, but Pete pulled me roughly away, reinvented another wheel, attached the two of them to a bicycle frame that he had also reinvented and together we pedalled back down the learning curve as if the devil were after us. I looked over my shoulder. The devil was after us.

'Faster,' I screamed. Downwards we flew, past the lowest common denominators who backed away in fear, past the level playing field where someone was moving the goalposts, back towards the sanctuary of the old economy when, without warning, a vehicle appeared in front of us with flashing lights and blaring siren. We were going too fast to stop and we crashed slap bang into the ambulance at the foot of the hill.

Pete was thrown from the bike, performed a double somersault and a single dead-cat bounce then lay as still as stone.

'A health professional, a health professional,' I screamed, 'my kingdom for a health professional.' I rushed to Pete's side and cradled his head in my hands.

'Pete, Pete,' I whispered urgently, 'use your communication skills to me.'

But it was no good. Pete's window of opportunity had closed for ever. He had reached his bottom line.

Or else say nothing

'I just love writing,' she said. 'Don't you just love it, Joe?'

'No,' I didn't say, 'love is not the verb I'd use, my chickadee.'

'And if there's one thing we writers need,' she said, 'it's feedback, isn't it?'

'If there's one thing we need,' I didn't say, 'it's feeding. Big and juicy feeding with dripping hunks of meat and roasted vegetables in gravy thick and warm as blood.' But while I didn't say all that I could see what was coming as clearly as the wench roped to the railway tracks can see the looming cow-catcher and hear the rumbling wheels and smell the whiff of fate and her kohl-darkened eyes grow wide as side plates, as soup plates, as an entire dinner set, and she writhes and shrieks and squirms in an orgasm of terror so delicious and so vulnerable that you just know the hero of the day will come galloping out of nowhere and — but where was my hero? I had no hero. I was alone and doomed. This woman's wheels would slice me into rashers. I was done for.

'So I was wondering, Joe, if you would care to', and here she paused, the executioner's axe catching the sun at the moment of stillness at the top of the swing, and she smiled a smile which no doubt she thought of as beguiling and which I did not consider beguiling, 'if you would care to cast an eye over a little something I've written.'

'Why of course,' I didn't say, 'and at the same time would I care to take a pair of knitting needles heated over a bunsen burner to the point of incandescence and slide them slowly up my nostrils before tapping them home with a cabinet-maker's hammer? Would I care to? Oh God.'

'Well,' I said.

'I always read your column, Joe, and I've got one of your books, so, well, you know.'

'Oh yes, I know,' I didn't say, 'I know exactly what you mean. I recognise your iron logic, the same logic that decrees that every time I buy a packet of frozen peas I can summon Mr Wattie round to dig my veggie garden. Yes, how reasonable. Yes, of course, right.'

'What sort of writing?' I said.

'Oh Joe,' she said, 'it isn't any *sort* of writing. It's just writing, you know, it just comes as it is, don't you find that? That it flows, and you really don't know where it comes from.'

'No,' I said, 'I don't find that at all. I find it hard.'

'I do think,' she said, 'writing ought to be spontaneous, don't you?'

'Yes, yes, of course,' I didn't say. 'In much the same way as I think the designing of an aircraft carrier should be spontaneous or the building of walls or the . . .'

'I think it might amuse you, Joe.'

'All right,' I said, kneeling and sweeping the hair I haven't got to one side and laying my neck upon the block, 'I'll have a look at it.'

'And don't spare me,' she said, 'I want you to be ruthless. Tell me what you honestly think or else say nothing.'

'I'll tell you what I think or else say nothing,' I said and rose to go.

'Oh, can't you read it now,' she said, 'here and now? It wouldn't take a minute.'

I took it home. I take a lot of stuff home. I don't know why.

By which of course I mean I know exactly why. I lack the courage to say no. And besides I know why people write.

Words are common property. They're all we have to wring a little meaning from the world, to get some sort of grasp on what and how and why. We want to say things. We are too much alone. We want to understand and, perhaps even more, to be understood. And so we write. It does us good. It acts as therapy. It is the keeping of a diary. It is an exercise in thought. Momentarily it stills the endless whirling of a random world and pins a bit of it down.

From private to public seems such a tiny and obvious step. The diary is words on paper. The book is words on paper. What's the diff? The diff is, well, I took her writing home and laid it on my desk and shunned it for as long as I could shun it and then late the other night I picked it up and read it and made myself a cup of coffee and read it again. And then I put it in an envelope and posted it back to her.

She rang me up. 'But Joe,' she said, 'you didn't say a thing.'

And I could think of nothing to say but sorry.

Natch

Take several gallons of water and dump some sodium laureth sulphate into it, along with cocamidopropyl betaine, propylene glycol, butylene glycol, and a liberal slug of ethoxydiglycol. Add other polysyllables to taste and sprinkle with sodium chloride. Mix, heat, stir and cool, then bottle the result. What you've got is a lot of shampoo.

But before you stick it in boxes and pack it off to supermarkets in the hope that the unwashed millions will make you rich by hauling it from the shelves, you must first christen the stuff. And as you dunk it in the font, what name will you intone over its chemical complexity? Exactly. Got it in one. You'll call it 'Naturals'.

And so would I. And so, more importantly, did the nice people at Colgate Palmolive. They called their shampoo Naturals, and I've just bought a bottle of it and read the list of ingredients.

But before the Colgate Palmolive legal team come rumbling over the horizon waving writs, eager to prove in a court of law that all the ingredients of Naturals shampoo are indeed natural, I am happy to admit they may be right. I am willing to believe that somewhere in Thailand — which is where, by the way, they make their shampoo, for reasons of pure philanthropy and without thought to cheap labour — there are limpid pools of ethoxydiglycol to which the antelope come down shyly of an evening to bathe and sip.

I am willing to believe it because nature abounds in chemicals. Indeed nature is chemicals. Even as I am writing this, the ghost of fifth form chemistry has whispered in my innocent ear that sodium chloride is nothing more nor less than table salt, a substance as natural as malice. Quite what salt is doing in shampoo I've no idea, but neither do I care. The stuff seems to clean my hair all right. No,

I have no beef with Colgate Palmolive. My beef is with the word natural.

Natural. Everybody loves natural. It seems like the word next door. A pretty thing with vowels in all the right places and well-proportioned consonants, but also a word so deeply wholesome that you would happily hire it to baby-sit.

But you would be wrong. Natural's a slut. It's the loose woman of the lexicon. Take a tour through the backstreets of the dictionary and you won't find a harder-working whore. In the world of advertising there's barely an executive who hasn't made use of little Miss Natural, who hasn't in some dank alley hugged her flexibility to his black and greedy heart.

Advertising executives love to lie with her because natural has become a synonym for good. Natural means grass and trees and sky and sunshine, gentle birds and quivering delicate antelope. But what we seem to have forgotten is that natural also means bubonic plague. Natural means leprosy and scorpions. Natural means death, drought and prunes.

The opposite of natural is unnatural, by which we mean man-made. And herein lies an oddity. We've come to think that man-made stuff is bad stuff. We couldn't be more wrong.

As Thomas Hobbes famously observed, and as I have never tired of repeating, the life of man used to be nasty, brutish and short. What made it so was nature. Today, by and large, our lives are pleasant, civil and long. And what has made them so is man. Nature gave us smallpox. Man wiped it out. Nature gave us tooth decay and man has given us dentists. Dentists are unnatural.

We have not always been foolish enough to believe that nature is purely nice. It was only in the early 19th century that people began to cherish the untouched bits of the world. Drips like Shelley wrote odes to the west wind while everyone else took shelter from it. Wordsworth went into raptures over daffodils but had less to say about poison ivy. What they both needed was a week in the mountains in nothing but their underpants. And so do we.

Because then perhaps we might see through the nonsense. When we saw shampoo, or a tub of margarine or an underlay of magnets advertised as natural, we would scoff. The word has slept around too much. It has lost all meaning. It has become merely a nice noise.

Quite why this should have happened I can't tell you. I could hypothesise about the myth of Eden. I could speculate on collective guilt or on the ignorance of urban man. But I think I'll just go and rub salt in my hair.

Murder your darlings

'Murder your darlings,' advised Sir Arthur Quiller-Couch, but I didn't have to. Meridian Energy murdered mine.

Sir Arthur was writing about writing, an activity that's always kept a herd of charlatans in business. Bookshops abound in books explaining how to write a best-selling novel, most of them written by people who haven't written a best-selling novel. But still they sell to the wistful, like home-exercise gear to the fat and the lonely.

Sir Arthur's advice is sound but he didn't follow it. He wrote prose so purple you could paper a brothel with it. And anyway the idea wasn't his. He cribbed it from Old Doc Johnson. 'Read over your compositions,' wrote the warty dyspeptic doc, 'and wherever you meet with a passage that you think is particularly fine, strike it out.' Wise counsel, but 'Murder your darlings' is neater.

So there I was this afternoon knocking out darlings at a rate of knots, prose so exquisite that it curled my toes, when Meridian Energy pulled the plug. The desk lamp died. The computer screen fizzled up itself in half a second and lay dead. The dishwasher stopped. The bloodshot eye of the answerphone went black. The house, which I would have described as silent, fell silent. The clock on the oven was blank. Time was in abeyance. Only the weak autumn sun kept at it.

I couldn't work. No one could e-mail me. Though the phone on my desk was dead, the one in my bedroom, for reasons I can't even guess at, worked. I rang Meridian and got, to my astonishment, a human voice, a voice belonging to a customer services operative most promisingly called YouarespeakingwithBeckyhowcanIhelpyou. But it transpired after a brief chat that she couldn't. Yes, she said, she was aware there was an outage. I bit my tongue. No, she said, they didn't at this moment in time know the cause of the outage.

I bit it harder. No, she said, she couldn't tell me at this moment in time when power would be restored. I tasted the metallic tang of blood.

'Okay?' she said cheerfully.

I felt the weight of futility. 'Okay,' I said, 'in fact just dandy.'

'Thank you,' she said, 'for calling Meridian.'

And that was that. I had been tossed back a couple of centuries, to a world of rushlights and open fires which I didn't have and bed at dusk which I soon would. So I did what I always do when stuck and took the dog out. Stopping at a café en route for a flat white necessity, I met a sad woman fleeing, like me, a powerless home. She told me she had been doing her accounts on computer when suddenly all the numbers disappeared. She asked what I had been doing. I said I had been breathing life into darlings, darlings that made my toes curl, but I don't think she was listening.

I left her mourning her figures into a short black and went up the hill with coffee and dog to sit for a bit on a rock with thoughts, then back down again to the silent house and a strange sense of impotence.

I couldn't type; I couldn't cook the bacon sandwiches I'd planned for dinner. I had perhaps two hours of fading light, 800 words to write and a body to feed. And the world seemed simpler. That is all. The chickens out the back still strutted, and the dog curled undisturbed by the gas fire that, by a magnificent piece of design, won't work without electricity. The house seemed to exhale and relax. Fewer things could intrude on me. The news I didn't need to know would be less able to reach me. The tinsel of the internet, the endless blurting of the e-mail, the phone calls asking me if I cared to address the ladies' social club could not get through. The hush was deep and ancient. The world is too much with us, wrote lumbering Wordsworth 200 years ago. He could not have guessed what the 21st century would bring, how it would stretch out so many tentacles to wrap around our lives and squeeze the silence out of them. I sat and read and then as the light thickened I put aside the book and simply sat.

Fizz and wallop. Lights came on. The dishwasher reignited. The phone rang. I made coffee and booted the computer into life. The screen was blank. Meridian had murdered my darlings. Gone, all gone. I hadn't even heard them scream. I bet that never happened to Sir Arthur Quiller-Couch. The livid green letters of the oven-clock were blinking HELP.

■ Grammar with teeth

I taught for twenty years. Now I'm doing it again, part-time for a month or two. Nothing's changed. I stand in front of classes and I try to interest them in words. I speak of nouns and verbs and how they reflect the world. I praise the power of simplicity. I say that language is thought, that language is what separates us from the beasts, that shoddy language is a crime. I rant and I clown and I sweat but it doesn't seem to do much good. Most pupils just wait for time to pass. They want to be away and doing. I often think I'm wasting my time. I can rely on only one person to be interested and it seems absurd to drive all the way to school in order to interest myself.

Education is a curious business. And today on this heavy summer Sunday I was going to write about it. I wanted to detail the folly of the NCEA and the bankruptcy of educational theory and the misconception of the nature of the child. I would use a lot of abstract nouns. My tone would be earnest and adult. But then the puppy arrived. I had agreed to look after it for the day. The puppy put paid to earnest and adult.

When people buy a puppy they see it as a bundle of adjectives. That snub little muzzle is cute. That tottering run is endearing. Those big brown eyes are adorable. But the buyer soon discovers that the adjectives are only a sales pitch. A puppy isn't adjectives. A puppy's a verb. It does stuff. And it learns by doing stuff. For a puppy, to be and to do and to learn are the same verb.

I looked after the puppy for eight hours. During those eight hours it stopped being a verb for approximately five minutes. Those five minutes happened to coincide with the five minutes that I was being a verb. I was restraining the puppy.

A puppy is crammed with vitality. Inside its tiny frame I could feel the verbs squirming. Restraining it was like trying to hold a bag of corks under water.

Abstract nouns don't interest a puppy. Nouns such as education or language or thought are no good because they can't be bitten. What a puppy wants are concrete nouns and this puppy found concrete nouns all over my house. And having found them it bit them in order to learn what they would do.

The shoe didn't do a lot but it tasted faintly of cow. Cow is meat. Meat is good. The puppy chewed the shoe until I got up from the computer and did a verb, whereupon the puppy transferred its attention to another concrete noun. This noun is twelve years old and called Jessie. Jessie is experienced in the ways of puppies. She's a good teacher. The puppy nipped her. Jessie growled. The puppy stood back a moment to absorb the lesson and then decided not to. It nipped her again. Jessie snapped the air an inch from the puppy's nose. This time the puppy absorbed the lesson. But the lesson it absorbed was specific rather than general. The puppy learned not to bite this particular concrete noun. But it didn't learn not to bite all concrete nouns of the same class.

Another concrete noun of the same class was lying on the sofa. His name is Baz. Baz is not experienced in the way of puppies. He is three years old, 35 kilos, as fit as an orchestra of fiddles and a great killer of possums. The puppy was roughly the size of a possum.

The puppy leapt onto the sofa and bit Baz's ear. Baz did nothing. The puppy bit his cheek. Baz tried to shake the puppy off. The puppy held on. Baz sighed and got off the sofa with the puppy hanging from his cheek like a toothed pendant. I have known several teachers like Baz.

Baz lay down. The puppy was delighted. It discovered a world of prepositions. It walked around Baz and burrowed under him and jumped onto him and clambered over him and bit into him.

To distract the puppy and to rescue Baz I led them into the garden and turned on the hose. The puppy let go of Baz in order to bite the stream of water. But the water acted more like a verb than a noun. It refused to stay bitten. The hose proved a far more satisfactory noun. And then the puppy saw the chooks. Here was food on the move. Here were nouns that did stuff. Suddenly there were verbs everywhere: run, chase, scatter, bark, squawk, fly. I contributed a few verbs myself. Bellow was the first of them, followed by pursue, lunge, miss, slip, fall and swear. The puppy loved it.

And so it went on. The cat was met and barked at. A milk carton was chased and seized and thrown and chased again. And whenever things grew dull there was always Baz to assault. The puppy met a multitude of nouns and committed a multitude of verbs. It learned a lot and it was happier than any kid in school. And all without a word. It was an education.

SOBS

'Miss Biltong,' says the headmaster, leading us down a corridor that smells of disinfectant and caged hope and gym shoes, 'is the longest-serving teacher at SOBS. Nevertheless she is . . . I'm sorry? Oh, of course, silly of me. SOBS is the School of Business Speak. Living as I do within the cloistered calm of SOBS, I find it easy to forget that not everybody in this world is a FOTA.

'Anyway, as I was saying, Miss Biltong is . . . I'm sorry? Oh, there I go again. Fan of the Acronym. I do apologise. But, as I was saying, I don't think I would be exaggerating to say that Miss Biltong's influence stretches into every boardroom in the country. Her catechisms of business language are based on an idea by Flann O'Brien, an Irish writer, who filched the idea himself from the Catholic church. But the content of Miss Biltong's catechisms is all her own. Once learned, those catechisms are never forgotten. Give Miss Biltong a company director at the age of seven, and he is hers for life.'

The headmaster pauses at a classroom door, and gestures at the honours boards above it. In the faded gold lettering I recognise the names of some of this country's most distinguished captains of industry.

'I believe,' says the headmaster, his ear to the door, 'that we are in luck. Miss Biltong is just beginning a catechism class.'

Through the door comes a firm but elderly female voice, intoning a greeting in a sing-song pattern familiar to all who have suffered through primary school.

'Good morning, human resources,' says the voice.

'Good morning, Miss Biltong,' comes the sing-song echo.

The headmaster opens the door sufficiently for us to file into the back of the room. A woman of mature years, to whom time has not been kind, stands before a class of children. They have the bright eyes of the young, she the tweed skirt of the old. Her hair is done in a bun. She seems frail but authoritative.

'So Theresa,' says Miss Biltong, the light glinting from her steel-framed spectacles, 'choose a number.'

'Twenty-seven, Miss Biltong.'

'Splendid. Business Language Catechism 27 it is. Are we all ready?'

'Yes, Miss Biltong.'

'When you become company directors, will you be paid?'

'No, we shall receive remuneration.'

'How does remuneration relate to wages?'

'Very nicely.'

'Does your company ever spend a lot of money?'

'No, it has a capital expenditure programme.'

'Is it a meaningless capital expenditure programme?'

'No, it is a significant capital expenditure programme.'

'By what nautical metaphor do you undertake this significant capital expenditure programme?'

'We embark on it.'

'What's the time?'

'An obsolete word for time-frame.'

'What are checks?'

'The first half of balances.'

'What's the difference between . . . Yes Stephen, what is it?'

'May I be excused, Miss?'

'Stephen, Stephen, Stephen, when will you learn? Can anyone help Stephen? Yes, Theresa?'

'Stephen hopes to achieve a leaner structure by natural wastage.'

'Very good, Theresa. And Stephen, the answer's no. We have a catechism to complete. So, what's the difference between checks and balances?'

'No one knows.'

'Do we ever pay off debt?'

'No, we don't.'

'What age-related activity do we apply to it?'

'We retire it.'

'What redundant phrase can we affix to the end of every sentence?'

'Going forward.'

'How often should we use the term robust, going forward?'

'As often as possible without reference to its meaning.'

'Do businesses expand?'

'No, we grow them.'

'What is it now, Stephen?'

'Please Miss Biltong, I've think I've achieved a leaner structure by natural wastage, going forward.'

'Has the market bottomed out, Stephen?'

'Robustly, Miss.'

'Very well, my little human resources, this seems an appropriate moment to pause for morning break. You may use the level playing field, but, please, no one is to move the goalposts. And no climbing on the regulatory framework. Is that understood?'

'Yes, Miss Biltong.'

'You may go.'

The happy children scamper from the classroom and the headmaster turns to us with a look of gratification.

'As you can see, gentlemen,' he says, 'there is hardly a company report written in this country that does not owe something to Miss Biltong. QED, I believe.'

Talking lousy

Lousy Language is booming. According to the Society for Lousy Language, which administers the sport and has recently incorporated the Cliché Club, which was stony broke, and snapped up the Inappropriate Simile Society like a rat up a drainpipe, anyone can play. A spokesman for the Dead Metaphor branch of the society said that they welcomed new players with open arms.

And it is with the variant of the game called Dead Metaphors that most beginners start. The key skill a beginner has to master in order to play is to learn to use metaphors like key skill without thought to their meaning. After that he needs only a handful of exhausted similes and he's in like Flynn.

Some players are content to spend their lives at this level, but those with a natural propensity for Lousy Language soon realise that dead metaphors are two a penny. So they specialise. A popular early specialisation that many people like at the beginning is Redundancy and Repetition. It can be played over and above the basic fundamental game of Lousy Language and has proved so popular that there's now a great big club entirely devoted to it.

But even Repetition and Redundancy can pall and grow dull, and rather than lingering within its limited confines most serious Lousy Language enthusiasts head off in search of Milton's fresh fields and pastures new. A few fetch up briefly in Novelty Coinages, a small and specialised competition dominated for the last three years by a single player. His threepeat of successes understandably daunts newcomers who are afraid of becoming perpetual cellar dwellers in the Novelty Coinage league. And when they further realise that today's novelty coinage is tomorrow's dead metaphor they often choose not to put in the hard yards.

They have plenty of other options. A few find pleasure in the Euphemisms competition although the disadvantaged and underprivileged sometimes find it challenging. A more popular choice is Mixed Metaphors. Here many Lousy Linguists find that they can really branch out and spread their wings. Indeed some of them are hooked on mixed metaphors just as soon as they dip their toe in the water. And once hooked they're up and running. The danger that the Mixed Metaphor player must always beware is thought. If for one moment he pauses to reflect on the meaning of his metaphors his game will collapse. Any suspicion of thought must be nipped immediately and ruthlessly in the bud before being kicked firmly into touch. Otherwise the player will find that he's cooked his goose by shooting himself in the foot.

He can even find himself shifting accidentally into the highly specialised field of Unintentionally Saying the Opposite of What You Mean. Numbers in this game are literally exploding. It is impossible to underestimate its popularity.

The Society for Lousy Language is keen to stress that Lousy Language is more than just a game. Proficiency in any one of its thousand variations can significantly enhance employment prospects, most obviously in journalism and broadcasting. Many amateur Lousy Linguists have gone on to become highly paid sports commentators.

But Lousy Language opens doors to many less expected fields. The civil service, for example, is crammed with Lousy Linguists. According to the society spokesman, Wellington boasts more players of a Lousy Language variant called Obscurantist Stuffing than any socioeconomically comparable urban environment in the country. And many of them are in positions that afford substantive remuneration. They have to hire a porter to lug home their fiscal envelopes.

The Lousy Linguist also has the world of commerce at his feet. Once he has learned to monitor strategic developments going forward, or at least in the medium term, then the sky's the limit. In other words, said the spokesman, Lousy Language games are the ideal training ground for the managers of tomorrow, and he cited the example of Mr Christopher 'Chris' Moller as a model for all aspiring Lousy Linguists.

'Here is a man,' said the spokesman, 'who has had a glittering career in industry and has now risen to the head of the Rugby Football Union and SANZAR. But he has never forgotten his debt to Lousy Language. Here, for example, is the reply he gave only last week to a question about television revenue. "To suggest that a drop in one market is going to translate to a 50 per cent drop in the total global revenue for SANZAR is a very long bow to draw."

'Forget the redundancy of "total global",' said the spokesman, wiping joyous moisture from the corner of one eye, 'forget the misuse of translate, and concentrate on the bow metaphor. There you see a master at work. Could anyone beat that image for sheer impenetrability? It goes beyond cliché. It climbs to dazzling heights of meaninglessness. I gawp at its genius. It represents everything that we at the society stand for. But was Mr Moller satisfied? No he wasn't. He went further. With a skill that leaves me speechless he improved on the unimprovable. "It was a very wide miss of the goalposts," he said. Beat that.'

Good as a rich monk

A nice corporation rang me. They wanted me to write a little something for them. 'We'll pay you,' they said, '75 cents a word.'

I liked that. ($2.25.) I liked that a lot. ($3.75.) I liked that so much that a surge of liking rose within me, a tsunami of liking, towering tall and voluminous and green as greenbacks, then breaking warmly over me and receding to leave a mass of creamy suds of loveliness, knee-deep and swirling in my bank accounts.

Had that last sentence been written for the corporation, it would have been worth $34. That's more than fifteen times as valuable as the sentence 'I liked that', which says as much, and says it better. Although now that I've used 'I liked that' twice, its value has doubled. Well, actually, I've now used 'I liked that' three, no, four times, so it would have raked me in a total of $9. I've done jobs where I earned $9 an hour. Oh, I liked this job. I liked it a lot.

What a doddle. Fancy a coffee? Let me write you a coffee. There, I've written you one, the frothiest cappuccino. No, don't thank me. It was a pleasure. Want chocolate on the top? Or rather, would you like a little chocolate sprinkled on the top? There you go. At 75 cents a word that's all the chocolate you could possibly want.

To coin a phrase, I would be phrasing coins. This was money for jam, and even more money for a sugar-laden fruit preserve. To enrich it, and me, still further, I had only to add 75 cents worth of pectin. Or of arsenic. It's all the same to me. 'What's the value of words?' asks the man of action. 'Seventy-five cents each,' say I.

This had to be the only job in the world where 'seventy-five cents' was worth $2.25. And 'two dollars twenty-five' was worth $3. But 'three dollars' was worth a mere $1.50, which is only half the value of 'a mere dollar fifty'.

It felt like a form of magic. By typing 'dog food' I fed my dog. If I wanted to treat her to a dried pig's snout, of which she is inordinately fond, I had only to write a dried pig's snout into existence.

Here was the world inverted. The world is things. We gave the things names. Now I had only to name the things to earn them. For sure it would take a while to write myself a house, but not so long as it would take to build one.

And I liked the way that the length of the word didn't matter. For one thing, I had always thought that I was worth as much as that ghastly vamp Madonna. Now 'I' was. And for another thing, I prefer short words to long words. Long words are like cushions. Short ones are like fists.

And with this scheme I would quite rightly earn as much for 'gut' as I would for 'stomach', or for the even primmer, pseudo-medical 'abdomen'. I liked that. I liked that a lot. It gave me a good feeling in the gut.

But every silver lining, apart from being worth $1.50, brings a cloud. The cloud this offer brought was called inflation. Because I now understood, and grasped, and comprehended, the reason for that awful form of language so often found in corporate and bureaucratic worlds.

I've fumed, not to mention raved, and even fulminated, against such language many a time (and oft) but now it all came clear. Those corporate and bureaucratic boys and girls must be paid by the word.

How else to explain the substitution of 'at this moment in time' for 'now'. How else to justify the 'window of' that always serves to introduce a corporate opportunity.

The best prose is spare as a monk's cell. A single chair and table. Walls as blank as honesty. The sort of prose that Orwell wrote.

Such prose is ill rewarded. Orwell coughed himself to death on some Hebridean island. Writers should be paid, not for the words they write, but for the words they cross out. They never will be.

Meanwhile here was my invitation to the corporate boardroom, its armchairs stuffed with adjectives. Waiters simpering through the throng, one hand held deferentially behind the back, the other toting a laden tray of Latinate synonyms and rich adverbial modifiers. 'Take all you want,' says the host, urging me to gorge on the stuff that clogs the arteries of prose and stills the little beating heart of truth.

Orwell would have scoffed at the offer. I took it. Every man has his price, and mine is 75 cents a word.

I wrote the piece, doing my best to quell the urge to pad it. I sent it in. They turned it down. 'It might upset some customers,' they said.

How did I feel? I felt good. Good as a monk.
'But we'll still pay you for it,' they said.
How did I feel? I felt very good. Good as a rich monk.
It was, as I said, a very nice corporation.

Lucy mon

Oh golly gosh, I'm having trouble with my eyboard. The letter ' ' seems to have got stuc.

I found this out when I sent an e-mail to Andy and he wrote back instanter saying 'What's a mon?' I wrote back saying 'mon' was a form of address in Scotland, normally preceded, for reasons that eluded me, by 'hoots'. 'Fair enough,' wrote Andy, 'but why are you living the life of one?', which puzzled me a bit until I had a pee at my previous e-mail.

'Sorry,' I wrote immediately, 'having problems with the letter ' '. Didn't mean mon, but rather mon, you now, one of those religious chaps that lives in a convent', and Andy wrote back 'Don't you mean monastery?' to which I replied, 'Not if he's a lucy mon, I don't.'

I touch-type of course. It would be unprofessional not to. But I loo at the eyboard at the same time, because one can't be too sure in this precarious world. Belt and braces, that's the way to go. And besides, how else am I supposed to now where the letters are?

The consequence is, of course, that I don't loo at the screen, and I fire off e-mails to Andy with no 's in them. As soon as he pointed out the problem, I tried pressing the . I pressed it again and again and again. Once or twice it worked (see), but generally not a dicy bird.

In one way it was great fun. It threw up all sort of strangenesses that refreshed, I felt, the tired old language. 'Dicy bird', for example, brings to mind the great Condor of Fortune that once soared above the Andes. The Aztecs sacrificed ids to it in the hope that it would bless them with the shelter of its wings, instead of dumping on them from high in the sy.

And the missing ' ' breathed fresh life into old joes.

Patient: 'Doctor doctor, I thin I'm a leptomaniac.'

Doctor: 'Have you taen anything for it?'

The missing ' ' could have altered the course of history. 'iss me, Hardy,' says the dying Nelson, to which Hardy replies, 'Of course iss you. Who did you thin I thought it was?'

'No,' groans Nelson in extremis, 'I meant "iss me". Iss me now, Hardy, before it's too late. Please.'

'Shoot him, Lieutenant,' says Hardy. 'We can't let the crew see him lie this. He's gone completely boners.'

(Of course one can programme a computer to do fun stuff automatically — by telling the machine to replace the letter 'e' with something infantile like 'bottom' and then I typbottom a linbottom or two for fun, though I admit that it soon grows a bit tirbottomsombottom.)

Anyway, I suppose things could be worse. Imagine if I was writing a novel and I also lost the letter ' ', number four in the blooy alphabet, and I ha a main character in the novel whose name was ic. It would mae life very har inee.

I have got a 'd', fortunately, but the ' ' really has got stuc, and though, as I say, it is fun in one way, it is also disastrous. Because when I told Andy that I'd been living the life of a mon I was speaing the truth. I've been monish because I'm writing a boo. It isn't a novel about Dic, but it is 85,000 words long and it's due at the publisher in four days. I'll get there, I thin, just, but it's been tough. I actually haven't had a drin for twenty-seven days, which is, I believe, the longest drought since about 1971. The liver thins it's in clover — though in four days' time it's in for one hell of a shoc.

But with the polishing still to be done to the text I've now got a problem. It's all very well to write a column with no ' 's in it, but I can hardly whac this sort of thing off to the publisher. Should I just eep on eeping on, and try to sirt round all the words with ' 's in them, or should I try to fix the eyboard? And if I try to fix the eyboard, what if it all goes wrong and I only compound the problem. I've got this really trendy computer that won't tae a dis, so I can't mae a copy of the text. I could lose the lot. Six months wor up in smoe.

But I've got this little aerosol of stuff that advertises itself as 'the toolbox in a can' and perhaps if I just give the letter ' ' a teensy-weensy squirt, lie so

Five and a half intimates

A woman rang me. She was organising a book festival. Would I run a workshop, she said. No, I said.

I said that I had done workshops and found that I did all the work. My workshops were lectures.

Well then, she said, would I like to give a lecture? I said I would be happy to talk about my favourite books. She said that would be dandy. I give the talk this evening. Last night I thought I should do something about it.

By counting the books on a shelf and then multiplying by the number of my shelves, I estimated that I own 1200 books. I've read almost all of them, but I'll read very few of them again. I keep them because I think they make me look clever. They also insulate the house.

I toured the shelves with a notebook, writing down the names of favourite authors. My shelves are roughly alphabetical. By the time I'd reached 'L' I'd filled two pages. 'L' was particularly fruitful: Lanchester, Larkin, Harper Lee, Laurie Lee, Levi, Levin, Lively, Lodge . . . I made a cup of coffee, sat on the dirty sofa, thought a bit, looked at my list and scrunched it. It was not a list of my favourite authors. It was a list of authors I liked, like an address book. What I wanted was the intimates.

Just as you have countless acquaintances, several friends, but only a very few people that you would run to in times of trouble, so it is with authors. There are a few, a very few, whose books I return to time and again. Just to think of reading them is to feel a sense of indulgence, like sinking into a hot bath of milk. Books as comfort in a spiky world. Books as succour.

I started a new list. I included only the books I'd read at least three times. In the end I had a dozen. I asked myself who the true lovers were, the writers I would like to curl up with on the dirty sofa that very minute, and deep in whose words I would happily spend the day. I culled more from my dozen, each with a pang. I was left with those I just could not cross out. There were five and a half of them.

The five were Evelyn Waugh, Philip Larkin, Albert Camus, William Shakespeare, Laurie Lee. The half was Thomas Hardy.

I do not pretend they are the best five and a half authors in the world. Shakespeare is the best five and a half authors in the world. Shakespeare is the best hundred and five and a half authors.

Of the others, Waugh was a vicious bigot, Larkin a misery, Camus a poseur, Lee a romantic and Hardy a clumsy doomster.

They're all men and they're all dead. Five were English, one French. But what counts, I think, is that I first read each of them in my late teens. That's the volatile age, the age of greatest intensity. Time is never so rich again. It's the age when the fledgling bird shuffles onto the branch and wonders if it can fly.

None of these authors taught me. None of them showed me anything new. Rather they coupled with my mind. Each fitted a bit of my head like a plug in a socket. Each gave words to something I had sensed, apart from Shakey, who gave words to everything I had sensed.

In *Decline and Fall*, Waugh showed me a hard and glittering world of knaves and suckers, a world where the amoral did things and the nice suffered the consequences. And he made me laugh. In the first half of *Brideshead Revisited* he drowned me in love like honey. In the second half he didn't convert me to Catholicism.

I lived in the suburbs. Larkin showed me the suburbs. He stripped off the comforts to reveal a skeleton of desperation. I had sensed that desperation. To see it clear thrilled me. It relieved the desperation.

Camus showed me random. He showed me that things happened only because they happened. There is no thread. I had already sensed that all the threads were false. Camus gave me the courage to believe my disbelief.

Laurie Lee, well, he went walking in Spain. And though I doubt the details of the book — he wrote it almost twenty years after the event — he did the job in words so vivid that they seared my mind. And from those words I reaped a sense of coloured purposelessness, of beauty in the arbitrary sideshows of the everyday. I still suspect him of romanticism, but to cross him off would be to deny the way his words seduced me then and still seduce me now.

Hardy made me cry. And Shakespeare, well, he made me wonder how anyone since has found anything to say.

I'm looking forward to giving the lecture. It will be the purest self-indulgence. If no one comes to listen to it, I shall give it to the empty chairs.

Mean

I gather that the World Trade Organisation has held 'meaningful discussions'. That's good to know. But what does meaningful mean in this context, and in particular what does it mean for you and me? These are the questions I mean to answer by means of this column.

In the first place, and to the relief of everyone, the meaningful discussions appear to mean that the Doha Round is still alive. Doha, of course, doesn't mean Doha. Doha means Cancun. But if the meaningful discussions mean what they appear to mean, then it won't be long before Doha stops meaning Cancun and starts meaning somewhere else.

What will that mean for somewhere else? Well, first off, it will mean the gravy train chugging into town. Of course the gravy train means neither gravy nor a train. What it means is a free lunch, and, as we all know, a free lunch means the opposite of a free lunch. It means an expensive breakfast, an expensive lunch, an expensive dinner and several expensive cocktails with cherries in, plus a snack from the amusingly expensive minibar, all of it paid for by someone else. And someone else, ladies and gentlemen, means the taxpayer. And the taxpayer means you and me.

So I think we're entitled to know who exactly will be eating the free lunch that you and I have paid for. And it's a question I mean to answer in a manner that will leave you in no doubt of my meaning. The suits, ladies and gentlemen, the suits will be eating our lunch.

Of course, suits don't mean suits. Suits means the men and women who wear suits, or rather the men who wear suits and the women who would wear suits if they were men. But because they're not men they wear trouser suits instead of suits. A trouser suit means a pair of trousers and a jacket, as opposed to a suit, which means a pair of trousers and a jacket. If that distinction means nothing to you, forget it. I'm not here to quibble about meanings.

So, when I say suits I mean the men and women who represent their countries at the World Trade Organisation. These men and women have been chosen by the elected governments of their respective countries, chosen, in other words, by the chosen, with the word chosen in that last phrase having two slightly different meanings.

(I am excluding for the sake of simplicity the non-democratic countries. In their case the suits means the people chosen by the unchosen or the self-chosen.)

So, having clarified those meanings, what does it all mean? Let's start with the meaning of the World Trade Organisation itself. World obviously means world. Trade, equally obviously, means the rules that restrict trade. And organisation means the forum in which they have meaningful talks about free trade.

Free trade means different things to different countries. The United States of America is a champion of free trade, by which it means subsidising its own farmers. New Zealand is also a champion of free trade, by which it means not subsidising its own farmers. What does this mean? This means a need for meaningful discussions.

But meaningfulness is not only to be found inside the World Trade Organisation. There is plenty of meaningfulness to be found outside it. Because any meeting of the World Trade Organisation invariably means protesters.

Protesters mean to break into the meaningful discussions that the World Trade Organisation is holding. What the protesters are protesting about is globalisation, and we all know what globalisation means. Globalisation means McDonald's. Globalisation means big American corporations exploiting people by selling them things they want.

The protesters are on the side of the poor countries. They believe that the World Trade Organisation means to destroy the traditional life of those poor countries. But it is important to note that by protesters I do not mean the people who actually lead that traditional life. Those people are far too poor to travel to Cancun to protest.

It is not clear what the protesters mean to do if they manage to break into the meaningful discussions. But they never do manage to break in, because between the protesters and the World Trade Organisation stand the riot police. The riot police mean business.

Of course, business used in this sense does not mean business. The business of the riot police means hitting protesters with sticks so that the World Trade Organisation can carry on its business. Not that business in this sense means business either. The business of the World Trade Organisation means holding meaningful discussions.

The real meaning of the word business is industry. Industry means making things to sell, which means trade. Business, in other words, consists of organisations that exist in the world to trade. And it is essential to understand that organisations that exist in the world to trade are not represented at the World Trade Organisation. It's none of their business.

I hope you have found this discussion meaningful. If you wish for more I would advise you to acquire a copy of *The Meaning of Meaning* by I.A. Richards, a pioneer in the study of semantics and a keen amateur auto-proctologist.

Do you care?

Do you care? Oh good. Me too. I care like billy-o. After all, this is 2004, and we've transcended all that eighteenth-century nonsense about cultivating one's own garden and letting others cultivate theirs. The theme of the twenty-first century is caring. Caring, my darlings, is in.

I am a whirlpool of caring. I suck into my caring vortex everything that nice, caring Judy Bailey or even nicer and more caring John Campbell instruct me to care about. The Ukraine, high country tussock, chlamydia rates in Laos, lice in Laos, problem gamblers, melting icecaps, type two diabetes, type ten diabetes, I care about them all with such intensity that I sleep only eight hours a night.

And of course I'm not the only carer in this warm-hearted world, and neither are you. Caring is everywhere, praise be. Here's a story of caring.

There's a track on the Port Hills. My dogs frolic up it most days and I lumber after them, my bronchials squeaking like a nest of newborn mice. Every so often I stop on one of the several bluffs along the track to admire the view and to smoke the mice into silence.

The bluffs in question are outcrops of basalt where I stand and get a titillating sense of vertigo at the thought of tripping and plummeting to the valley floor and certain death. But I haven't plummeted yet. My caringness, you see, extends even unto myself.

At the bottom of the hill where the track meets the road there's another bluff. It's a man-made thing in the form of a retaining wall, and if I were to trip over the edge of this bluff I would plummet to a certain sprained ankle. For the wall is 4 feet tall.

But even though this bluff is the lowest on the track by a factor of twenty, a deeply caring protective barrier has recently been erected across its top. The barrier is built of swimming pool fencing. This is apt, because the swimming pool fencing act is one of the most caring pieces of legislation to emerge from Wellington for many a long while. I keenly await its sequel, the sea, river, lake, pond, creek, puddle, bath, basin and dog's water bowl fencing act.

But how do I know that this barrier is a caring barrier? Because it says so. Across the top of it there's a strip of the sort of tape that policemen use to cordon off an accident scene. But this tape does not say 'Accident' on it, or 'Keep Out unless you're an important shaven-headed detective'. This tape says 'City Care'.

Not 'City Maintenance Department'. Not 'Ministry of Works'. Not 'Dirty Municipal Jobs Inc'. But 'City Care'.

Presumably the people who work for City Care are selected for caringness. Not, how big are your biceps, o labourer, but how wide is your heart? I wish I'd seen the wide-hearted ones erecting this barrier, cooing to the 4-inch nails before easing them into place with care and a 16-ounce claw hammer.

Time was when nobody cared. In my youth, for example, if you didn't have a mother or father you had a guardian. That name told you all you needed to know. Guardians were the callous overlords of Dickensian orphanages. When not beating their charges' backsides into biltong, they were sieving the fortnightly gruel ration to remove any traces of nutrition. But that was then and this is now. Guardians are gone and in their place have come caregivers. Indeed, since it is not all that long ago that I was a youth, it is just possible that some of yesterday's guardians are today's caregivers. The same people, but oh what a change of heart. Now they enwrap their little charges in the warm duvet of care.

Consider medicine. It used to be an inhuman business of science and pills and knowledge, the doctor a remote brute, his treatment mechanistic. But not any more. Medicine's become healthcare. The name implies sugar on every pill and an attitude like melted toffee. While the surgeon saws through your thigh-bone he plays a CD of Simon and Garfunkel.

And only the other day I saw the caring Stephanie 'Steve' Chadwick on television, promoting her caring act of parliament that banishes smokers from pubs. She insisted that smokers were poor people who needed help. She cared, you see. What's more she had overwhelming support from what she called healthcare practitioners, among whom she included herself. For 'Steve' is a midwife.

Picture a midwife and you may see a crone with a face like a boot sole hauling out the new-born, slapping it into life and then rattling grimly off on her black bicycle to the next haulage operation. But not any more. 'Steve' and her caring colleagues now practition healthcare and the name tells us that everything is different. Words are all. Change the name of something and, hey presto, you change the thing itself. Now doctors care, guardians care, labourers care. Their names guarantee it.

Though at the same time I can't help recalling a pop group that went by the name of The Grateful Dead. A year or two ago the leader of The Grateful Dead died. A sorrowful spokesman announced that the surviving members of The Grateful Dead were, and I quote, devastated.

Poor things. I hope someone cared for them.

Fifty thousand an hour, money-makingly

'O Harry,' said Hermione introductorily, 'I've got this cracking idea for a new plot.'

'Good,' said Harry Potter. 'About time.'

'Why do you say that?' asked Hermione interrogatively.

'Well,' said Harry, 'according to the text I'm only fourteen, but in real time I'm in my early twenties and after all those scrapes we've been through together, Hermione, I've got to know you really well and, frankly, my wand . . .'

'O Harry,' interrupted Hermione blush-sparingly, 'you silly beast. Asexuality's a convention of children's literature and so you're going to have to wait till after the final book in the series which probably won't arrive for another year or two. Do you think you can hold on?'

'I'll try,' said Harry leg-crossingly.

'Meanwhile,' said Hermione subject-changingly, 'we need a new plot. Some of the critics have been giving us a bad time. They say the books are clunkily written . . .'

'What?' interrupted Harry clunkily. 'What do they mean, clunkily?'

'And,' continued Hermione apparently non-Harry-hearingly, 'that the whole of our story is simply a corny battle between good and evil using time-worn cliché-ridden medieval imagery.'

As she spoke a silvery-blue dragon reared coincidentally onto its hind legs, writhing with all its might and spitting fire from its vicious-looking fanged mouth, the sparks raining down on its scaly hide.

'Is that all?' asked Harry.

'By no means,' said Hermione. 'They also say that Hogwarts is parodic nostalgia, a sort of Billy Bunter with magic, and that most of the incidental characters speak like Spitfire pilots in black and white films.'

'Whoa, there,' shouted a moustachioed wizard illustratively as he struggled to restrain the dragon on a stout leather leash, 'just look at her plume of fire. Isn't she a beauty?'

'So what do you say to that, Harry?' asked Hermione point-makingly.

'Fifty thousand copies an hour,' said Harry, 'is what I say to that. We're selling fifty thousand copies an hour. The critics are just . . . are just . . . help me out, Hermione.'

'Green with envy,' said Hermione outhelpingly.

'Precisely,' said Harry. 'They're just green with envy. But what's your new plot element?'

'Well,' said Hermione well, 'I think we need a new evil character, so I've come up with a German.'

'Oh, now that *is* a good idea,' said Harry. 'That fits in nicely with our air of fifties-style Britishness. But what's this character's name? Names are everything in our business. We've got Voldemort, who translates, though no one seems to notice, as "flight of death", we've got the posh romanticism of Hermione, the deliberate irony of the ordinariness of Potter, allied to the royal hint in Harry, the Anglo-Saxon consonantality of Hagrid with its intimations of witchcraft, the straightforward demonology of Griffindor, the black and predatory connotations of Ravensclaw, the comic inversion of Warthogs, the. . .'

'Ratzinger,' said Hermione papally.

'Crikey,' said Harry, 'that's good and nasty. Tell me more.'

'As I see it,' said Hermione, 'Ratzinger sings to rats. He's got a cellar full of rats and he sings instructions to them whereupon they rush out on murderous errands. It's great colour stuff, all German and efficient and sinister.'

'I like it,' said Harry.

'But at the same time Ratzinger belongs to a worldwide organisation led by a frail old man who suddenly ups and dies. All the club elders then go into a huddle and choose Ratzinger to take over. They announce their decision by sending smoke out of a chimney.'

'That's a bit far-fetched, isn't it?' said Harry. 'Do you think people will swallow it?'

'You bet,' said Hermione wageringly. 'But the best bit's still to come. Ratzinger changes his name to something nice and puts on all this medieval finery and then, guess what?'

'What?' said Harry.

'He denounces us. Effectively he declares war on Hogwarts. He says that the stories of our adventures are "subtle seductions".'

'Subtle!' exclaimed Harry. 'There's nothing subtle about Harry Potter.'

'Ah but,' butted Hermione, 'the whole point is that he's a competitor. His organisation runs doctrinal schools like ours and deals like us with imaginary forces to which it gives powerful names, and it sets great store by ritual incantations, and it dresses up a lot of its pronouncements in a dead language that only insiders can understand, and it reveres a book of ancient pronouncements, many of which, it must be said, are contradictory, but still it's a powerful force, and though the organisation doesn't officially believe in witches and wizards it nevertheless condemns them as dabblers in the occult which it also officially doesn't believe in, though it did once, and . . .'

'It sounds,' said Harry, 'a pretty mixed-up outfit.'

'But a powerful one,' said Hermione.

'Fifty thousand copies an hour powerful?' asked Harry.

'Of course not,' said Hermione, 'and that's the point. It would love to be fifty thousand copies an hour powerful which is why Ratzinger's having a go at us.'

'Green with envy, then,' said Harry. 'Like all the rest of them.'

Teaching

When I was a child, teachers were drooping things. They had leather patches on the elbows of their jackets, wilting moustaches and halitosis that could kill gorse. The male teachers weren't much better.

The only career decision I ever took was never to teach. I went on to teach for twenty years. Teaching is simple and intuitive. It is a vocation, like acting. Both are performance arts, and neither can be taught. At teacher's college, where I ostensibly studied phys ed, the only thing I learned was that nine out of ten white males float. And I am the tenth.

The two indispensable qualities for teaching are enthusiasm and an affection for kids. Thereafter it's a question of being true to your own nature. I am weak. If ever I pretended to be a disciplinarian, the kids giggled.

All teaching theory is bunkum. What works for one teacher won't work for another. And the contemporary orthodoxy that every child is a self-motivated student and the teacher a mere facilitator of learning is the silliest theory of all. If you subscribe to it, you have never taught.

I'm pleased I don't teach any more. I've done my bit. And it's a job for the young.

The tongue-thing

So, the lassie has a thing through her tongue. It is a silver thing, a sort of dwarf weightlifter's dumb-bell, and she has developed the charming knack of making one end of it protrude between her lips and then wiggling it from side to side. Thus she has added her bit to the popular art of body-piercing, an art much practised among primitive peoples. Indeed the number of holes in this girl's flesh and the tonnage of silver bangles dangling from them may well denote high rank, but today I am concerned only with the dumb-bell through the tongue.

And I am not alone in being concerned with the dumb-belled tongue. The nasty principal of this girl's high school is also concerned with it, so very concerned that he has told her to remove it. She refused. He suspended her from school.

Enter the lassie's father, frothing with indignation as protective fathers of vulnerable children understandably tend to do. And, of course, he sat her down, told her in forthright terms to remove the dumb-bell, apologised to the principal and sent the lassie to bed without any supper.

Or so we would have supposed. But we would have supposed wrong. Instead, dear papa gave her a pat on the back and a tube of Brasso for the dumb-bell and then informed the fascist principal that his daughter would remove the dumb-bell only over dad's dead body, and while he was still breathing she would continue to attend school.

The nub of dad's argument was that the school had contravened an inalienable human right, the right to freedom of expression. His daughter wanted to wear the tongue-thing; the tongue-thing was, indeed, a profound expression of who she was, and the bossy little schoolmaster had no right to crush her individuality.

Well, now, it has been a hot summer. Let us suppose the daughter had chosen to attend school naked (except of course for the tongue-thing, which I would imagine is pleasantly cool in the mouth when the wind is from the nor-west). Would dear papa have let her? Would he have crushed her free spirit?

Or were she to decide to go to live with baboons in whatever ghastly country baboons live in, or to become pregnant, or to insist on eating only cat-biscuits, would papa nod his head, smile, pat her on the back and say, 'that's my girl'? He would? Then he is nuts.

No doubt dad would argue that his daughter is doing nobody any harm by piercing and embellishing her tongue. Ignoring the possibility that she may not be doing her tongue a fat lot of good, on the face of things he would seem to be right.

But how faces lie. Let us consider the tongue-thing from the point of view of the school's principal. If he allows the father's argument and admits the right to the tongue-thing he will be in no position to reprimand any child who breaks any convention. Freedom of self-expression will be the catch-cry, and soon the principal will find himself in charge of a school where anything goes. Or rather he won't be in charge of it at all.

The result of that is easy to imagine. Parents will remove their children. The school will shrink and then sink and leave not a wrack behind.

We hear an awful lot about rights. Father insists on his daughter's right to express herself. At the same time he implicitly assumes her right to an education. Both rights are indeed enshrined in law in New Zealand. Neither is a natural right. Both are artificially created by an artificially organised society. They are not so much rights as privileges.

If dad is unconvinced by this distinction I invite him to send his daughter to North Korea having first taught her a few choice phrases of self-expression about the president of that country. The authorities would certainly remove his daughter's tongue-thing. Whether they would bother to extract it from her tongue first is less certain.

Or let him send her to Eritrea to insist on her inalienable right to eleven years of education at the state's expense. They love a good laugh in Eritrea.

The rights that this gentleman is insisting on are rare in this world. Most people do not have either of them. They are to be cherished, and should not be invoked for the sake of an infantile whim. *De minimis non curat lex*, which translates loosely as 'stop whining about tongue-pieces, darling, and thank your lucky stars you live in a wealthy democracy'.

And then finally there is the question of age. Father insists that his daughter knows best. At what age did she start knowing best? At fifteen, or ten, or five? Or was she pretty clued-up in the womb? And if she knows best, if she is capable of making adult decisions for herself, then what need has she for school? School is a place of training. His daughter does not apparently need any form of training. Whatever she does is right.

I have just discovered that one may not become president of the United States until one is 35 years old. The hoary old birds who knocked up the Constitution clearly thought that if you have lived that long you have enough experience to talk sense. How wrong they were. Witness several presidents and one New Zealand father.

Prizing advice

Some while ago I took up golf and I wrote, 'Nothing in life has so confirmed my fear that I have reached middle age.' I apologise for quoting myself here but, more importantly, I apologise for being wrong. For five minutes ago a phone call proved me wrong. It seems that I am not in middle age; I am in old age. In shuffling slippers I have rounded the final corner in the great race and am tottering towards the tape before an empty grandstand. The timekeeper yawns, glances at his watch and cocks his finger above the button that says stop. I am as old and slow and wrinkled as a tortoise. I have a spine like a stick of chalk. I mumble through gums, suck eggs and snooze. Soon I shall snap like a water biscuit.

I know all this because the man who telephoned me, you see, was a school principal. Would I, he asked, care to address his school prize-giving?

I have seen school prize-givings. In thirty-something years in schools, a dozen of them spent learning little and twenty of them teaching less, I have seen them all. I have heard a swag of boring bishops. I have heard a herd of entrepreneurs, smug with suits and wise with wallets, returning to the scene of the crimes of childhood and telling lies. I have heard famous sportspeople mumble platitudes about passion and dedication and hard work paying off, and the need for that horror of horrors, goal-setting. I have heard the fat-chested cock of immodesty crow loud and long about yesterday. I have sat through a man telling 600 children that at the age of fifteen he suddenly developed an unquenchable fascination with parrots, the breeding and showing thereof, and he urged the children to do likewise. I have endured military men encrusted with medals for having sent younger men to their death, and I have heard them say that life is a battle and that it pays to have God on your side and a couple of tanks. I have heard them all and I have even, God help me, smiled politely at their jokes.

The children haven't. The children have yawned, fidgeted, stirred, scratched themselves, fingered the cigarettes in their pockets, eyed the exits manned by teachers with folded arms and have switched their brains into neutral and their ears into stops. And now they will yawn, fidget, stir, scratch, finger, eye and switch in front of me. And they are wise.

For to what does the mind of a crusty oldster turn when invited to address children? As inevitably as a weathervane turns to the wind, it turns to advice. And in no field of human endeavour has so much air been vibrated to so little purpose as in the giving of advice. Advice is a refugee; everyone wishes to pass it on but no one wishes to receive it.

And is the advice of the old worth listening to? Are parrots, the breeding and showing thereof, the key to life? Do God and tanks make good allies? Is it wise to set goals? I do not think so. Nor do I think that in the years I have lived I have learned very much of value to pass on. I remain the ignorant fool I always was. I may walk more slowly and suffer worse hangovers, but I continue to make the errors I made as a child. I have just got better at hiding them. Character is destiny, said Novalis and I am with him. It's what happens to happen, said Larkin and I am with him.

And there, in those last two sentences, you have it. Over the years I have collected a few nuggets of other people's wisdom. I have not surveyed the map of my experience and seen the world afresh. I have just stumbled from hap to mishap, read a few books on the way and picked up some pretty phrases like a bright-eyed, dull-brained magpie.

But let us suppose otherwise. Let us suppose for the moment that

I had the wisdom of the ages and the wit of David Lange. Would it profit the world that I went to the prize-giving, reared to my feet to insincere applause and cast my wisdom about me like a grain to fall where it will, some of it lodging perhaps in the heads of a few of the little darlings dragooned into sitting in patient rows before me, and, having lodged, sprouting into a beacon that will guide them through the dark alleys of their lives to come? No, it would not, for three simple reasons: one is that grains cannot sprout into beacons, the second is that the children would not be listening and the third is that nobody acts on advice.

I know so. For in the twenty years of teaching I have dispensed tons of the stuff. I have run two boarding houses and sprayed advice about me like a fountain. None of it did any good. The most salutary experience occurred when a boy in Canada came to talk to me after the others had gone to bed. He brought with him a toothbrush. We chatted about the toothbrush, then he told me that his mother had multiple sclerosis. He told me that she was deteriorating. He told me that he was afraid that she would die. He cried. And I could think of nothing to say. When he had said what he had to say he left.

In the morning I sought out a colleague whose wisdom I valued. I told him what had happened. I told him how hopeless I had felt, how I'd found nothing to say, no advice to give.

The wise man told me that, on the contrary, I had done the best thing. I had listened and my silence was the best advice that I could give. And he was right, of course. And now that I think of that story I realise that, if nothing else, I have written my prize-giving speech.

A call to arms

Whoa! Rein the horses, stop the wagon train, form a circle, shelter the women and children, load the muskets and prepare to do battle. (On second thoughts, just shelter the children: the women of today are up to it.) The vandals have come down from the hills and civilisation is under threat. (On third thoughts might as well let the children have a go too. If they can put up with body piercing they can go to war. If anyone needs shelter today it's the men.) But it's time to kill or be killed. If we lose this one, well, who cares? It will be all over and there will be nothing left to fight for. Sound the bugle, sing heigh ho, for this is it, the big one, the decisive engagement between culture and barbarism, and there's something scary but pleasing after decades of decline to have the enemy in plain view. Now at last we have something to shoot at. The years of endurance are over and courtesy is long gone. These are raw days. The enemy has a name and a form at last. It is called the Bee Gees.

You've heard the story. Students of English at the University of Cambridge sit a compulsory paper on the subject of tragedy. That tragedy is the only compulsory paper deserves an article on its own with a fat dose of irony, but now is no time for irony. Now is the time for cold steel.

Those who set this exam have stooped to baseness. After years of blameless academic purity — 'Ibsen's tragic vision was predicated on the image of disease. Discuss'; 'Address the notion of literal and metaphorical blindness in the tragic oeuvre' etc — they have let down their guard and the subculture of inanity has thrown a right hook through the gap. That right hook is the Bee Gees.

The walls of academe have crumbled, eaten out by the maggot called relevance. And that maggot has crawled onto the exam paper in the form of the following words:

> Tragedy
> When the feeling's gone and you can't go on
> It's tragedy
> When you lose control and you've got no soul
> It's tragedy.

Words written by the Bee Gees. It is tempting at this point simply to take sides, to throw in one's lot with the Mounted Battalion of the Educated Few and rally beneath a standard on which is embroidered the legend, 'We shall not dumb down'. The Bee Gees represent everything that education is supposed to drag us out of.

They are a pop group — nasty — they are impossibly wealthy — nastier still — and they cause men and women of unimaginable poverty of mind to form 'fan clubs', groups of such unmitigated awfulness that we must needs be protected from the possibility of infection by shrouding them in inverted commas.

But though the temptation is strong, it ignores the fact that the Bee Gees' words make a rather good question. They invite debate and disagreement and that is what exam questions are for. Consider Macbeth — by Act V (oh, that lovely educated V) he has lost the power to feel the virtuous emotions of pity or grief — has lost, in short, his soul — and can go on only as a murderous automaton. That indeed, as the Bee Gees suggest, is tragedy. Meanwhile Mrs Macbeth has lost control and cannot go on in any way at all. She flings herself from the battlements. That too is tragedy.

Ah ha, perhaps so, scream the defenders of the faith, but the Bee Gees didn't know that. They just flung a few emotive words together, found that they rhymed and sang them. And besides, the masses who writhe and squirm to their 'music' (more disinfectant punctuation) pay no attention to the lyrics of the songs. Those lyrics are merely noise, an anodyne addition to the simian rhythm of the drums and that crudest of instruments, the electric guitar. The Bee Gees know not what they say. They gibber like parrots, but are incapable of consecutive thought.

Well, perhaps so and perhaps not. Nevertheless I think we should note the fundamental irony in all this. The great tragedians, whose work we revere but don't read, were the Bee Gees of their day. Look at the size of the theatres in Athens. Four-fifths of the population rolled up to see Aeschylus's latest blood-spattered epic. Or consider the impoverished groundlings at Shakespeare's Globe with their bad breath and worse armpits. The ancient tragedians were popular. Popular does not mean bad.

But I argue against myself. I have been trained in cultural supremacy. My education obliges me to take arms against a sea of Bee Gees. Don't shoot till you can see the whites of their teeth.

Cosh the teacher

'More and more people,' said the woman on the radio, 'are becoming addicted to gambling. What we need is education in schools.'

Well, the first lesson in the School Cert gambling curriculum is easy to imagine. It would consist of 'don't'. I find it harder to imagine the second one.

But as it happens gambling is already taught in schools. It's called maths. The school I attended even ran an advanced gambling course. It was called the sixth form common room.

There we played poker with huge intensity for tiny stakes. Our chips were copper coins. If silver appeared on the table a crowd gathered to gawp at the high-rollers.

The star of our poker school was a dour little creep whom I shall call Cosh. Cosh, I suspect, had the odds written on the inside of his spectacle frames. There was certainly plenty of room. Before betting he considered, then reconsidered, then slid the coin forward with such gaiety of heart that it scored a groove in the tabletop. He then paused with his finger on the coin to reconsider his reconsideration. If he let go of the coin he did so in the manner of an Old Testament prophet offering his first-born for sacrifice.

If Cosh laid a bet, the wise threw in their hands. That Cosh went home most evenings with a pocket so stuffed with copper that he limped, says nothing for our wisdom and everything about gambling.

I haven't seen Cosh in years but I do know that he went into insurance and I am told he is now rich. I haven't seen Dave Collier in years either but I bet he isn't.

I loved and feared Dave because he made things happen. To paraphrase Clive James on one of his childhood friends, Dave would have a good idea and shortly afterwards you heard the sirens.

When Dave played poker it was like the weather in Patagonia: you never knew what was coming next but it was sure to be extreme. Easily bored, Dave bet on every hand, normally in inverse proportion to the strength of the cards he held. His cunning lay in the word 'normally'. Dave lost a lot but when he won he won big. Once he bluffed Cosh out of several silver coins. It must have felt lovely.

Because of their natures I am confident that neither Dave nor Cosh is now a gambling addict. But statistics suggest that someone I went to school with is. Let's call him Smith. And if Brighton Grammar School had formally taught a course on the dangers of gambling would it have saved Smith? No, it wouldn't, any more than losing money to Cosh did.

Compulsive gambling is ruinous. It devastates families, careers and happiness. But teaching its dangers in school is as futile as most overt moral education. Ninety per cent of moral education happens in the home and it happens when we're young and it goes in through the skin. Next to nothing goes in through the ears. Sermons don't work. They never have and they never will.

The woman on the radio would no doubt argue that what she wanted was not sermons on gambling but information about it. But even if we ignore the fact that children instantly spot the moral fist in the informative glove, what is there to learn about gambling?

In our sixth form common room there was only one lesson to learn and it wasn't a difficult one. It was that Cosh and the odds were the same thing and in the long run you couldn't beat either.

Common sense tells every gambler that the odds are against him. Addicts ignore that common sense. Their reasons for doing so may be diverse, compelling and tragic but when common sense has flown out the window, moral education won't charge to the rescue through the door. Addicts deserve help and compassion and I expect the woman on the radio does far more to help them than I do. But to suggest that school could have saved them is wrong.

Every schoolkid today can draw you a beautiful picture of a cancerous lung. And a fair proportion of them are so skilled that they can colour it in with one hand while lighting a cigarette with the other. Those same children are also infinitely better informed than I was about the dangers of alcohol yet if you believe what you read in the newspaper they are also infuriatingly better supplied with the stuff.

And we've had sex education for several decades now and the remarkable result seems to be a generation far more likely than their parents to contract gonorrhoea and chlamydia and far less likely to be able to spell them.

He was my English teacher

He's dead. Jack Smithies. My English teacher. Of cancer. I got an e-mail today. Went off in his sleep. I've written about him before but I can't let his death pass without doing something. He was my English teacher.

I had other English teachers of course, but they didn't matter. They made no splash in my pond. There was one who got us to depict the legends of King Arthur in strip cartoons. In the seventies that sort of thing was in vogue. I couldn't see the point of it then and I can't now. Jack Smithies never did stuff that was in vogue.

After Mr Strip Cartoon came Ernie. Ernie was ancient and he taught me nothing. He took two years to do it. I can still recall the way Ernie spoke, as if someone had pulled his tongue a little bit too far forward and at the same time wedged something semi-permeable in the bridge of his nose. His was an easy voice to imitate. No one imitated Jack Smithies.

Ernie, bless him, made us parse sentences according to some strange scheme of his, but I never got it. I grasped the patterns of grammar only by doing foreign languages. Ernie also found Chaucer funny, or at least he made a point of explaining to us why Chaucer was funny, although Ernie himself never laughed at the jokes. Nor, as we spotted, did he explain the sex jokes. Then one fine day Andy Grant told Ernie that Chaucer wasn't funny. Ernie grew angry in a way I hadn't seen before. He was a placid beast but suddenly he was fury made flesh, bellowing at Andy and swinging his withered arms. Now *that* was funny. I don't recall Jack Smithies ever being angry.

Two years of Ernie must have meant a period a day for forty weeks a year. That's 400 or so hours of teaching and nothing has stuck but his failures. Ah well. He tried. Rest his bones.

Further back still lie a string of primary teachers — women in tweed skirts, Miss Coghlin, Mrs Lake and one with warts. They did spelling tests, I suppose, and dreary foundation stuff, and I remember that Miss Coghlin cared about handwriting.

I always hated my handwriting. It said too much about me. I seemed unable to lie with it — not with the words I wrote, of course, they were always available to lie with — but with the way I shaped the letters. However much I tried to jazz my handwriting up with fancy Russian d's or capital F's written backwards like continental 7's, the shapes I made on the page still seemed to shout the immutable truths of my weakness of character. All the same, those women, those sturdy women teachers, they seemed good then and they still do now. But they didn't excite me. Jack Smithies did.

I did English at university. My director of studies was Nervous Tony, a distinguished medievalist, peeved not to be a professor, secretly sliding his laceless shoe on and off under the desk while telling me of Gawain and the Green Knight, pronounced 'kernikt', or reciting chunks of *Piers Plowman* from memory. No fun there. We didn't get on. I wrote a couple of bad short stories about him and his nervousness. I've written nothing but good things about Jack Smithies.

Nervous Tony farmed me out to a woman I liked. We still correspond. She came to my room for hours at a time, told me about her folk-singing husband, about growing tomatoes, about lesbians, about milk churns. She smoked my smokes, drank my coffee and was the first adult woman I ever saw as a real frail person. But though I liked her, I did little work for her.

After her I was deemed educated. They stamped my passport and let me loose. No English teachers since.

The ones I've noted didn't teach me much English. But then, once you've learnt to spell and punctuate there's not much left to learn. Or at least not much that can be taught.

And Jack, my English teacher, the one who counted, the one who did make a splash in my pond, didn't teach me much either. No lapidary phrases, no moral precepts, no startling insights. He just showed me some writers, and showed that he liked them. It was Jack who introduced me to Larkin. But I'd have found Larkin anyway.

So why did he matter? I don't know. Perhaps my mind just meshed with his. Anyway, he made me laugh. Not by telling jokes. Not by telling stories. But by, well, being Jack. He made a difference to me that I can't begin to define. It was largely because of him that I went on to study English. And it was largely because of him that I taught English for twenty years.

And now he's dead. Twenty-four hours dead. By the time you read this they'll have burned or buried him. Burned, I expect.

The values of Minscum

Calloo callay, of frabjous day, the world is coming right. Two minutes past the yardarm this morning and I poured myself a snorter, sat down with the paper and discovered that the police are going to be issued with Tasers. Tasers are stun guns.

Henceforth, drop litter in the street and Constable Bigfoot will reach for his holster. 'Hold it right there,' he'll bellow. If you make a run for it, whoompha. Three hundred thousand volts will leave you squirming on the pavement begging for less.

Magnificent news, of course, but that was far from all. I turned the page and, well, let the article speak for itself. 'The Ministry of Education will introduce new values to the national curriculum . . . As part of a ministry curriculum review, a comprehensive list of values to be taught in schools has been put together . . . including honesty, respect and responsibility . . . Ministry Senior Curriculum Manager Mary Chamberlain said teachers wanted more advice on what values to teach.'

Call me a crusty old conservative but my heart leapt. There's nothing it likes more than a few old-fashioned values. It was the work of a moment for me to seize my snorter glass and hie me down to the local secondary school, locate its eaves and drop from them, applying my glass to the wall and my ear to the glass. And this is what I heard.

A previously valueless teacher was addressing a class of eagerly attentive fourteen-year-olds.

'Good morning, class of eagerly attentive fourteen-year-olds,' he said.

'Good morning, Mr Previously Valueless Teacher,' they chorused as one, that one being the winsome Samantha Plainbody. The remainder of the class were busy at the back being dishonest, disrespectful and irresponsible with an assortment of educational paraphernalia.

'We have a visitor this morning, children. Her name is Miss Ministry Senior Curriculum Manager. Say good morning.'

'Good morning, Miss Ministry Senior Curriculum Manager,' said Samantha.

'Thank you for your warm welcome,' said Miss Ministry Senior Curriculum Manager. 'I know my title's a bit of a mouthful. Please call me Minscum. That's what my friends call me, and I just know we're going to be friends.'

Deftly raising an umbrella to ward off the rain of expletives, condoms, syringes and other educational paraphernalia, Minscum continued undeterred, aware that the little darlings could hardly be blamed, having all been raised in a moral vacuum into which she was about to release the life-giving air of

'Values, children. I'm here to talk to you about values.'

'What's them, Miss?'

'That's a really good question, er . . .'

'Weedpusher, Miss.'

'Weedpusher, thank you very much for your contribution. Values are things that you've been deprived of by your dysfunctional upbringing. But now the Ministry of Education is going to rectify the deficiency with an ongoing integrated values programme initiative which in half an hour a week will undo all the harm of your formative years and rewire your skulls entirely so that you'll become sound members of the community and pay your taxes cheerfully, thus enabling the Ministry of Education to continue such vital work as paying Waikato University to survey teachers and parents in order to find out the value they place on values. Isn't that exciting? Anyway, children, values are what used to be called morals.'

'What's them, Miss?'

'That's another really good question, er . . . Runtface, and if you just put your beer down for a second I'll explain. Values are the things you used to go to Sunday school to fail to learn. They are concerned with right and wrong.'

'What's them, Miss?'

'Goodness, what a lot of excellent questions you're coming up with, children. You are a very bright class. How sad your intelligence is unmatched by your values. Still that's what I'm here for, to lead you through the moral maze and to release you from the torture of relativism.'

'What's them, Miss?'

'I think that's enough of your really good questions just for the moment, children. Let me ask you a question instead. Who's heard of honesty?'

'Me, Miss, me, Miss, me, Miss,' rose a mighty chorus.

'Excellent,' exclaimed Minscum. 'I can see I underestimated you.'

'We was lying, Miss.'

'Oh dear, lying's terribly irresponsible and disrespectful.'

'What's them, Miss?'

'Well, now, irresponsible means not accepting that there are consequences to your actions and disrespectful means . . .' but Minscum never managed to explain what disrespectful means because the previously moderate flow of missiles swelled to a torrent that rent the cloth of her ministry umbrella. Minscum fled the room, acquiring as she went a collection of minor bruises that she would eventually show off under Any Other Business at the next meeting of the Values Curriculum Development Subcommittee.

'There,' she said, when she and the Previously Valueless Teacher had gained the sanctuary of the corridor. 'I think, if I may use a sporting metaphor, I've done the hard yards. I'll leave the squidgy ones to you.'

'Thank you very much, Ministry Senior Curriculum Manager,' said the Previously Valueless Teacher. 'I'm sure everything will be just fine now. Enjoy your return flight to Wellington and keep up the good work.'

'Oh, and this may come in useful,' said Minscum, handing the Previously Valueless Teacher a Taser.

More tosh

The Education Ministry has revealed its draft new national curriculum. I can't tell you how excited I am.

I came to teach in New Zealand a couple of curriculums ago. My subject was English, which had always seemed straightforward to me. I taught the little darlings anything I liked, warping their minds as I saw fit, and then as the end of year approached I taught them to pass the exam.

From the New Zealand curriculum, however, I discovered that there were seven 'modes' of English. One of these was viewing and another was shaping. I didn't know what these meant. After I had read the guff about them I still didn't know what they meant. So I taught English as I had always taught English which was more or less how I had been taught English, and no one seemed to mind.

One curriculum later, the seven modes of English were discarded. Some people had made a nice living explaining them, and textbooks had been written around them, and teachers had been sent on courses to learn about them, and then they disappeared. No one ever admitted they were absurd. They just got dumped, and the people who had made a nice living from them jumped onto the next gravy train of educational theory.

Since then I'm pleased to say that I've lost track of changes to the curriculum. But I've just had a look at the new one on the ministry's website. It's very pretty. It will have cost millions of dollars. Those dollars have bought a lot of abstract nouns, and those abstract nouns will make as much difference to children as the seven modes of English did.

The new curriculum identifies five 'key competencies'. (And yes, I did want to stop reading at that point, because language like that acts on my gorge in the same way as rancid meat does. But I swallowed hard and read on.) I discovered that the 'key competencies' (the inverted commas are no longer necessary but I am using them as disinfectant) are 'managing self', 'relating to others', 'participating and contributing', 'thinking' and 'using language, symbols and text'.

Where do I begin with this stuff? Well, let me begin with where school begins. It begins with a five-year-old child. The draft new curriculum calls this child a student, but you and I know better. The child is a child, an infant that has spent the five most formative years of its life somewhere other than in school. Let's call this child Mary.

Mary's nature, at the age of five, will be pretty well established. Ahead of her lie 13 years of school. They won't make a massive difference to her. Puberty will. Television, advertising and the internet may. The friends she makes may. But school won't.

Mary will be at school for about seven hours a day for about 190 days a year. In other words for the next 13 years she will be at school for roughly 15 per cent of her time. And she will be under the direct influence of the school for an even smaller fraction of that time. Most of that 15 per cent will be spent taking an intense interest in her friends or in herself. In other words, school can't do much. And it certainly cannot and will not teach her to 'manage self', whatever that may mean.

Schools are not moulders of character. They do not create good citizens or sane people. Genes, families and society do that, or fail to. Schools may try to patch up damage but they are capable of little more than first aid.

Nevertheless schools are good things. They have a straightforward and important job to do. First they must teach Mary the basics of language and maths. If they do that well, then Mary is fitted to take part in the world. Then they must give Mary a chance to do things that she wouldn't otherwise have the chance to do: to play music or games, to dissect literature or mice.

The specific details of what's taught don't matter much. If you don't believe me, recall your own days at school. Boyle's law, the valency of potassium, the effects of glaciation, Shakespeare, have all rotted to a general compost.

But if you're lucky there is something that didn't rot. That something will not have been the curriculum you were taught. Nor will it have been character-moulding moral instruction. It will have been an enthusiasm. And that enthusiasm will have been generated by a teacher. You can name that teacher. Other pupils at the school at the same time would name a different teacher, but for each of you there was one that mattered. That teacher will have had a passion for his or her subject. That teacher will have lit a similar passion in you.

It is teachers that matter in schools. The rest is fiddle-de-dee. The millions of dollars spent on the new curriculum won't create a single happier, wiser or more responsive Mary. But teachers will. Pay them more and let them get on with it.

A lot like us

According to a magazine I picked up at the dentist's, children say the darnedest things. So, where do I start with this tosh? Well, why not start with some of the darnedest things that children actually say? Such as, 'Yo bro, give me your lunch or I'll beat you up.'

Or, 'Totally wicked and awesome.'

Or, 'Seven years! That's a bit stiff, your honour.'

Or, 'Thanks for the lunch, bro, which was totally wicked and awesome. But I'm still going to beat you up.'

The notion that kiddiwinkies are all cute little parcels of benevolence with a tendency to malapropisms is an obvious delusion. And the opposing notion, that they are all murderous thugs, spoilt, selfish, untutored, overprotected, overfed, overmuscled and overrunning a society that is incapable of controlling them, is a delusion just as obvious.

Kids were my business for 20 years. They didn't provide much income. School teaching is viewed as a profession more or less on a par with zoo keeping. It's the business you go into because you took an unhealthy pleasure in school yourself, or because you feel a sense of missionary zeal, or because you can't think of anything else to do.

Teaching did cure me, however, of any sentimentality about children and of any fear of them. The curious truth about children is that they are a lot like us.

But they do provide zest. Even their lethargy is zestful. That zest is infectious. It causes time to pass swiftly. And even though I whooped with delight when I managed to quit teaching in 1998, and even though a herd of wild horses on dietary supplements wouldn't drag me back permanently to the classroom, I do miss the little darlings. If nothing else, they made me laugh. Not by saying the darnedest things, nor yet by telling me jokes (oh, children tell jokes so very badly), nor yet by being staggeringly ignorant, but simply by being fresh, erratic bouncers through the early years of life.

So when, recently, in crabbed middle age, hermitic, thwarted, misanthropic and cross, I was asked to go and chat to some schoolchildren, I accepted. I didn't fall, I hope, or at least not entirely, into the old trap of thinking I might have something useful to tell them. I did have lots of useful things to tell them, of course, priceless things, the fruits of 50 years of breathing, but at the same time I knew exactly how much attention the solipsistic darlings would pay to those fruits. Children don't want to be told useful stuff, any more than you do, indeed, less.

No, the main reason I accepted was selfish. I wanted an infusion of the muddled zest of the young. And I wanted to laugh.

The kids shambled into the library. Some were earnest imitators of adults. Others had made unfortunate choices with their hair. Teachers were stationed around the perimeter of the throng like snipers. And I was a guest speaker.

Oh, God, I've seen guest speakers in school: poets (ow), dignitaries (ow plus), distinguished former pupils (ow squared) and advocates of sexual health with their hearty frankness (ow to the nth degree with bonus interest). But, in compensation, I've also known the effect they've had on kids, which is zip.

I thought I'd start strong. I hoped I might excite them a bit. 'You,' I said, picking a girl near the back. 'What's the difference between you and a gibbon?' She looked as if she'd been shot, which was gratifying. She said nothing.

'Come on,' I said, 'what's the diff between you and a gibbon? DNA says that you are 99.9 something per cent identical to a gibbon, so where lies the difference?' The girl looked at me with the full-moon eyes of wonder and perhaps disdain. But at least she wasn't yawning.

'No ideas?' I said. 'So if you chanced to see a gibbon in the street you would mistake it for a human being?'

The girl continued to stare at me in silence. But others piped up. I listened to all of them cheerfully, then shot them down. Until one boy said 'language' and we were away. Or at least I was. I plunged into a rant about language, its relationship to thought, its fundamental importance to learning and therefore to civilisation, the need for fresh language and the perils of tired language. I asserted that anyone with some control of language was in a position to do better thinking and better things than his yo-bro coeval. We had a rare old time, or at least I did, and during the hour that I was there I didn't actually notice any kid sleeping or leaving, and several argued badly but with vigour, and I worked myself into a lather and I think it was all right.

'Right,' I said, as I wound things up. 'Anyone got any last questions?'

The girl I'd originally selected, and who had still not spoken, put up a hand. I was delighted. 'Yes?' I said.

'What's a gibbon?' she said.

Kneeing Zucchini

I no longer teach, so I ought to stop banging on about education, but Sue Bradford doesn't teach either and she's been banging on a lot.

What has excited Ms Bradford is corporal punishment, though I prefer to call it kid-walloping. Kid-walloping is in the news because a Christian school wants to do some.

The school has written to parents asking if they mind if their kids get walloped. I don't know whether the parents mind or not, but I do know that Ms Bradford does. She minds terribly.

'A full investigation must be launched to ascertain whether any child has been assaulted by staff and if so prosecutions must be considered. I believe this is a disgraceful policy, which will encourage abuse of children. I am appalled that any organisation that is tasked with the welfare and education of young people would consider it a desirable discipline option.'

The Christian school (an obvious oxymoron, but let that pass) is not upset by Ms Bradford's opposition. The headmaster said that he needs to wallop some kids because he's in the business of exercising God's law. In other words, the headmaster is deluded, dogmatic and potentially dangerous, but the parents at this private school chose to send him their kids, so that's their problem.

I attended a state school where boys were occasionally caned by the headmaster. In my class there was an irritating and pompous child whom I shall call Zucchini. Zucchini had a strange metabolism. If you kneed him in the crotch, his nose bled. He resembled a slot machine. In went the knee down there and out came the blood up here. It was so amusing that kneeing Zucchini in the crotch became fashionable. In consequence, Zucchini suffered more than even he deserved. I never kneed Zucchini but I remember finding it funny. A few found it addictive. Only Zucchini dissented, and his vote didn't count.

Somehow the authorities learned of Zucchini's plight. Three of his assailants were summoned to the head's study. They were caned. Now let's return to Ms Bradford's words. She described corporal punishment as 'assault'. Wrong.

Kneeing Zucchini was assault. The caning was something different. Zucchini was not at fault. Zucchini's tormentors were. Zucchini could not have avoided his fate. Zucchini's tormentors could have, simply by avoiding Zucchini.

According to Ms Bradford, the caning that Zucchini's tormentors received was likely to 'encourage abuse of children'. Well, its immediate effect was precisely the opposite. The perpetrators left Zucchini alone. They may not have become his best friends but they did stop kneeing his groin.

But perhaps Ms Bradford is thinking longer term. Perhaps she means that the intoxicating delight of caning would soon turn any headmaster trigger-happy, so that he would end up rampaging through the school, brandishing his bamboo much as Ms Bradford brandishes her liberal credentials, and beating children indiscriminately just for being alive. To which all I can say is that our headmaster didn't.

But then again, Ms Bradford may mean that caning would turn us, the children attending that wicked school, into child-abusers. It didn't. Nor, while I'm at it, did the caning teach its victims violence. They were already experts.

Ms Bradford is 'appalled' at the thought of children being 'assaulted' while ignoring the truth that children regularly assault children. She also ignores the truth that children regularly assault teachers. Only this week there was talk of teachers striking because of the danger to their wellbeing from the children they teach. Yet Ms Bradford's attitude implies that children are all vulnerable little diddums. The truth has obviously got lost somewhere.

But Ms Bradford does not have a monopoly on being appalled. I am appalled that any child should assault a teacher. I am appalled by a child saying 'Don't touch me. I know my rights' when that child has shown no respect for the rights of others. I am appalled when a teacher can't teach well-behaved kids because ill-behaved kids won't let her. I am appalled when kids emerge from school unable to read or write after 10 years of expensive education. That's what I call child abuse.

The notion that kids are little balls of innocence who would all grow into loving angels if only we adults didn't warp them, is bizarre, romantic, self-deluding nonsense. It takes only one visit to a kindergarten during playtime to dispel. The idea was formulated by that old dingbat Jean-Jacques Rousseau in about 1750 and discredited shortly afterwards. Yet somehow it persists as today's sentimental orthodoxy. It is the same delusion that impels people like Ms Bradford to call pupils students, as if every one of them were a self-motivated scholar. (Though it is interesting to note that when someone is threatening to wallop them, they stop being students and become children again.)

Kid-walloping won't come back into New Zealand schools and it wouldn't make much difference if it did. What would make a difference, however, in the endless debate over education, is a bit of honesty about the nature of children. Oddly enough, they're just like us.

Domestic and personal stuff

Where did the grand romantic sweep of life disappear to? It disappeared into the little things, like worrying about money and wrestling with duvet covers. Whenever I write about such little things I get letters from readers saying yes. The bathroom is a particularly fertile source of material. It is the place of most alone, where we come face to face with time and self and the disappearance of the grand romantic sweep.

Be the boss

Don't give in to technology. Stand up to it and beat it. Never forget that it is the slave and you are the master.

My bedroom light fizzled then died. I padded to the cupboard to fetch a replacement bulb.

One week and three trips to the supermarket later, I remembered to buy one. The dead bulb had held sixty watts, so I bought one containing a hundred. It should last almost twice as long.

I stood on the bed. Mine is a dead bed. It has sagged into the shape of a rowing boat. I straddled it, balancing on its gunwales with the ease of a trawlerman in a gale. I reached up for the light bulb.

Raising both hands above one's head does little for the balance. It is why trawlers don't have electric lights. Nevertheless I removed the light bulb. I did this by not letting go of it as I fell. The glass came away nicely in lots of little pieces. Some of them even had blood on them, making a decorative effect on my snowy bachelor bed linen.

Close technical inspection revealed that I had indeed removed the bulb. What I hadn't removed is what home handymen call the metal thing that fits into the thing. I headed for the toolbox for pliers.

One week and three trips to the supermarket later, I remembered to buy a pair of pliers. They were made in Taiwan with green plastic handles and they cost agreeably little. They were of a variety called 'Heavy Duty'.

I played trawlerman again. The thing that was stuck in the thing came out with a sharp crack. A chunk of the thing it was stuck into broke off. The pliers broke too. Undaunted I inserted the new bulb. It lit up.

A hand full of working electricity unnerves me. I leapt down into the rowing boat, deftly catching the bulb as it fell. I turned the light switch to off, climbed back up on deck, slid the bulb in again and twisted it into place. It fell out. Peering into the thing I saw that the bit of the thing I had broken off was the bit of the thing that held the thing on the light bulb in place. It wasn't just a light bulb I needed. I needed an entire new thing.

One week and three trips to the supermarket later, I remembered to find out that the supermarket doesn't sell things. I needed to go to a specialist thingmongers. I thought of getting a man in, but pride said no. The wallet agreed.

The man in the electrical bits shop smiled when I explained in technical terms exactly what I was looking for. It was the smile of one expert to another, a sort of electrical freemasonry. In no time at all he unearthed exactly the right thing. 'That's exactly the right thing,' I said. He smiled again and both the other assistants smiled too. I liked the electrical bits shop.

Electrical repairs require one big decision. If you don't turn off the mains you risk death by electrocution. If you do turn off the mains you have to reset the clock on the microwave. And on the video, and on the oven and on the bedside table. I always choose death by electrocution. Apparently it's swift and you get to look like Rod Stewart.

Pausing only to write my will, I fetched a screwdriver from the toolbox.

One week, three trips to the supermarket and one to Placemakers later, I had acquired a gift pack of fifteen screwdrivers with blue plastic handles. They were made in Taiwan. I was ready.

Our physics teacher was called Glegg. Glegg was strange. He told us that electricity consisted of a chap called Mr Volt standing in a box. Mr Volt spent his life pushing barrels out of the box and round a circuit. The barrels were called amps. I bore this in mind as I applied my screwdriver to the things that attached the wires to the thing. In the style of all good electricians I also screwed my eyes up and stopped breathing.

Glegg also taught us that there were three wires. One was the live wire, one was the earth wire and the other wire was another wire. They came in different colours. I couldn't remember the colours.

It didn't matter. There were only two wires attached to the thing. Both were black. Electricity has obviously changed.

When I detached the broken thing the light shade fell off with it. I put it aside and attached the new thing to the wire. It was easy. I inserted the light bulb. It stayed inserted. Dismounting the trawler deck I started breathing again and turned the switch. The light went on. I tried not to smile. I failed badly. I wished I had Glegg's phone number. I went to put the light shade back. I found that to put the light shade back I needed to detach the new thing. I put the light shade on the floor and went to bed. Masterfully.

Cars and frying pans

Cars are like frying pans. The key to both is to do nothing to them.

All food can and should be fried. The best frying pans are those big black French jobs that strain your wrists. In the hands of a trained chef they can kill burglars.

If you let such a pan mature, and in particular if you let a decent depth of fat develop in it, it will fry anything. If after several months the fat becomes so deep that you lose sausages in it, then the solution is to eat takeaways for a couple of days while the fat solidifies. It can then be turned out onto a plate and cut into squares. Crunchy Cholesterol Slice is its proper title, and it is best buttered.

The fatal error with frying pans is to wash them. Water affects their chemical composition, making the potassium ions covalent. This means that, after washing, the surface of the pan has thousands of microscopic hands reaching up like those waving sea anemones on coral reefs which are common on television but rare in Lyttelton Harbour.

Crack an egg into a washed pan and all the little hands will clutch onto the electrons in the eggwhite. The egg will stick to the pan like superglue, the only difference being that the bond between the egg and the pan will be strong.

It's much the same with cars. I know quite a lot about cars. I know that red cars go faster than other cars and that men don't drive automatics. I know that driving fast is safer than driving slowly because an accident is a random happening in a random place and so the less time one spends in any random place the less chance one has of meeting the accident lurking there. I also know how to put petrol in, although not how to stop it regurgitating over my shoes, and I know that cars, like frying pans, work better if left alone.

But the society of meddlers have other ideas. Because my big red car is a few years old, the powers of this land, advised no doubt by the brown-suited troglodytes at Occupational Safety and Health, have decreed that every six months when the monster is purring with efficiency it has to be taken to a garage to be mended. This happened to me only two weeks ago. As usual they gave my car a WoF. As usual I gave them just under $1500.

When I got the car back it was immediately evident that they had done an awful lot of work on it. The driver's seat had been adjusted, no doubt to render the mechanic's weekend joyride more comfortable. The mirror had been adjusted too, presumably by the feet of the mechanic's girlfriend.

Further evidence that they had worked long and hard, so to speak, on my car was the fact that it wasn't going as well as when I took it in.

A glance at the docket explained a lot. For a start it explained why mechanics are all young. Having worked for ten years at that hourly rate they retire.

The rest of the docket had all the lucidity of the instruction manual to a Korean VCR. There were words like grommet.

Anyway, true to the frying pan theory, a few days after the car had been fixed, little red warning lamps appeared on the dashboard. I found them quite decorative and ignored them. If you pander to a car's whims it will soon have you opening the bonnet every five minutes.

The car stopped. I turned the key. The engine made the noise of a man flicking through a telephone directory. Then it fell silent.

Now there are two types of car owners. The first type is those who left school early. Such people crawl under stopped cars, adjust the grommets, strip down the carburetor manifold, suck petrol through the sump gasket, spit it out manfully and make the car go.

The other type is the educated few. We are strong on the ontological insecurity of nineteenth-century novelists. When our cars stop we ring the AA as soon as we have finished crying.

My AA man was a charming chap called Chris. He opened the bonnet as if it was the easiest thing in the world, fiddled a bit, then did exactly what I would have done; he fetched a hammer.

At this point I offered to help. After all it was my car and if anyone was going to swing a few blows into the bodywork I had first claim.

To my surprise, Chris tapped gently at a complicated bit of the engine. To my even greater surprise he didn't make the car start. I think Chris may have stayed on too long at school.

The trouble was the alternator. Obviously, Chris summoned an alternator man who soon told me all I wanted to know about the alternators fitted to Subaru Omegas, which was that they cost $150.

It was dark. I offered to hold a torch for the alternator man. He told me not to bother; he could change an alternator in the dark. And he did.

When I got home I fried some eggs, bread and peas and sat down with a nineteenth-century novel for a good long think.

Baking nuts

There comes a time on a Sunday when the body craves something more substantial than aspirins. And it was at just this time last Sunday that I read an article about baking biscuits.

Grandmothers bake biscuits; I don't. I have never filled my tins.

But the article featured a recipe for ginger nuts. I love ginger nuts. Bite into a dry one and it's an even money bet whether tooth or biscuit will break first. Dunk a ginger nut in coffee, however, and it becomes a delicious confection which is easily spooned from the bottom of the cup. I read the recipe, I salivated and I decided I would bake.

Having ransacked the larder for ingredients, I rang a woman who knows. She told me that no, I couldn't really do without eggs or ground ginger. Nor could I substitute noodles for flour or beer for golden syrup.

I had to have baking soda too, apparently, but she reassured me that even if I never baked another biscuit my baking soda would not go to waste. I could clean my bath with it.

The woman who knows doesn't know my bath. Anything that could clean that bath has no business in biscuits. It would be more at home in a warhead.

My trip to the supermarket cost me a smidgen under fifteen dollars. I calculated that my home baking would power into profit after 500 biscuits.

In measuring 100 grams of butter the bathroom scales proved unsatisfactory, but all great cooks are innovators. On the 27th of July 1975 I took six wickets for forty-seven against Eastbourne, and was presented with the ball. It has travelled round the world with me.

A cricket ball weighs five and a half ounces. I tickled the calculator and found I needed two-thirds of a cricket ball of butter, one and a half cricket balls of sugar and one and three-quarters of flour.

After that it was a simple matter of placing the cricket ball in a bowl in the right hand and ingredients in a bowl in the left hand and seeing which way I leant.

I had to cream the sugar and butter. I presumed that cream meant beat. Creaming proved an efficient method of bending forks.

After five minutes of creaming I had whipped up an arm full of lactic acid and the dogs had whipped up an enthusiasm for airborne lumps of sugared butter.

Add one tbsp of golden syrup. Golden syrup is not divisible into tbsps. It is not divisible into anything. However high you lift your tbsp it remains linked to the golden syrup tin by a rope of sagging sweetness. In the end the dogs solved the rope problem.

Sifting one and three-quarter cricket balls of flour from a height proved to be fun. Some of the flour landed in the bowl. Rather more landed on my black dog. When she sneezed she looked like the inside of a Christmas paperweight.

Creaming time again, then a pause to revive the creaming arm and straighten the creaming fork, before rolling the sludge into twenty-four golf balls and laying them on the baking tray I hadn't got. Improvising with tinfoil was genius, but transferring the foil to the oven proved costly. Balls roll. The dogs got seven of them raw.

Then all I had to do was turn the light on in the oven, pull up a chair and watch my balls become nuts. They sweated a little, then slowly, beautifully, they darkened. As the biscuits flattened, I swelled. As the surfaces crackled like the picture in the recipe I burst with pride.

Twenty-five minutes later I drew from the oven seventeen perfect gingernuts. I laid them on the wire cooling tray known as the kitchen bench, and dashed to the phone to boast to the woman who knows. She was out.

Having hauled the dogs off the bench I cooled the eleven gingernuts by blowing on them. Then I picked one up. It was as hard as an ice-hockey puck, a tooth buster, the real thing. I made a coffee, I dunked the biscuit. It disintegrated. I did a little jig. After forty-one years I had filled my tins.

Twenty Yak

There comes a moment in the life of any smoker when he knows with sudden certainty that he will never smoke another cigarette. This moment normally occurs in hospital and is followed by a dramatic fall in body temperature.

When I enter Mastermind, smoking will be my specialist topic. I took up smoking at just the right age and did not, as so many of my contemporaries did, give up when we moved on to secondary school. I also smoked for all the right reasons; viz. sex, sport and poverty. Anyone who knows me now will confirm my prowess in just over 30% of these. In other words, then, I reckon I know a thing or two about smoking.

That, however, was until today. For today I rang the editor of *The Press*. I'll rephrase that. Today I rang THE EDITOR OF *THE PRESS*, an august gentleman, immune to capital-letter flattery and sporting one of those Frank Nobilo beards of stubble which I've never quite understood. What I don't understand is how they tend them. Is there some sort of shaver like a ride-on mower that is sold only to golfers and prominent, stately editors who are no doubt also nifty with the five-iron?

Anyway THE EDITOR OF *THE PRESS* and I got chatting, as one does with editors, about cigarettes, and HE said some frightfully kind things about my rate of consumption. Was HE a smoker, I asked. It turned out that THE EDITOR OF *THE PRESS* was an ex-smoker, which I've always thought, as I told HIM, to be the very best type of smoker. How, I asked, did he stop? And HE said, 'Yak.'

See what a pithy man HE is. Yak. It's a beautiful answer. Economical, trenchant, enigmatic, editory. I was impressed. THE EDITOR OF *THE PRESS* didn't get where HE is today by beating about the bush. Ask HIM a straight question and HE'LL say, 'Yak.'

It transpired that Yak is a brand of Nepalese cigarette popular with the more suicidal Sherpas. A few beards ago THE EDITOR OF *THE PRESS* was in Nepal — well-travelled too, you see — and faced with a cash-flow crisis. American cigarettes were beyond his pocket and Yak, though less than a dong for a packet of twenty, were, as HE put it, 'guaranteed tonsilitis'. So HE gave up. Just like that. There's character. There's strength. There's what this country needs a bit more of. And that's exactly what I told HIM, in a most unobsequious man-to-man way.

But for those of us who flounder a little lower on the evolutionary ladder than editors, stopping smoking is less straightforward. I've had a dab or two at it myself. I could never get a decent drag out of those patch things, and the chewing gum stuff was so bitter that I had to have a coffee to take the taste away, and as even the simplest chemist knows, coffee grounds + H_2O (heated) = unquenchable lust for a cigarette.

Of course, one can go the organic route. I have in front of me the 'Wise Woman's Tips for Giving up Smoking.' They include, 'Bring home a flower', 'Eat a wild salad — even if it's only one dandelion leaf', and, top of the list, 'Take an oat-straw bath'. All great fun as I am sure you agree, but in my 'garden' it's hard to know if you've got the dandelion before the dogs have, so I just brought a flower home and ate it. This necessitated a coffee to take the taste away.

Sprawled in my oat-straw bath with *The Press* and twenty Rothmans I saw an ad in the personal column. 'Stop smoking the easy way . . . Hypnosis.'

Now, I owe a lot to my mother. She taught me how to know when a sponge is cooked, which strangers to accept lifts from (the wealthy ones), and a method of gripping the carotid artery that I have never seen bettered. (On the famous night when she caught the burglar *in flagrante* and the spare bedroom, the police had to ring around for his dental records.)

What my mother never told me, however, and finding it out for myself has cost me time, money and tears, was to shun all people with framed diplomas on the wall.

The hypnotist's wall was more diplomas than wall. Pride of place went to an ornate little number reading, 'The Bulawayo Centre for

Hypnosis, Naturopathy and Proctoscopy. Weekend residential course. Pass with distinction.' It had a big red seal.

I paid $70 to the hypnotist, who was wearing a golf-club sweater but didn't have a proper beard, and then I conned him. I did this by pretending to be hypnotised when I wasn't. I closed my eyes and breathed slowly and spoke robotically. He was completely taken in.

The moment it was over I went straight round to the dairy for twenty Yak. They were out of Yak, so I had to settle for Camel on the grounds of their similar exotic shagginess, and then I lounged against a lamp-post opposite the hypnotist's diploma-laden house and smoked ostentatiously. It was one of those moments of triumph, rather like talking man-to-man and straight up with THE EDITOR OF THE PRESS. Such things make life worth living.

Love for lunch

Today I had lunch with a psychiatrist. This is not a behavioural pattern that I have previously exhibited — partly because I have known no psychiatrists but also because I have not thought well of their trade.

In twenty years of teaching I saw a number of disturbed children packed off to the couch. It rarely seemed to do them much good. In general, I found that if anything mended the kids it was time and if nothing did then it was the legal system. My impression has always been that the brain is a dark, mysterious ocean, and that psychiatry is a blind fisherman in a very small boat.

Nevertheless this particular psychiatrist proved lively company at a party and we agreed to meet today in one of the more fashionable bits of downtown Christchurch. As I waited for her I sipped my beer and watched the crowd shuffling past in the winter sunshine. Perhaps it was the effect of my lunch-to-come but rather a lot of them looked mad.

The psychiatrist arrived fifteen minutes late, smiled like the sun, sat and did not apologise. I silently admired the ploy. We ordered gewürztraminer and a dish of bits of fish.

The conversation soared. We discussed meditation, Sanskrit vowels, chaos theory, sixteenth-century philosophy, twentieth-century philosophy, the growing prevalence of depression, the nature of joy, the popularity and value of Prozac and whether bacteria could be happy, all with a formidable sweep of lightly held knowledge to which I contributed several ums. I also refilled her glass twice.

And then we got onto love. Now I know a bit about love, and I said so. On the inside of my locker at school I had a photograph of Geoff Boycott. There was something about the way he held his bat, something about the sweet stretch of flannel over thigh pad that sang to my fourteen-year-old soul.

The psychiatrist looked quizzically at me over a slice of blackened monkfish but I persevered.

And then, I said, over the horizon came puberty, marching strongly and letting nothing obstruct it. And with it came love.

She asked me to describe the symptoms of love.

Moping, I said, featured prominently, along with self-pity, grinding despair, sulking, moonlit vigils and a curious addiction to reading and writing poetry. Would she like to hear some?

Despite the monkfish she shook her head with some vigour, reached for a prawn and asked if I still suffered these symptoms.

With a tolerant smile I explained that I had grown beyond such emotional intensity and had indeed been free of the effects of love for at least two years.

The prawn went South, pursued by a swig of gewürzt. 'And you call this love?' she asked.

I asked her what she would call it. She told me. There were several phrases. The least offensive was preoccupational emotive attachment.

Oh, I said, and I meant it to sting, but she swept on.

She acknowledged that to some extent psychiatrists were indeed fishing blind in a dark ocean, but there were some well-lit bits. You could, for example, dose people up with something mildly radioactive in the bloodstream, then get them to think certain types of thoughts and, with the help of a machine, study the bits of the head that were being used to think these thoughts. Every sense impression, she said, every feeling, every thought in the end is just a chemical reaction in the head, an influx of serotonin across the synaptic cavity or whatever. Now, she said, it was a curious coincidence but a colleague of hers was studying the sort of infatuation I had described. And her colleague had found a drug that seemed to cure it. The stuff was called — and I wrote this down to get it right — trifluoperazine.

She paused for effect and a morsel of snapper.

I said that I thought they should put trifluoperazine in the water supply. It would have spared us, for example, Donny Osmond or Boyzone. With trifluoperazine the Beatles today would be dodgy mechanics in a Liverpool backstreet, Tom Jones would be buying his own underwear, Winston Peters wouldn't get a single blue-rinse vote, Lady Chatterley could have got some knitting done, *Death in Venice* would have had a happy ending, someone would have punched Leonardo di Caprio and Lolita could have got School Cert.

'Yes indeed,' said the psychiatrist, and left me with the bill. It was $60.

Small stuff

There's a book called *Don't Sweat the Small Stuff*. I haven't read it because it's a self-improvement book and no self-improvement book has ever improved anyone except the author whom it often improves to the tune of several zillion bucks. But the title of this book intrigues me.

If, as I imagine, it advises the reader not to get swamped by trivia, but rather to keep his entrepreneurial eye forever trained on the horizon of opportunity where the big stuff roams, then I think it's hogwash. Big stuff sounds good but means little. 'Life,' said somebody, 'is just one damned thing after another.' Truth, such as it is, lies in the small stuff. It is always with us. The stuff like letter boxes.

When I bought my house it came with a letter box. It was a wooden letter box and a frail one but it did the job. It safely held the fizzing hate-mail and the accusations of dud grammar. It held the cheques I receive for writing stuff, and it even held a magnifying glass to read them with. The only thing my little letter box wouldn't hold on to was love letters. They dissolved like edible underwear. Perhaps they were written on edible underwear. Or perhaps the jealous dogs got to them first. But otherwise the letter box was sound.

Then one night its little roof blew off. I set to work repairing it with some fine wire nails and a dainty cabinet-maker's hammer, and in no time at all I had returned it to what it started as — which was several pieces of wood. They made good kindling.

Warm but letter boxless I took a catering-sized jam bucket and nailed it horizontally to a post.

Back indoors I wrote 'letter box' in my 'Things to do' book. The 'Things to do' book is my way of handling the small stuff. When there's something I've got to do I write it in the book. When I've done it, I cross it out.

The aim of my life is to cross out all the small stuff. Then I can put my feet on the windowsill and gawp at the big stuff as God intended. But I never cross everything out. In fact my 'Things to do' book reads like an inverse autobiography. My successes have all been crossed out but my failures stand tall. They're as persistent and shaming as genital warts. The letter box is one such.

Every day for two years my letter box has reproached me. 'You are idle,' it mutters, 'I am a jam bucket. Get a letter box. Everyone else has got a letter box.'

And because I've got a bad letter box, I notice that everyone else has got a good one. Fired by envy, I have become a connoisseur of letter boxes. I have noticed, for example, that three models dominate the suburban letter-box market — The Grim, The Gruesome and The Twee.

The Grim is the stalinist letter box. It is built of thin sheet metal painted anonymous cream. It's square as a shoebox, and smooth as a Martian's skull. It has a slot in its forehead and nothing else.

The Gruesome purports to be decorative and is normally to be found amid psychotically neat borders of flowering annuals. It consists of a metal stake sunk into the ground, a crossbar extending from the top of the stake and the kite-shaped letter box dangling from it like a corpse on a gallows.

The most popular design is the Twee. The Twee is wooden and looks like a miniature Swiss chalet. Under its steeply pitched eaves there's a triangular slot for newspapers, beneath that a compartment for letters with a flap at the back and beside that a compartment to house the lovely, bulky, promising parcels I never get.

And yesterday I bought a Twee. I wasn't looking for it. I chanced upon it outside one of those second-hand shops that sells dirty pieces of sadness. The price was right and the Twee was mine.

Back home I dug a hole and sank half a railway sleeper into it. I packed the earth around and trod it down. The thing stood firm. I placed the Twee on top of it and nailed it into place. I didn't hit my thumb and the Twee didn't split. I put lots of nails in. I shook it. It stood as solid as the Treasury. I tore the jam bucket from its mooring and threw it away.

Every five minutes I returned to check my letter box. Its firmness thrilled me. Its neatness delighted me. I kept opening and closing the flap for the joy that was in it. The postie arrived. She handed me a bill. I asked her to put it in the slot. She put it in the slot. I opened the flap and there was the bill. It was a fine moment. It was good small stuff.

In my 'Things to do' book I crossed out 'letter box' and wrote 'pay bill'.

Einstein's bus

According to Einstein, time can travel at different speeds. I think that Einstein must have frequented bus-stops, for nowhere in the universe does time travel more slowly than when waiting for a bus. Bus-stops are built in the gap between tick and tock.

But you can learn a lot from bus-stops. At the bus-stop on Norwich Quay I have learned that there is a group called the West Lyttelton Thugs. They have carved their title into the bus-stop bench. I have also learned that James Burwood is a victim of phonetic language teaching. 'James Burwood was hear 1999,' wrote James. Or I presume James wrote it. It is of course possible that one of the West Side Thugs wrote it so as to get James into trouble. Perhaps James beat one of them in a spelling test.

But whoever was hear I know how they felt. Waiting for a bus is as frustrating as impotence. There's nothing to do but hope that the bus might come. James was hear in 1999 but it doesn't say how much of 1999 he was hear for. It is raining and it is cold and I feel as if I have been hear for about a yere.

Only the graffiti entertains me. 'Welcome to Lyttleton,' says the wall of the shelter, 'watch out for inbreeding.' I am watching out, but all I can see is the wind and the rain and the grey-brown sea, the rusting trawlers, the blackly shining street and one old woman limping through the puddles. Every other Lyttiltonian is wisely at home, drinking gin by the heated indoor gene-pool.

It's the Queen's birthday. By now she will have opened her presents — oooh look, an eviction notice. So thoughtful, Charles, but really, I couldn't possibly — and the party games will have begun. Right at this moment they may be pinning the tail on the fiancée. Ever the loyal subject I hold my own party game. I spy with my little eye something beginning with 'n'. No bus.

I would welcome any sign of life. Where are the West Side boys when I could use a bit of thuggery? Whear is James Burwood? Not hear, just as I would prefer not to be. I would rather be at home but, as I say, you learn a lot from bus-stops. I am learning that next time I go to town for a night out I should not take my car. For now I have to go back to town to fetch it in the bus that doesn't come. The rain drums on the shelter and drips darkly down the metal. The timetable behind its perspex cover is obscured by condensation. The future is unreadable.

I approve of public transport. It makes such sense. Put fifty people in a bus and leave fifty cars at home. Less petrol, less smog, less noise, and far fewer cars to get in the way of my car. For though a bus is more worthy, I shall keep to my car. People throughout history have dreamed of a vehicle that takes you wherever you want to go while you sit down. They called it a flying carpet. We call it a car and we like it. But mine is in town. Someone should invent a car that comes when you whistle.

A bus-stop may have made a physicist of Einstein, but of most of us it makes a philosopher. For what is life if it isn't waiting for a bus that doesn't come? Shakespeare could have written a play about it. Beckett probably did. My life centres on an absent bus. It is the transport of delight which hasn't arrived, the prayer unanswered, the dream not yet made diesel. 'O Big Red, I am gathered here together in the presence of weather and the absence of car. Look down, I beseech thee, on this thy wet servant. O Big Red, where are you?' And suddenly the bus arrives. The sense of impotence evaporates.

The bus's windows are misted, its driver friendly, its seats barren of people. The engine strains, the bus accelerates and time accelerates with it. On the wall a red hammer. 'In emergency remove hammer to smash glass.' All emergency notices make me want an emergency.

The bus trawls through the suburbs collecting people who climb aboard and shake themselves like dogs. At Cathedral Square the rubber doors release me back into the rain, but I am purposeful now, in command of time and destiny, hurrying to where I ditched my car. As I turn into Hereford Street I am seized by the fear that the car will have gone. But there it is, mute and stationary with the brute patience of a mere thing. Time means nothing to a car. For most of its life it merely waits. But for me now it is my wish fulfilled, my independence restored, the best possible present on the Queen's birthday and there in the sodden street I want to hug it like a long-lost sister.

Lie lie lie

As every schoolboy knows — no, that won't do. We can't say that phrase any more. For a start we can't say schoolboy, implying as it does that there's a difference between the sexes — and we can't say sexes either because it inflames their adolescent passions. The truth, of course, is that the only thing that makes adolescence even remotely tolerable is that there *is* a gulf between the sexes and that hormones widen it by the hour and that inflammation is fun. But truth is out of fashion.

We can't say schoolchildren either, because it demeans the little darlings. It defines them by their youth and by the place that is failing to educate them, and thus tramples on their frail self-esteem.

No, we have to call them students and so induct them into the modern world by giving them their very own first little lie to play with. Students study. Now go spy on the teenage bags of testosterone barrelling and boasting down the street when school is out about five minutes past midday on a weekday afternoon and try to imagine them doubled over a book.

Nevertheless, as every student knows — no, you see, it still won't do, the problem being that you can't rely on them knowing anything. The whole grab-bag of chunks of literature and gobbets of knowledge that used to be considered indispensable has been hurled from the third-floor window of the teachers' training college. All truth has become relative and we have become scared of misleading youth and thus we condemn the little sweeties to a life of fumbling guiltless rootless discontent.

But there is one thing that we can teach tomorrow's citizens before plucking them from the teat of education and tossing them into the wicked world to make what way they can. We can teach them how to respond to telephone surveys. More precisely we can teach them what to do when they're heating a tin of sausages and baked beans and the phone rings and a woman asks to speak to the person in the house who is over the age of eighteen and who buys instant coffee.

The options, of course, are several of which the most obvious and appealing is to be staggeringly rude. It is the wrong option.

The right option is to whoop 'That's me, honeybun, you're talking to him', crook the phone between ear and shoulder, tip the beans and sausages onto a plate and prepare to tell lies. Lying to questionnaires is everyone's duty as a free-born citizen. It's enormous fun and it distracts attention from the sheer awfulness of the beans and sausages. Have you seen those sausages? There are about four to a tin and each is the colour and size of the severed finger of a drowned dwarf. But not the texture. Oh no, the texture is of goat's brain, parboiled with a pinch of gelatine.

The survey woman will ask you to rank each of the following brands of instant coffee on a scale of one to five, where five means you would crawl over burning hymnbooks to get a sniff of it and one means that you wouldn't touch it with asbestos gloves. Now's the time to lie. Tell the most monstrous whoppers. Confess a passion for that appalling powdered parody coffee that tastes like an old people's home in New Plymouth.

But be sweet to the woman who is asking the questions. It is not her fault that she's landed with the job from Dreadsville. She's stuck at home with the kids and she's got no money. The people who have got the money are the slab-faced executives who grind up the New Plymouth old folks' home and try to convince you with execrable and mendacious advertising that the stuff is drinkable.

Play them at their own game. One glance at their advertising confirms that they think the public has a delta minus brain that can be duped by pictures of a svelte woman cradling a steaming cup of their horrorbroth which is solely responsible for her having got her hands on a hunk of a hubby, two cherubic children and some nauseating furniture. Confirm their misconception. The questions asked will be transparent. Tell them what they want to hear. Convince them their advertising works. Lie lie lie.

With any luck the result will be a preposterously expensive advertising campaign based on the survey, a campaign that will lose them a lot of money. And so, because you have spent ten minutes lying down the phone, the survey woman will get paid, you won't notice the taste of the sausages and someone in head office might just click that telephone surveys are an unconscionable invasion of privacy. In other words, everyone's a winner — which, as it happens, is one of the few things that every modern schoolboy knows.

■ Hope and pile-cream

I have developed an allergy. I had suspected it for a while. Last night I conducted a clinical trial to settle the issue for good or ill. It turned out ill and so did I. I woke this morning stuffed with phlegm, filled a few handkerchiefs and headed for the pharmacy as soon as it opened. There for the usual amusing price I acquired a box of pills to add to the collection in my bathroom.

A bathroom is a beauty parlour and a doctor's surgery. Every bathroom cabinet contains only two types of stuff: things to make you sexy and things to make you well. If the well-making things exceed the sexy-making things the owner is over 40.

The only lockable room in the house, a bathroom is a place of confession where we strip away our disguises and the poor bare forked animal comes face to face with itself. The bathroom is a place of loving and loathing, a place of hope and pile-cream. And the things that accrue in a bathroom tell a raw and honest biography of its owner.

As infants we have no need of pills or bathrooms. The world is a playpen and dirt is a friend. Our bodies are as pliant as rubber and our teeth whiten themselves. Wounds heal while we watch. Then comes adolescence. Strange things happen to the body, self-consciousness becomes a tyrant and the bathroom saga begins.

A teenage girl needs a bathroom of her own. Acres of unguents are essential to her mating game. Ditto the boys with their aerosols and hair gels, all bought in the hope that beauty comes from the chemistry lab. Wrong of course. Beauty comes from being young. It is one of life's neater ironies that we realise this only when we aren't young.

The advertisers play on youthful insecurities, hooking the children as easily as summer mackerel. It's a very good thing. Making kids spend money on cosmetics they don't need not only trains them for a consumer society but also grants revenge to adults whom time has robbed of everything but commercial cunning.

Once the storm of adolescence has abated, the bathroom cabinet becomes a chronicle of the war with time. Women fill their cabinets with replenishing agents and anti-wrinkling cream; men with Steradent and toupees. And one by one, as the years tick by, the medicines arrive. And having arrived, they stay. Each tells the story of a skirmish with the ultimate enemy. They are battle trophies, or perhaps charms against recurrence, or just agents we think we can trust in the war we must lose.

In my own bathroom stand penicillin which once saved my tonsils, Cataflam which eased my back, and Mylanta which did battle with a curry and lost. There's also a packet of slippery elm. I cannot imagine why I have kept it. It recalls a long-distant Sunday of diarrhoea when the local pharmacist was closed and I dared not risk the journey into town. I went to the healthfood shop. I was a desperate man and though slippery elm did not sound like the right sort of stuff I was assured that it was. It wasn't. Emphatically.

And now my bathroom cabinet has gained another trophy, a packet of anti-histamines to counter my new-found allergy. My only other allergies are to wasp stings and ironing. I discovered the wasp sting allergy when I was 20. A wasp zapped my neck and by the time I reached hospital they had to widen the door to get me in. To counter the swelling the doctor pumped adrenalin directly into my veins. It felt like running out onto Eden Park before a hundred thousand fans who loved me. I have spent the last 20 years deliberately vexing wasps.

But my new allergy is less agreeable. Indeed it is cruel. Indeed, I suspect that the President of the Immortals is toying with me. You see, I have always felt that youth isn't everything and that there are consolations to ageing. Youth may be the time of love and poetry but it also ignorance and acne. And though the medicines may proliferate in my bathroom cabinet and though stiffness may become a memory for everything except my joints, nevertheless there is much solace to be found in the years of decline. There's solace in siestas and silence, solace in sitting and watching, solace in not having to compete or pretend, solace in knowing and not fretting about my long catalogue of weaknesses, and an abundance of solace in the occasional glass of something bracing. But on this spring morning which is as pretty as youth, I discovered for sure and for ever than I am allergic to red wine.

A tale of two mice

Time passes and things change. And I find it is always the little things that tell the story best, that toll the gap between then and now. Little things like mice.

I remember with sunlight clarity waking on a sofa 20 years ago with a regulation hangover. The sofa was vinyl, the pillow a stinking cushion, the blanket a stiff and dust-drenched rug and the house a dump.

We called it Beirut. Friends rented it on the grim fringe of a huge city, amid streets where litter slapped the ankles and where children had shaved heads, feral eyes and mothers to whom chance had been cruel in every way and had scored its cruelty into their faces, their clothes, their body shapes.

But dawn reaches even such a suburb as this and even such a house as Beirut. It filtered down to this living room, this vinyl sofa, this rented temporariness and woke me. Unknown numbers slept upstairs, but I was alone below. The bladder was vocal, the throat scarified, the head like a stifled groan. Half awake I watched as the sun pierced the dirty windows, sidled across the room and lit a vast second-hand TV with an indoor aerial, a tubular chrome chair, a wrong-height table, and a mouse.

A mouse the same colour as the carpet. And I lay still to watch it. It was aware of my presence but not as a life form. I was furniture. I was terrain. It was alert but not nervous, a tiny suburban antelope on the carpet's Serengeti. I watched until the ache of the bladder became like a shriek of a saw on a nail and I had to get up. The mouse disappeared not when I moved, but at the exact moment when I decided that I would move.

By the time I had used someone else's toothbrush, drunk a pint of water and made an instant coffee (I was a hardened sleeper in other people's houses in those days and could find the coffee in any kitchen in the Western world) and returned to the vinyl and the rug, the day was dirtily under way and the mouse a memory, a dawn encounter that had felt like a strange privilege. A communion of sorts. Something tinily good. That, as I say, was 20 years ago.

The memory bubbled up last week because a woman sent me a mousetrap. She comes from Whangarei and the mousetrap from the United States. Kind Mrs Whangarei had heard me on the radio saying that I was battling mice.

I always know when there's a mouse in the house because the cat stares at the fridge. It can stare at the fridge for hours. Mice go behind the fridge because there they find house-crud. House-crud is hair and toenails, grease and crumbs. It gathers only in houses. You never come across house-crud in a forest. And while the mouse frolics in the crud the cat sits attent with its tail wrapped around its base like a draught excluder.

Across the back of the fridge there's a sort of lattice. I can only guess at its purpose but to a mouse it's a climbing frame. During the night the mouse hillaries up the lattice and onto the roof of the world and finds bread and cheese. The bread's in a plastic bag, the cheese in a mousetrap. If the mouse goes for the bread it runs a slight risk of suffocation in the plastic bag. If it goes for the cheese it runs no risk at all. My mousetrap serves as a feeding station. The only mouse it ever killed was noticeably elderly and had the build of Buddha. I suspect it died of shock. Every other morning I have found a bare trap, ravaged bread, a dandruff of droppings and the cat still staring at the Kelvinator.

Until, that is, Mrs Whangarei sent me her dread engine. It is called

The Better Mousetrap. I presume that the factory that made this trap is easy to find because the world will have beaten a path to its door. The trap is made of grey plastic, admirably simple in design and as touchy as a feminist.

I baited it last night and went to bed. In the morning the cat was asleep on the sofa. On the floor a blob of mouse innards. On the fridge a triggered mousetrap. In the mousetrap a spread mouse. Its back-end looked like the ragged muzzle of a blunderbuss. Or like Beirut. The mouse had not had time to assume a look of surprise.

And it seems to me that these two stories, in their every detail, illustrate more clearly than anything else I could write, the gap between youth and middle age.

White rectangular domestic things

Glory be to God for dappled things, said Gerard Manley Hopkins, going on to sing a hymn of praise to feathers on a thrush's chest and speckles on a trout. And that's just fine by me. I like those things a lot, or quite a lot, or somewhat anyway. But though I'm happy for the thrush and trout, as far as I'm concerned it's glory be to God for white rectangular domestic things. You know the things I mean, the tomb-like metal boxes coated in enamel by a process I can only guess at, the boxes that stand mute and patient round the house, the things we notice only when they go kaput and then because they very rarely do. I mean the washing machine. I mean the stove and tumble-drier, and, most glorious of all the glories owing unto Him on high, the fridge. They also serve who only stand and hum.

The fridge is loyal and steadfast as a dog that doesn't need to go for walks — although admittedly in one of Owen Marshall's lovely stories there's a fridge that wanders through a farmhouse kitchen, driven by its lurching motor, cubical and android and tethered by a leash of brown electric cable, but even then it's not a threat to flesh, just idiosyncratically quaint.

My own fridge never wanders. For fifteen years I've fed it with a tiny quantity of lifeblood from the national grid and in exchange it's kept its faith with me. It may have come, I don't recall, with densely worded guarantees protecting me from shoddy workmanship, but if it did that guarantee has long since disappeared and rotted in some unremembered place, and all the while the fridge has chuntered on, a self-containing cube of chilliness, a geographic region in itself, distinct and unaffected by the vagaries of weather in the world beyond. Somehow, unlike the other stuff about the house, it doesn't seem to gather dirt. For though I never run a cleaning cloth about its walls, it stands amid the squalor like a virgin in a brothel.

For sure appalling crud collects beneath it, stuff that's greasy brown and sticky, stuff that takes a day of scrubbing with a brush to shift — or 30 seconds' licking from a dog — but to blame the fridge for that would be to lay the blame on Downing Street for sheltering Tony Blair.

It's got no catch upon its door. I don't know how it does it but it opens with the application of a feather touch and it closes with a gentleness that couldn't hurt the fingers of the frailest child, and yet when closed it's sealed as surely as a sleeping eye. Not even that most daring of adventurers, the ant, can pierce the fridge's seal. The ant that undissuadably infests all places that it shouldn't, the ant whose six incessant legs will one day tread the earth in meek supremacy, the ant that feasts on scraps and dust and eyes of corpses, the ant that seeps through cracks as thin as hairs, the ant that dies unmourned in millions devoted to its species' greater good, the ant that can move boulders from its path and men to tears, can't penetrate my fridge's silent gentle seal.

A fridge is testament to men. By men I don't mean man in general, I mean men, specific men with names and families, men who over the long centuries have fathomed how to wrest a metal out of rock, who've somehow found the way to manufacture plastic, who've buried taps in trees and sauntered from the forest with a cup of rubber, who've harnessed electricity from lakes, who've played with brains and fingers to construct a motor that just goes on going on.

Yet I, though born and raised in the most technical of centuries, am capable of none of these extraordinary things. I take them as my due for being me. I sip the sweat that poured from others' brows and never give my deep dependency a second thought, reserving for myself the right to pout and sulk and squeal that I'm hard done by, that I fall upon the thorns of life and bleed, without acknowledging that I am blessed with ease and plenty and a fridge.

Why, even 50 years ago a fridge was rare as honesty. In those days milk went off and butter melted, a fish in summer lasted only hours and salmonella flourished. If summer food was to be tasted in the winter it had to be preserved and rendered sour with vinegar or salt, or boiled or pickled, dried or cured or sealed in great preserving jars like surgeon's specimens. Those ancient arts no longer matter much. The fridge has done them down.

So Gerard Manley Hopkins, Jesuit and poet, glory be to God for thrush and trout indeed, but I beg leave to add the fridge is cool.

Lotsadeadredindians

Nicols Fox has written a book called *Against the Machine* in which she puts the case against labour-saving domestic gadgets.

Some years ago her clothes-drier broke down and she was forced to peg clothes on a line. 'I discovered that the trip outside to the clothesline forced me to interact with the day in a new way . . . Now I hang clothes outside every day, even in the Maine winter.'

Ms Fox is especially harsh on dishwashers. She recalls her idyllic childhood in backwoods America — I forget the actual name of the place but Lotsadeadredindians will do — where 'my mother and grandmother and I used to wash the dishes together in the kitchen and we had a lot of really good conversations in the process. They passed along stories and lessons for life . . . washing dishes wasn't just washing dishes. It was a kind of event.'

For Ms Fox, the dishwasher not only discourages such intergenerational exchange but also 'robs you of the only interesting aspect of dishwashing which is how to get off that piece of cheese that's stuck to the plate'.

A bestseller in paperback, *Against the Machine* has now been made into a play. And in a scoop I present the first scene.

Location — a kitchen in a log cabin in Lotsadeadredindians.
Cast — Nicols Fox as a girl and Grandma Bristlechin.
Action — the dishes.
Grandma Bristlechin: Why look you here, my child.

Nicols: What is it, Grandmama?

Grandma Bristlechin: Just you look at that. Oh me oh my, if that ain't the most interesting piece of cheese I've seen stuck to a plate in many a long year I'll eat the rim off my stetson and boil the rest of it into an apple-pie for Thanksgiving.

Nicols: Grandmama, can I ask you a question in the interests of pursuing an intergenerational conversation?

Grandma Bristlechin: You go right ahead, my child, while I gets a-scraping with this here knuckle bone that's somehow become exposed through 103 years of washing dishes.

Nicols: What's menstruation?

Pause.

Nicols: Grandmama?

Grandma Bristlechin: What is it, my li'l potato dumpling?

Nicols: I asked you an intergenerational question in order to give you the opportunity to pass on a story or a lesson for life and you didn't say nothing, Grandmama.

Grandma Bristlechin: Well, bless me, my child. I guess I just got too carried away with this here interesting morsel of cheese.

Nicols: Grandmama, why was I given such a ridiculous Christian name?

Grandma Bristlechin: My, you're full of questions for a li'l girl. Any fuller and your freckles'll pop off and your dungarees bust and that's not something should happen afore the apples are safely in the barn and . . .

Nicols: Is this a story or a lesson for life, Grandmama?

Grandma Bristlechin: There you go again, child. Why not go ask your momma. She's outside at the clothesline interacting with the day.

Nicols: But Grandmama, there's three foot of snow on the ground.

Grandma Bristlechin: Once a woman discovers pegging out there ain't no snowdrift in the whole of Lotsadeadredindians gonna put her off her daily interaction. But maybe by rights you should be fetching her in now afore she comes over all brittle again. *(Exit Nicols.)* Whoa, steady there, my child. What with all that energy of yourn you'll be a-tripping over the chain that's bound me to this sink for 103 years, the chain I do love so much I bless every li'l festering ulcer on my pretty ankle.

(Re-enter Nicols dragging her stiff blue mother whom she props against the dado.)

Nicols: Grandmama, what's a dado?

Grandma Bristlechin: There you go again, asking them questions of yourn. I swear there's more questions in you than there's crackers in that there weevil barrel.

Nicols: It's just the stage directions told me to prop Mother against it.

Grandma Bristlechin: Oh my child, move her this minute or she'll be a-dripping again and drenching the wainscotting.

Nicols (thoughtfully as she moves Mother to the larder): Grandmama, when I grow up I'm going to write a book and I'll become famous and rich and then I'll buy you a dishwasher and . . .

Grandma Bristlechin (snatching up her granddaughter and rubbing her fiercely across her chin until she draws blood): Now there'll be no more of that devil's talk from you, my child, or I'll be washing your mouth out with pork fat and sourdough, do you hear me? Where did you go learning them dirty words like dishwasher from? Why the dishwasher ain't even been invented yet and to tell the truth I ain't rightly sure it should be. Anyway I won't be having none under my roof, nor any of that clothes-drier business I heard you whispering about with young Jack Thimbleshift under the haybarn the other day. I'm onto you my girl, don't you worry.

Nicols wriggles out of Grandma Bristlechin's grasp and runs off stage right defiantly screaming, 'Clothes-drier, dishwasher, other labour-saving devices' while Grandma Bristlechin reaches calmly under the sink for her Smith & Wesson .303 and takes careful aim offstage. Curtain. Under the curtain a puddle forms as Momma thaws in time for Scene 2 in which Nicols begins to revise her position on gadgetry.

Land you can play with

Cold rain drilled the roof all day. I didn't notice when it stopped. Now, mid-evening, my duties done, I am horizontal on the sofa, head propped on a dirty cushion, a fat book on my chest. My dog has wrapped herself twice about the gas fire, singeing her belly-fur. The deep luxurious cocoon of winter.

There seems too much light at the window. I roll off the sofa, push back the blind. Snow. Dropping past the window in big, slow flakes. My heart lifts like a child's heart.

I have never believed that the Eskimos have eighty-seven words for snow. You need only one word. Snow. Listen to it. It sounds like snow.

Snow settles here perhaps twice a decade. It's the guest that visits rarely, surprisingly, and everywhere, in slippers. It takes a known landscape and makes it new.

And you have to be the first to defile it. I can no more resist snow than I can resist the best people. Boots, hat. My dog rises and stretches. She doesn't know what's beyond the door. She has seen snow only once before. A puppy then, she danced and snorted in it, unable to grasp the nature of the world new-made. I open the door and we stand at the threshold of the white world like two children. Like Adam and Eve.

She hesitates, sniffs the snow, advances into it and then we're off up the untouched road. As we climb I turn to look at the black wet marks of my boots and her paws and I think Robinson Crusoe. Then on to the hills.

Snow is land that you can play with. I toss a snowball. It hits a bush and disintegrates. My dog rushes to fetch it and cannot find it. I toss another. She jumps to catch it in the air, bites it and I hear her jaws clash. She sneezes and shakes her head and her body writhes with the game. I toss more and more. She leaps for each one, and bites through it.

The snow falls on my sweater and melts into black. It falls on her fur and stays white until she shakes it off. It is falling in big wet flakes. Further up the hill it forms miniature drifts in the grass. It bends the stems of ragwort, the brushes of broom. Though my hands are numb I cannot resist its texture. I throw snowballs at fenceposts. I strike the branches of trees and then scamper backwards out of the mini-blizzard, shaking myself like a dog.

On the hills deep silence, a giant muffling. I think that I can hear the snowflakes landing. And underfoot the stuff squeaks. Through the cloud the moon shows phosphorescent-oily. The snow won't let the light sink into the land. It tosses it back and gleams. The hills are sharp-edged.

I stop to look down over the white roofs of Lyttelton. I can hear children emerging to squeal and slide and fall and cry. The snow is a better and more unexpected gift than Christmas.

Over a fence and a ridge and then down the side of a silent valley to visit my old dog's grave. I've piled rocks there. I don't disturb their cap of snow. I stand a while. The wet has seeped through my boots, soaked my socks, is starting to numb my toes. I don't much mind. The feeling is as memory-laden as a smell.

The snow has stopped. I urge it to start again. Going back down the hill my boot whips out from under me and I am suddenly heavily on my back. Jarred. Up-ended like a circus clown. Snow's anarchic, a worldwide banana skin. It sends trucks slewing, sends wheels spinning suddenly useless. With heavy slow insistence it breaks our cables, saps our power, defeats us, makes us fools.

I am not hurt. Snow tossed me over but broke my fall. I lie a while. My dog waits with animal patience. At the foot of the path a house. Guests are leaving. The open front door glows golden like a Christmas card. Voices are excited by the snow. 'Be careful now. Be careful.' The snow magnifies the sound, reflects it as it reflects light. I put my dog on the lead. There's a puppyish zest in her.

While we've been up the hill a mass of people have trodden the road, all doing as we've done. The snow is soiled and ruined slush. Past a house where a neighbour sits with his son. They have double glazing, never draw their curtains. They are watching television.

Rain starts to fall, pitting the snow. In the morning it will have gone.

Dreams on wheels

My mother drives a hatchback. It's the sort of car in which you have to press the throttle to find out if the engine's running.

Two months ago my mother was taking me for a drive when a sports car overtook us. It was a sixties MG, all bucket seats and adolescence revisited. Like all sports cars it was designed to appeal to men too old to play sport.

As the MG passed, my mother sighed. 'Oh,' she said, 'I'd just love one of those.' My mother is seventy-nine. Naturally I was appalled.

I had thought my mother immune to whim. She belongs to a

generation that did not indulge itself. Women like her wore printed cotton frocks and devoted their lives to rearing large families on carbohydrates and a single income.

To learn that even my mother could lust in secret for a car, underlined a truth of affluent society. Every vehicle is a wheeled aspiration. Every vehicle reflects its owner.

Most young men want a motor bike. A motor bike equates to freedom. It is the horsepower that snaps the apron strings, the oyster-knife that shucks open the world. It is wind in the hair and a throb between the legs. Whether or not a young man gets a motor bike depends on how much his parents dislike him.

My own motor bike was a moped. It went up hill quite well if you pedalled it. I loved that bike. I used to sing on it. I sang songs rich with adolescent grief or adolescent rapture. I bellowed my new-found manhood to the overarching sky. Once I swallowed a wasp. It made me crash. I had no excuse for my other crashes.

There are three ways to stop riding motor bikes. One is to do yourself damage. Another is to grow up. The third is to yield your motor bike to the police. I took the third option. As a result I missed the next phase of motorised life — the young person's car.

Young people drive heaps or phalluses. The heap is cheap, is poverty on wheels. It has rust, and vinyl, and keyless entry through the rear passenger window. You can sleep in a heap, or have sex in it, or tell lies about having sex in it. The heap is yesterday's car for tomorrow's people.

The phallus is tomorrow's car for today's hooligans. It's an enclosed motor bike. Based on designs for Apollo XVI its bonnet is longer than its passenger cell. It has fat tyres, gulping air intakes, a boombox, a fiercely farting exhaust and a spoiler at the back. The spoiler is named after the parents who paid for the car.

But the bike, the heap and the phallus are just rungs on the ladder towards middle age. Middle age is compromise and so is its car. That car is a saloon. It's the motorised equivalent of clothes from Farmers. Though manufacturers take pains to promote the differences between saloons, the whole point of them is their similarity. Practical, sensible and dull as a suburb, saloons refuse to poke their heads above the parapet of conformity.

But there are alternatives. Those who have encumbered themselves with a vast brood forsake even the aerodynamic hints of a saloon. They acquire a people-carrier. It's a nine-seater semi-bus. It battles through the wind towards the future. The people-carrier announces to the world that the owner has surrendered all claim to independent personal life.

More assertive is the four-wheel-drive all-terrain recreational vehicle. Rectilinear and butch, it resembles a shipping container on stilts. The owner still wants to compete. On the front a monstrous pair of bullbars to scatter rampaging herds of supermarket trolleys.

Beyond the all-terrain butchness comes the executive smoothness. Smug as a bank account, sleek as a suit, it glides from home to office, climate-controlled, equipped with everything, a motorised Switzerland, self-contained, neutral, unassailable, purring with pleasure at itself.

But all is vanity and in the end the king of the road is time. Time makes people old and as they grow old they shrink. Their cars shrink with them. They shrink to those strange elevated narrow cars. They shrink to hatchbacks.

So when my mother said she yearned for a sports car, I gawped. I had never dreamed that she dreamed. But magnanimity is everything. 'Mother dear,' I said, 'old age should do as old age wishes. Mortgage the house, squander my inheritance, scour the country for a pink MG and scandalise the neighbours. Set the net curtains twitching and the tongues aclack. You are only old once. Follow your dreams. Buy that car.'

My mother looked at me. 'But I couldn't get in or out of it,' she said. So all, in the end, was well.

At two drunks swimming

As any safety enthusiast will tell you, drinking and swimming don't mix. And as any drunk will tell the safety enthusiast, nuts.

The safety wallah will say that out of every thousand drunks who go swimming, one drowns. The drunk will say that he's never seen a thousand drunks swimming.

Anyway, there were only two of us, so it was a statistical near-certainty that the drunk who drowns was still in the pub. Well, actually, there were four of us, if you include the dogs, and we did.

The trip to the bay was the barman's idea. My other excuses are that I was drunk, that my dog likes swimming, that I like swimming with her, that it had been a hot day, and that it was midnight.

The problem with a hot day is that it doesn't happen at midnight. A southerly had risen. The waves were a couple of feet tall and fringed with cream. But we were committed, and the dogs were exultant.

The barman stood on the rail of the jetty in his trendy swimming togs. I stood on the bottom step of the jetty in my sky-blue Warehouse underpants. The barman finished his cigarette, tossed it into the sea in a glowing arc and followed it. I finished my cigarette, tossed it into the sea in a glowing arc and stayed where I was.

The coolest man I ever saw was standing on the high board above a French swimming pool, smoking. He had the body of a decathlete. People were looking up at him. He knew they were looking up at him. When he neared the end of his cigarette he wrapped his tongue round the filter, withdrew it into his mouth and dived. Then he surfaced, rolled onto his back, unfurled his tongue and carried on smoking.

From the water the barman called his dog. The dog is young, loyal and stupid. While I stood admiring the goosebumps on my arms, it bounded past me and launched itself. Dogs dive badly. They start paddling before they hit the water. And they land on their bellies.

The smack when the dog hit the water made me wince. The dog did not wince. It was away, black and happy in the black water.

I was not away. I called to the swimming barman to count down from three. On three, I crouched. On two, I breathed in. On one, I swung my arms back. On go, I stood up again. The barman said something provocative. I dived. The water was surprisingly warm. My sky-blue Warehouse underpants came off.

My dog appeared beside me, her legs frantic under the water. She snorts as she swims, but she can swim for miles. I can't.

All females float. Nine out of ten white males float. I am the tenth. If I lie still in water I sink. Apparently most black men sink too. I suppose that is why you see few black swimmers in the Olympics.

At the same time, you see lots of black runners. The conclusion to draw, I suppose, is that if you're a white man being chased by a black man, you should head for water. If you're a black man being chased by a white man, run. And if you've got one white parent and one black parent, you should be fine.

I didn't suppose all this at the time. I was trying to swim towards a raft anchored in the middle of the bay. It went in and out of view with the waves. I got mouthfuls of salt.

I lost my dog behind a wave and I worried about her. Then I felt a twinge of cramp in my calf and I worried about me. The raft seemed a long way away.

I hate seaweed. When it slithers against my chest it reminds me of the depths of black water below. I do not like to be so reminded. I can think of few deaths worse than drowning. People say that your life passes in front of your eyes. Perhaps it does, but with water in my airways I doubt if I'd sit back with popcorn to watch it. Anyway, I've seen it before.

People also say drowning is peaceful. I don't know how they know. And of all the opposites of peaceful, one of the most emphatic is having water in your airways.

I veered towards the shore. I couldn't see my dog, or the barman's dog, or the barman, or any pleasure in what I was doing. I wanted solidity under me. I was fighting the water and panic.

I heard barking and saw my dog on the path above me. That made the last ten yards easy. I hauled myself onto the rocks like something primeval evolving. My dog fussed about me. I picked my way along the gravel path towards my clothes, naked, teeth chattering like a typewriter, acutely aware of being Lear's 'poor bare forked animal'.

The barman had swum to the raft and back.

'Great, wasn't it,' he said.

I said I'd been scared.

'Yeah,' he said, 'great, isn't it.' And I had to admit that it was. Afterwards. Scared is good, afterwards.

A cup of Eros

There are two things you should do with coffee: drink it, and give thanks for it.

And there are two things you shouldn't do with coffee: boil it and do research into it. For coffee is a good thing and there are few enough good things in this world and we should leave those good things alone.

But now some people have done research into coffee. I use the word research loosely, but not half so loosely as I use the word people. These people are intrusive, lab-coated, myopic, killjoy, thwarted pseudo-scientists. Some of them are necrophiles with bad breath. The rest are less appealing. I could, if pushed, be quite rude about these people.

These people did their research (and you just know that they pronounce research with the stress on the first syllable, which is as sure a sign of depravity as using a Walkman) and they came up with findings. Researchers never just find things. Instead they come up with things, in the manner of the extraordinary man who recently stuck his head under water for six minutes and came up with a world record. When interviewed on television he said he felt ecstatic.

I don't know if the coffee researchers are capable of ecstasy. If they are I wouldn't like to see it. But I have seen the findings they came up with, and the nub of these is that coffee makes men, but not women, irritable.

Well, ha. It is seven in the morning. Beside me is a pint of coffee thick enough to hold the teaspoon upright. It is my second pint of the morning. And I am irritable. But to conclude from this scenario that the coffee caused the irritability is like concluding from a glimpse of a baboon that life in the jungle turns your buttocks purple.

The only reason I am irritated now, irritated to the point of incandescence, is that I have just read about this witless research.

I am not opposed to research. Research is merely curiosity, and curiosity will and should continue regardless of how many cats it kills.

But I am opposed to this particular research. I am not opposed to it because it makes women out to be more stable than men (though that, of course, is in tune with the ghastly zeitgeist), nor because it panders to a paranoia about what we eat and drink (though that, of course, is also in tune with the ghastly zeitgeist), but because its conclusion is wrong. It's as wrong as a Walkman. I can prove it. My evidence is me.

I run on coffee. I walk on coffee. I laugh on coffee. I play squash, chess and silly buggers on coffee. I am as addicted to coffee as I am to oxygen. And yet, as my dogs will verify, I am generally about as irritable as a nun on Prozac.

This research is simplistic nonsense. It implies that there are only two types of people, men and women. Drop a flat white into either, it suggests, and behold the consequences — a woman as serene as a floating wisp of summer cloud, a man so irritable that his buttocks turn purple.

The human being is a complex beast. Every ounce of serious research confirms this complexity. It confirms that the human brain is an underlit capital city and the researcher is a visually impaired tourist with a limp and no guidebook.

But not according to these researchers. For them the human being is as predictable as a slot machine. Into the man goes the caffeine and out of the man comes the irritability.

And as a result, say the researchers, men at work should refrain from coffee. It makes them less co-operative. Instead the men should cluster co-operatively round the gulping, farting water-cooler. Oh, spare us.

Has none of these researchers ever had a tough afternoon over his test-tubes, taken a break, poured himself a coffee, sipped at its muddy beauty, felt every muscle in his body sigh and expelled from between his hideously bearded lips a long slow aaaahhh of relief, releasing into the patient air every bitterness, every frustration, every ounce of the perilous stress-making stuff that weighs upon the heart? Presumably not. So he doesn't understand that coffee is magic. It is good and necessary magic, consoling magic in a spiky world.

And magic is perilous stuff. The researchers are fools to fiddle with it. For evidence I offer the myth of Psyche.

Psyche had a lover. His name was Eros. She did not know his name. He came to her every night after the sun had set and he left before it rose. In the intervening darkness he made love to her with an intensity that left her sighing with pleasure, radiant with pleasure, floppy with pleasure, as if, indeed, she'd just drunk three flat whites.

But pleasure wasn't enough for silly Psyche. One night she set a lamp beside her bed. When Eros came and did his stuff once more then fell asleep in her arms, she leant carefully across and lit the lamp so as to do research on her lover. A drop of hot oil fell on Eros's shoulder. He woke and he fled. And he never came back.

When your turangawaewae crumbles

For seven years the table stood on the deck. And for much of those seven years my dog stood on the table. From there she could watch the world pass by, and bark at it if it looked threatening.

The table was not an outdoor table. It was an indoor table that I had stolen from a former place of work. I stole it by accident but I kept it by design. I kept it because my dog liked it.

It was a ponderous thing that was never going to make it onto *Antiques Roadshow*. Its legs were not turned. Its top was an inch thick. Its joinery was crude. And it took seven years to die, seven years of rain and sun and frost and sometimes an inch or two of snow. The death was fun to watch, in a slow-fun way. The underside of the table top stayed the colour of timber. The topside turned the colour of a corpse. And ever so slowly, glacially slowly, the planks that made up the table top shrank and separated and began to buckle. Shortly before it died the table looked like greyly frozen sea.

My dog didn't mind. She continued to lie or sit or stand on it and bark at distant poodles.

Then a couple of months ago the table collapsed. I saw it happen. My dog stood up on it to bark and the table underneath her tottered. One joint gave way. That threw the load onto the other joints. They yielded one by one in accelerating succession. The table folded in on itself. It went down like a camel kneeling. It was the moment towards which seven patient years of weather had led. It was the inevitable climax, the tipping point, the point at which the forces of construction lost and the chaotic world won. Here was entropy in action.

My dog was unimpressed by entropy in action. She jumped off the toppling table and ran to me for succour. Her turangawaewae had crumbled. We all need succour when our turangawaewae crumbles.

I left the heap of wooden rubble where it lay. I liked the anguished silent randomness of it. I liked the way it sat in distinction to the straight lines of house and deck. But I felt sorry for my dog. She needed a place to see the world from. So after a week I built her one.

I measured major pieces in the pile of rubble and sketched a design in my head and drove to the timber merchant's. It was a daunting place. The men there had trailers on their utes and could reverse them. And they spoke about wood in a dialect I didn't understand. But a man with shorts and forearms took pity on me and spoke in English and redesigned my table plan and sold me the timber I needed and several tools I probably didn't. They included an electric drill. I'd always wanted an electric drill, but never found the excuse to buy one.

In the showroom was an outdoor table. It cost less than I had spent.

I am no carpenter, but I made a frame and it was almost square. I nailed the planks of my table top onto it and they held firm. I cut four legs and turned the table top upside down and screwed three of the legs into place so that they stuck up like the legs of a dead cow in a river. I screwed brackets inside the legs to hold them firm as the man in shorts had told me to. I put more screws in than I needed to because the drill had been expensive.

It was a chore to keep swapping drill bit for screwdriver head, so I stopped drilling holes. I just leant on the drill and drove the screw home. If the screw heads protruded I tapped them in with a hammer.

The fourth leg was a problem. My legs were not quite the same length. Nor were their ends quite square because I didn't have a tool to square them with. I thought a bit and then I turned the table the right way up, slotted the fourth leg into the frame, adjusted it until it touched the ground then held it in place with a couple of short nails. I followed the nails with a dozen long screws. Or at least I meant to. After five screws the drill screamed and smoked and died. I substituted nails for the remaining screws. Great big nails.

I shook the table. It stood firm. I decided not to lay a spirit level on it. I stepped back from the table and admired it. The fourth leg was a little askew, but I didn't mind. It had an honest look. I coaxed my dog to climb onto the table. She obeyed with caution. Then she sat down on the table. I sat on it too. I put an arm around my dog. Together on our turangawaewae we looked out on the world, defying the silent forces of entropy, and ready to bark.

Between us and dust

Otorohanga (pronounced 'North Island town of no account') has become a town of some account. It has appointed itself the capital of Kiwiana. The locals have bedecked their humdrum main street with giant versions of the things that make this country this country. It is a parade of predictabilities. There are sheep and kiwifruit and pavlovas and jandals and sheep. But apparently the tourists — that vast tribe of the bored who long for their holidays to end so they can go home and tell the neighbours how much they didn't want their holidays to end — flock.

In Otorohanga the English tourists can gawp at their own sheep, the Australians at their own dessert, the Chinese at their own gooseberries and the Japanese at their own footwear. For the jandal, that local institution, is as Kiwi as ju-jitsu.

In Great Britain the jandal's a flip-flop, in North America it's a thong, but in Japan it's simply what they've been shuffling around in since they first pushed rice into mud.

The very word jandal admits as much. It's a contraction of Japanese sandal. For confirmation I looked it up in the *Oxford English Dictionary* — not, I should point out, the *Shorter OED*, nor yet my old pal the *Concise OED*, but rather the granddaddy *OED*, the big one, the compendious everything of the most widespread language in the world, the twenty-volume took-a-century-to-compile *OED*. And there between Jan (January, abbrev.) and Janders (jaundice, colloq. obs.) I found, well, nothing. The *OED* doesn't recognise the jandal. But you do and I do, and so does the rest of the world.

For the jandal is a global thing. It is the world's cheapest footwear. From the steaming trash heaps of Sao Paolo to the teeming brothels of Bangkok, the jandal puts half an inch of foam rubber between the dominant animal species and the dust he sprang from.

And in the forty or so years since the leather sandal of Japan turned into the universal sandal of summer, it has evolved. Today the shelves of the Warehouse offer jandals with inch-thick soles, with contoured soles, with soles of little nipples. There are flowered jandals, velcro jandals, see-through jandals, jelly jandals. And none of these are jandals. They are too fancy. The true jandal is as minimalist as Japanese gardening.

It is a sole and a strap. The sole has an off-white veneer. The underside is anaemic blue or anaemic red. So is the strap. That strap is stamped with a crude motif and is held in place by three little plugs. And that's it. The lot. The jandal.

It's the shoe you're wearing when you're not wearing a shoe. It cannot be worn with socks except by holidaying bureaucrats and a toothless man I sometimes fish with. The jandal will carry you across blistering sands and melting asphalt. It is amphibious. It floats. It can be shed in an instant. It makes a serviceable door-wedge, an outstanding fly-swat and a fine noise against a fat thigh.

Running in jandals is a perilous art. Gripping the sweaty sole requires the toes of a gibbon. Few of us have the toes of a gibbon. Sooner or later the tip of the sole of a running jandal catches on the ground and curls back on itself and your impetus pulls the plug through the sole.

When you sit up and dust yourself down you find a flap of skin hanging from your big toe and the remains of your jandal hanging from your ankle. And that's that. The jandal is finished. Once the plug has pulled through, it will pull through again. You can push it back in, but for ever afterwards you will be walking on treachery. It is time to toss the jandal, walk barefoot to the beachfront store and part with another $1.95. But that's easier to write than to do.

For an old jandal is like a familiar lover. One side of the sole is still as fat as a steak, but the other has worn as thin as a slice of ham. The thing slopes as you slope. At the heels and the toes the white veneer has disappeared so it looks like a footprint in blue sand. The straps have moulded to a bulge in the shape of a heart, a heart that fits your foot and yours alone. To toss this out is an amputation. And what you're amputating is the best of your past. For you wore that jandal when the weather was warm and you were free and things were simple. Trashing a jandal is like burying a songbird of summer. Even in Otorohanga.

Hello, heat

Heat's back. Hello, heat. Laden with steam and indolence it swung down yesterday from the waistband of the globe, dumped its wet on the Alps then came to my house. It came like an oven-door opening.

I drew the blinds. The heat laid siege, slowly. It seeped through the cracks and went everywhere and stayed. It occupied the middle and the corners. It filled the space under my desk, made my feet slide on my jandals. It turned the dog's water bowl on the deck to the temperature of blood. It killed insects and sprinkled the water with the corpses. They floated like tiny screws of paper, wispy, spent, burnt.

My dog has a black fur coat. In the heat she was like Trotsky in Mexico. Unlike Trotsky she couldn't shed her coat. The air heated her up, flopped her down, opened her jaws and tweaked out her tongue. The heat drove her under the house and pushed her over onto her side, panting.

Down below in the port it made windscreens into fireflashes. It made vinyl car seats screamingly untouchable. It made supermarket bags pudgy.

I am a cool climate man. I don't mind warmth. But warmth isn't heat. Warmth is a kindness. Warmth says do. Heat says don't.

Hot countries are poor countries. Samoa is poor. El Salvador's poor. Sudan is very poor. In hot countries they put on long white cotton shirts and sit down. They sit in the shade with a hat and a beer and patience. Sit it out. Try not to bother. Sit it out. Heat bleaches and saps. Bleaches the land, saps the will.

At twenty-one I went teaching in Spain and met heat for the first time. It was heat like brass. I didn't know what to do. I didn't know to do nothing. I flitted from shade patch to shade patch. I taught in the Spanish summer as I would in a Danish winter. I taught till the sweat darkened the crotch of my trousers, till my neck boiled with boils.

The fan in my classroom broke down one morning. I was teaching six middle-aged women. They conferred, then took pity. They took me away to an underground bar and fed me beer and a cold omelette. They taught me fretlessness. It doesn't matter, said the women. Today it is hot. That is all it is.

The only hot countries that are rich are the countries with oil. They were poor countries for ever, but then the busy greedy pale men came from the cool places with equipment made of metal that grew too hot to be handled. The pale men drilled through the rock and laid pipelines, sucking the liquefied heat of the desert away to put feeling in the fingers of the north. The locals took the money and sat in the shade of their thick white walls to drink sweet tea and watch the pale men being busy.

Last year I went to Singapore. The heat there was wet. The air wouldn't take my sweat. It was too full. It was always an inch away from rain, sudden, brief and rampant rain that was warm and that drenched and then stopped. After it had stopped the island steamed. I hated all of it.

Yesterday I had to work. I worked badly, listless with heat. The keyboard was sticky. My head was torpid. Invention wilted. There was grit in the vees between my fingers. The desk fan skimmed ash from the ashtray. I gave up and drove the dog to the bay. The road ahead of us danced with black heat.

My dog ran into the water to shoulder depth then just stood there, reviving. One minute in water took a decade off her age. Cool again, she bounded through the wavelets like a spring-loaded puppy, like a lithe black dolphin.

Two women lay on their backs on towels, like starfish in bikinis, surrendering as if dead. Few men do that. I think some women are reptiles.

I swam with my dog. She snorts as she swims. I like to swim on my side to watch her legs working under water. Dogs don't really swim. Naturally buoyant, they just float and run. My old dog can swim for miles.

The soil of the path behind the bay was dried to talcum powder. The leaves of the sheltering trees, still pale green and spring tender, diffused the sunlight to something gentle. But you could sense the effect of the sun on them. You could sense them darkening, thickening, ageing. Two months from now they'll be leathery. Four months and they'll crackle underfoot.

Back home and the house was a vat of heat. I fed myself, fed my dog, then stripped and lay on my bed, sweating, riding it out.

Where do you go to?

Sleep's good, especially at Christmas, but going to sleep is better. I know nothing more delicious than sliding from wake into sleep. It's a letting go, a submission. You let slip the constructed self, the armour that you don each day to fight the world. As you fall asleep it slithers off as softly as a dress of silk. Even the hardest gang-man, the most shaven-headed, sex-tongued, greed-driven, hate-brimming, finger-jabbing, gun-stroking bully boy slides into softness each night, vulnerable as his own fraught psyche.

It's the journey into utter privacy, the time of most alone, like a hermit withdrawing deep into the darkness of the cave. And in the darkness up swims sleep. It's the oldest daily miracle.

How does it happen? How does the thug go to sleep? How do you? Do you count sheep? I doubt it. I have never met anyone who counts sheep. The conscious act of counting defies the rise of the mind that dreams.

I play cricket. Or rather every night I replay a little bit of cricket, a single moment that happened twenty years ago. I know exactly where the game was played. I can see the ground, the hedges that surround it, the long grass inside them, then the close-cut turf of the outfield half-bleached by the summer, the fresher green of the square, the mower's stripes, the pitch itself. Lying in bed, I can feel the sun of twenty summers ago on my forearms.

I am batting. A young man runs in to bowl. His shirt is flapping. He leaps at the crease and bowls. The ball is overpitched, a half-volley, juicy as a summer plum. The air is spangle-bright. I can see the gold lettering on the ball, the raised stitches of the seam. I lean forward, drawn to the ball with a sort of midsummer ease. My movement has the pace of flowing honey. Like honey it is sweet and simple. Body and bat are one.

The sound of the ball in the bat's heart is as rich as a church bell. No jarring. No sense of impact. It is like a caress, a channelling of affection, and the ball's direction simply reverses. The ball has come to me and then it has gone away from me as I have desired that it should. I haven't hit the ball, I have expressed it. It feels as natural and as languid as a dog's stretch, as a river's flow.

At a speed that surprises me the ball scuds across the turf as straight as the hand of a clock. Mid-off makes a hopeless dive at it. His floundering clumsiness occupies a different realm to the progress of the ball from my bat to the field's far edge.

I take a stride or two up the pitch, knowing I've no need to run but doing so for form's sake. The ball's speed, its impetus, is mine. I am attached to it as it travels. It owes its movement to me. Look, I did that.

Forty, fifty, sixty yards away now, and it is still running on the fuel I fed it through the simple arc and flow of my body and my bat. It crosses the boundary and plunges into the long and withered grass of summer, where it comes to rest, held by a mesh of tangled stems that binds it like a cradle. It's made a nest, like a small animal. I sent it there. And in my mind I join it there, in its nest of long grasses.

Its arrival upsets a tiny metropolis. It's the meteor that flattens New York. Ants, spiders, grasshoppers, a thousand insects I can't name, scurry for safety in the mulch of spent vegetation, frantic for the darkness and the rich moist soil. The ball waits. In my head I wait with it, waiting for the disturbance to subside in this miniature jungle.

Slowly peace returns. The spindly spider resumes its high-stepping progress through the stems, its arched legs as frail as its own gossamer. Ants go back to their co-operative business. Mites, woodlice and a million microscopic creatures re-emerge to scout and fossick through their tiny world. And I am among them, not moving, just seeing and being there, where no one cares or matters, where death is common and ordinary and regenerative and where no cricket scores ever penetrate, where no words are written, where no words exist, but where the endless web of brief and interdependent lives goes on going on. I sink into it. And as I sink the other self rises, the night-time self that can go anywhere with its strange alternative logic. I am asleep. Happy Christmas.

Nannies and billies

Ladies, would you like to meet men? If not, I don't blame you. But if so, come with me. I'll show you men. I'll show you a place where, as in the goldfields of Otago in 1860, men outnumber women by ten to one.

And these men aren't grizzled old miners with waist-length beards of sofa stuffing, men who lean scenically on shovels so that other miners can take sepia photographs of them to fill the museums of the future. No, these men are paydirt. They're nice modern men who wash and who apply under-arm deodorant just as the advertisers tell them to, so that they smell of rainforest. (Though rainforests, in my experience, actually smell of rotting vegetation and snakes, anacondas in particular. Anacondas stink. If you don't believe me, toddle down to the reptile house at your local zoo and have a sniff.)

Anyway, the men are nice men, and they're in a nice place. It's no Amazon jungle, this place, nor is it the nineteenth-century goldfield with huts and water-races and camel-coloured mud that can suck a boot off. No, this place is fluorescently lit, temperature-controlled, clean as an operating theatre and full of men. And stuff.

All sorts of stuff. Mushrooms, buttons, button mushrooms, washing powder (in which rainforest flavour is also available, so you can make your wardrobe smell like your armpits), baked beans, string beans, Lima beans, bean sprouts, beans from Africa, beans for Africa. It's a supermarket, ladies, and it's packed with men.

You shouldn't be surprised. Did you think it mere coincidence that the word supermarket is an anagram of sperm-u-krate? Yes, so did I.

But what you probably want to know is which supermarket. Which of the many supermarkets in Christchurch is the sperm-u-krate, awash with rainforest lovers? I shall tell you. Are you listening closely now? Are you intent? Are you keen and focused like an anaconda that has just spotted a goat?

Well, if so, beware. Goats are not indigenous to rainforests. Most rainforest goats are actually bait laid by snake-hunting German zookeepers. The idea is that the anaconda swallows the goat whole then settles into a post-lunch stupor. An anaconda is no sprint champion at the best of times, but with a goat inside it it can barely crawl. So all Herr Zookeeper has to do is amble up in his scoutmaster shorts and drop the snake into a hessian sack. No need even to feed it, there being already a captive goat to sustain it on the long flight to Düsseldorf.

But anyway, the supermarket. It's Woolworths. The big new Woolworths at Ferrymead. Go there at 8.30 on a Saturday morning and you'll find that the place is full of men. Bizarre but true. I've been there.

Last Saturday morning I watched the men. I didn't see a single shopping list. I didn't see a single dither. I didn't see a single man read a label or check for fat content. I saw only swift decisive movements, hunting raids, the bean tin seized and tossed into the trolley with the speed of a zookeeper bagging a snoozing snake. The trolley never stopped moving. These were men shopping with a purpose. That purpose was to finish shopping.

It was like Ruapuna with groceries. The more the men loaded the trolleys the faster they pushed them, partly because a loaded trolley corners better, but mainly because every item in the trolley meant they were one step nearer the chequered flag of the checkout and then freedom.

It was lovely. No foot-tapping waits behind aisle-blocking conversationalists. No squeezing past a woman scanning thirty-seven brands of identical pasta. No wayward steering. Only a silent masculine camaraderie of haste.

At the checkout, there were two men in front of me. Neither man flicked through a magazine backwards. As the groceries passed over the beeperscope neither man checked the prices on the little screen. And neither man seemed surprised to be asked to pay for his groceries. Both, indeed, were not only ready to pay, they were eager to pay. And of course, but of course, neither man wrote a bloody cheque.

No, each man was already swiping his discount card through the slot even as the checkout girl was asking if he had one. And each man answered the eftpos question about whether he wanted cash, even before it could be asked.

And having done the financial stuff, each man was already in position at the driving bar of the trolley, and moving off, when the checkout girl handed him the printout in the manner of a relay runner passing the baton. It was all so swift and wonderful.

So ladies, if you want to find men, men in abundance, responsible domestic men, try Woolworths in Ferrymead on Saturday morning early. But do so terribly carefully. You see — and I can't think of a nice way of putting this — I suspect that the men are at the supermarket at that hour of the day because, love you as they do, you aren't. So if you were to turn up in numbers, I think they'd smell a goat.

Nesting recruits

Friends of mine have just bought a house, poor darlings. I like them but I can't say that I like the house. Well, actually, I can say that I like the house. Indeed I have said that I like the house. I've said it several times and straight to their faces.

Were I a remotely honest man I would have said that the house was never a pretty thing and that anyway it had been buggered around beyond redemption by the previous owner. Someone had clearly given this man a hammer and chisel set for Christmas, and The Big Cheese, who is always fond of a practical joke, had chipped in by endowing him with an undissuadable belief in both his aesthetic judgement and his talent for carpentry. The results litter the house in form of chipboard shelves, an abundance of cupboards and a fence round the backyard that would baffle Escher. But have I said so? Of course I haven't. 'What a nice house,' I've said, and the new owners have gulped down the fib like starving Labradors. For one's first house is like one's first child.

They've got one of those too, only a month or two into its journey down the years, poor thing, and I can't say I've been completely frank about that either. The little critter's got about as much hair as I have, and a similarly battered-looking face, but that's where the resemblance ends. I'm as hungry for attention as the next man, but if you ignore me for three nano-seconds I don't crumple my face like a ball of wastepaper, writhe, bunch my fists, gather all my puny force into my lungs and emit a wail so potent that it would guide ships to safety in fog. That wail acts on every woman within a hundred yards in the same way as pheromones act on moths. Up to the cot they sprint like iron filings to a magnet, squabbling over the right to pick up and console the wizened little thing and offer it a one-sided conversation that begins with there there, moves through a forest of diddums, sweetypies and coochycoos and concludes with my departure in search of a bucket. Meanwhile the loveable little ball of wrinkles keeps the noise up for a bit, probably out of some instinctive presentiment that it's never going to have things this easy again. It's in the same position as a novice skier who's just been up the chairlift for the first time. With shaking knees the skier surveys the world and discovers that there's nothing ahead of him except seventy years of downhill horror.

And it's not just for junior that the future's downhill. Mumsy and Dadsy are rocketing in the same direction at a speed that's frankly appalling. Hitherto they've been rootless, profligate and very good fun, but now that they're building a nest those days are emphatically over. And roughly 50 per cent of them seem happy about it.

So are 100 per cent of their married friends, because these new recruits to the nesting classes have provided the old hands with the chance to get rid of stuff. A Niagara of unwanted and unwantable stuff is tumbling into the house from garages and lock-ups and spare bedrooms the length and breadth of Lyttelton.

It's a sort of reverse burglary. Everything that's cluttering up the houses of the established is being palmed off on the beginners. You should see the stuff. First came the furniture, tip-fodder every bit of it, broken-backed gloom upholstered in draylon, singing a song of suburban consumption that would make Leonard Cohen sound merry. And then came the other stuff, the small stuff. Teapots in the shape of chickens, spice racks, bent cutlery. Only this morning when I went round on request to bang a few 4-inch nails into the broken leg of a fifth-hand slat bed, a woman showed up at the house with a cardboard box. Inside the box was a fondue set with a flower pattern round its rim so indescribable that I'm not going to describe it. 'Can't bear to think of you trying to get by without one of these,' she said, more or less, then left at the speed of a city councillor leaving the back door of a brothel. Much of the stuff has already gone straight to the back of the DIY cupboards — God, you should see those cupboards, the design of them, the size of them, the sheer number of them — from which it will emerge only when some other poor sods get hitched and housed and sprogged, and my friends, now wise in the business of ownership, see the chance to pass it all on.

It's all too dreary to contemplate. I rang just now to see if hubby wanted to go for a possum hunt on the hills with the dogs and he said sorry, no, he was going, oh crikey dick, to Placemakers. To buy tools. It's all over. Ah well.

See me saw

There are tools, there are men's tools, and then there are chainsaws. A chainsaw is carnage on a stick. Whoever thought of the title *The Texas Chainsaw Massacre* could have stopped there. There was no need to make the film. Anyone could picture the pictures.

My neighbour is a manly man. He's got a chainsaw and I have coveted it. I have coveted it so hard I couldn't sleep. I watched him fell a tree last week. Brrrm, brrrm, yeeaow, crack, shudder, topple, BOOM. I find it hard to imagine a more manly sentence than that.

Having chopped the tree down the neighbour then chopped it up. Some time in the future the bits will turn into smoke and heat. Heat for nothing. I wanted free heat too.

My previous house had a gas fire. The gas came in chemistry-lab cylinders at $70 a pop which I didn't mind paying because I had no alternative. But my new house came with a log burner and I resented paying for wood. Wood is everywhere. The stuff grows on trees. I took to collecting driftwood from the beach and twigs from dog walks. But in the evening as I huddled round my twig heap I imagined my neighbour standing like an eighteenth-century squire with his back to a monstrous hearth, spreading his tailcoat to toast his buttocks, and I felt envy.

The solution to envy lay in the steep paddock behind my house where several trees had been felled and forgotten by the previous owner. Those trees were heat for the taking, heat for nothing.

Of the two assistants in the chainsaw shop, one was old and one young. When I stepped through the door they both recognised my manliness on the instant and raced to be first to make its acquaintance. The younger one won at a canter.

'I want a chainsaw,' I said, because that's how manly men talk. Terse, spare, emphatic.

'Good,' he said.

'Yes,' I said.

'What size?' he said.

'Big,' I said.

'Right,' he said and he rubbed his hands together in the universal sawyer's gesture indicating free warmth to come.

The chainsaw cost $1800. Protective chaps cost $200, steel-tipped boots $100, safety glasses $25, safety helmet $25 and banana-coloured ear muffs $20. The assistant also wanted to charge me $10 for a petrol can but I raised a manly eyebrow and he threw the can in for free. Most men just shop, you see, but manly men cut deals.

The chainsaw had a 25-inch bar. I liked that. Imperial measurements are manly. When I got the thing home the dogs barked at it. 'Good dogs,' I said, and donned my safety gear.

If you've ever carried a big chainsaw up a steep paddock wearing steel-tipped boots, helmet, glasses, ear muffs, a manly expression and a pair of chaps that seem to be made out of carpet, you'll know that it's warm work. You may also know that it's warm work walking back down a steep paddock to fetch the instruction manual.

The manual kicked off with forty-eight pages of safety instructions all of which I skipped apart from an amusing paragraph about the perils of white finger. Then page forty-nine explained that starting the engine was a simple business of depressing the compression valve, engaging the chain brake, squeezing the throttle trigger, adjusting the cotter pin spindle, calibrating the carburettor sprocket, then setting a steel-tipped toe into the handle of the chainsaw and tweaking the starter rope. And sure enough the mighty beast roared into life before you could say 'two pauses to demist the safety glasses and a mental note to self to ring the chiropractor'.

Stripping a trunk of branches proved entertaining. The chainsaw tended to seek out branches I wasn't aiming at. Then it would leap and roar like a stallion. 'Whoa,' I'd bellow in a manly voice, hoping that the neighbour would emerge to admire me. He didn't but it didn't matter. After little more than an hour I had stripped two yards of trunk. After that it was like slicing a giant salami. The engine roared, sawdust flew and a round dropped, neat as a hockey puck. I cut eight rounds then stilled the engine, laid the saw aside and just stood there, dripping sweat, sprayed with sawdust, my steel-tipped boots planted firmly on my own soil as the sun sank in the west. At my feet a pile of logs. In my heart a primitive satisfaction. I kicked a log. It rolled, gathered momentum, bounced like a tennis ball, cleared the fence, astonished a dog and crashed into the tin wall of the woodshed. The boom echoed round the valley and I felt good.

The logs lasted the whole evening.

The threshold of the ginge

I wish to propose a toast. On a Tuesday morning in snow-bound Lyttelton I am raising a glass with bubbles in it to the boffins of Louisville University, Kentucky. They are my US Cavalry. They may have arrived forty years too late to do my psyche much good, but I am still grateful. They have confirmed something that I have always known but that no one else has ever believed. I'm sensitive. I feel pain more than you feel pain. Now the boffins have revealed why. I'm sensitive because I'm a redhead.

I'm not a redhead any more. I'm a baldhead with wisps. But those wisps are the remnants of a head of hair that forty years ago was visible from space. It was the bane of my childhood. Goldlilocks, they called me, or Ginge or Carrot-top. As a child, if I wanted to hide from my mother at the supermarket I just burrowed into a display of oranges.

And I did want to hide from my mother because my mother wanted to take me to the dentist. As far as I recall, most of my childhood consisted of being dragged to the dentist, heels dug in like a recalcitrant puppy, wailing like a world-ranked professional mourner, and smelling faintly of oranges. I wailed and dug because the dentist hurt.

One family dentist was called Mr Wisher. I wasn't alone in dreading Mr Wisher. He was Victorian and brutal. His drill was operated by a bicycle chain that he wound with his spare hand. The waiting room door had a bolt on it.

But then we shifted to a twentieth-century dentist called Nice Mr

Mabberly. Nice Mr Mabberly gave anaesthetics and even asked what flavour you wanted. I always asked for strawberry and didn't mind the injection. But then he drilled and I did mind the drill. I minded because it hurt. 'Tut tut,' said my mother and Nice Mr Mabberly as they peeled me from the ceiling. 'It can't hurt. You've had an injection.' They were wrong. It did hurt. And now forty years on I know why.

'Redheads,' says Louisville University, Kentucky, and I'm quoting, 'need more local anaesthetic at the dentist than the general population.' And that's science. So suck on that, Nice Mr Mabberly. Suck on that, Mother (though I mean that in the kindest possible way).

The reason it hurt, according to the lovely boffins, is that carrot-tops have a special gene. It is Celtic in origin and it dictates that we have 'a lower pain threshold'. Bang right, boffins, and thank you. My pain threshold is subterranean.

At university I took up boxing. I did it mainly to prove to myself that I wasn't the wuss that everyone had told me I was because of my threshold. I impressed the trainer with my walloping of the punch bag and was the first of the novices to be given a bout. I can still remember my opponent. He was an aristo called Rupert. He had mouse-coloured hair. The bell rang and I hit Rupert. I hit him hard and repeatedly. Boxing was lovely and I was good at it. I was mentally lifting the world light-heavyweight crown, the cheque that came with it, and the label of 'wuss' from my shoulders, when Rupert hit me. He hit me on the side of the head and then on the nose and then on the side of the head again. 'Ow,' I said and then 'ow' and then 'ow'. Of course I should have hit Rupert back and I briefly considered doing so but it's difficult to hit someone when you've turned your back on him and covered your head with your hands. It's also hard to take aim when you're crying. I jumped out of the ring, went home and never came back. That night my pillow whispered 'wuss'.

It was the same with rugby. I liked rugby but I couldn't bear to be rucked. 'A little tickle-up with the studs', they called it. I called it excruciating. I would let people know it hurt. 'Wuss,' they said. 'Worse than wuss,' they thought. If only they'd known. If only I'd known.

In cross-country I used to get a stitch. A schoolmate who was good at running told me that the way to deal with a stitch was to keep running until it went away. Ha. Same as if you're stabbed on the way to work, the best thing to do is to carry on as normal. When I got a stitch I had no choice but to lie down in the mud like a dying lamb and bleat at the Great Ewe in the sky. 'Oi, Ewe,' I'd bleat, 'why me?'

How easy it would have been for the Great Ewe to tell me about my gene. But no. It took science to do that, as usual. Here's mud in your eye, Kentucky, and thank you.

Up Apophthegm Mountain

I'm a sucker for the big notion, the sort of thing you find in the *Dictionary of Quotations*. Give me an apophthegm like 'Life can only be understood backwards; but it must be lived forwards' or 'If you want to make God laugh, tell him your plans' and I'll swallow it whole and commit it to memory. For the next few days I'll also regurgitate it whole to anyone who'll listen. And a fat lot of good it does either of us.

For the grand notion never quite fits. It rings true in principle but it omits the detail that constantly muddies the picture, the sort of detail to which I woke this morning. Drizzle masked the hills, my nose was full of snot and I had a hangover that turned my head into the mental equivalent of television static.

I should have spent the morning working but instead I spent it reading the collected letters of a dead and gloom-drenched poet who lived, it seems, in perpetual drizzle. The letters are crammed with small stuff, stuff that mattered at the time but doesn't matter now, stuff like recalcitrant lawnmowers and the price of chops. But then suddenly he startled me with a nugget of big stuff. 'If my life were a week,' he wrote at the age of forty-eight, 'then this would be Friday afternoon.'

The words pierced the hangover and the snot and sank deep into the pink. Ooh, I said, with a delicious shudder of dread, and I laid aside the book.

For I too am forty-eight. I too am on Friday afternoon, and there's only the weekend to go. Oh golly gosh.

As for the week so far, well, all the important stuff happened on Monday, and I've forgotten the lot. It's all gone, all the stuff that dictated every subsequent event has shrivelled into oblivion. When I look back on Monday I see only a vague and sunny land of lala. Tuesday morning was more of the same, but then round about lunchtime up rolled puberty and the weather turned thunderous. There followed an intense afternoon of rich and self-indulgent despair, the air charged with threat and thrill. Nothing since has matched it. Wednesday I spent more or less drunk. Thursday was industrious, energetic and stable. And then came Friday. Friday proved surprising.

Early on Friday I went back to the land where I was born and caught up with old friends from school and university, all of us the same age. And I found myself moving from crisis to crisis. It was as if a switch had been thrown in every male head. Stable Thursday lives had suddenly turned into Friday chaos. Husbands of model diligence had eloped with feather-headed long-legged secretaries. Sensible stockbrokers who slept in ironed pyjamas had fled to the hills to be potters. Everywhere I went, careers were in abeyance and marriages were rubble.

Rather than being a holiday visitor, I became an itinerant counsellor, a shoulder for weeping on, a receptacle for the big questions. I enjoyed every minute of it. And the synchronicity of it fascinated me. It was as if everyone had woken independently to the awareness that this was Friday morning, that the peak of the week had passed and that if a life was ever going to amount to anything it had better start amounting now. It was a subconscious crack of the existential whip.

I saw most of the wayward ones again this year. They'd mostly settled back down. Marriages were patched, careers resumed, and everyone had snuggled down to a Friday afternoon snooze amid the welter of small stuff.

And that in the end is what's wrong with the grand notion. It's all very well to clamber up Apophthegm Mountain to take in the big picture, the tour d'horizon, the great sweep of things, but all too soon it's time to return to the place we belong, down among the small stuff.

All other life forms have the instinctual good sense to stay down there the whole time. You don't see ants wandering off to become painters or to have a final fling before the loins wither into silence. They simply keep on keeping on.

My aged dog has just lain beside my chair. She's twelve years old, which in dog terms is Sunday lunchtime. She neither knows nor cares. Food and hunting and other dogs still interest her, and that will do. The big stuff is a uniquely human interest and it doesn't get us far.

'We are unsuited,' wrote the same gloom-laden poet whose letters I was reading, 'to the long perspectives open at each moment of our lives.' However neat and appealing it may seem, the grand notion, the vision of one's life as a week, is less significant in the end than a hangover, snot, drizzle, a recalcitrant lawnmower or the price of chops.

Ah, winter

Ah, winter. You know how it is. Committed carnivore that you are, you eye the lamb leg in the supermarket chiller. It's on special. It's been stripped of its wool. It's been strapped by cellophane to its cradle of foam, foam designed to absorb any blood it might ooze so that we should not be offended. Beneath its stretched vellum of skin the purple muscle gleams with meaty promise. You stretch out an arm, so similar in design, and you grip the leg — oh, the sheer nutritional bulk of it, the brute indulgence — and you dump it into the basket. Your hunting is done for the day.

Back at the electrically run cave the rest is easy. Slivers of garlic? Forget them. Sprigs of rosemary? Forget them. Orange slices, olive oil, all fanciful stuff, forget the lot. Just strip the cellophane and foam and lay the limb without ceremony on the rack of the baking tray. The rack is vital. Everything else is a frippery.

Temperature? Ha. I don't know why ovens have dials. All things cook fine at 170. For how long? It doesn't matter. Two hours is good. Three hours is just as good. Four hours may be better. I don't know. I can't wait four hours. I want. After an hour the house is misty with lamb smell. That's the hors d'oeuvre.

But first you must spud. Spuds are essential. And spuds are easy. Get big spuds and cut them small. You can oil and salt the pieces if you like. It makes no difference. Into the other oven tray they go. Make sure there are too many. You can't have too many. Nor can you cook them too long. They take exactly as long as the meat takes. You want them cooked till the guts have shrunk. The guts of a spud are dull. The roasted exterior is cellulose made joy. (It may not be cellulose. I don't know. Neither do I care. I just eat.)

You're supposed to have another vegetable. I have gravy. Gravy is the best vegetable. I used to fear gravy. There is no need to fear gravy. A woman cured me of gravy-fear. The books are all wrong, she said. Here's what, she said. And I still do her what. It doesn't fail. It can't fail.

The house is fragrant with lamb. The dogs are clamped to the kitchen floor directly beneath the oven. You open the door of the oven to check your bounty. You don't look through the glass of the oven door because you can't look through the glass of the oven door. It is opaque with the great roasts of last winter.

The heat blast is like re-entry. It threatens to peel the skin from your face. You peer at the spuds. They are tan and glistening with hints of black. They have withered and shrunk. You wonder whether your too many will prove enough. But they are ready. So the meat is ready.

Extract the lamb leg on its rack. Say no to the dogs, say down. The skin has mummified, shrivelled to crispness. Don't pick at it. Resist, resist, resist. Lift the meat off the rack and lay it on a plate.

The base of the oven tray is a charred mess. Drown it. Drown it in water too hot to touch. Lots of it. Then swizzle it with something — a fork, a pencil, it doesn't matter. Dissolve the charrings. Tip the hot and peaty fluid into a saucepan. Add precisely one fistful of flour. Lots of salt. Lots of pepper. Turn up the heat to fierce. Boil it. Boil it till it froths. And stir as it froths. Stir like a crazy thing, with fork, with spoon, with pencil, though not with a whisk because you haven't got one and don't need one, just as you haven't got checked trousers and a tall hat and a white jacket that's hard to distinguish from one of those garments with which they used to hamper lunatics.

Turn off the heat. Let the gravy sit. It ought to simmer, but you don't know how to simmer. Who cares? You don't.

Carve the meat. How doesn't matter. Simply hack off the very best bits. They will never be as good again. Have them now. This is your rainy day. Any gristle, any fat, just toss it to the dogs. Spread the joy. We'll all be dead soon. Like lambs.

Smother the plate with hot meat. No china should be visible. Smother the meat with hot gravy. No meat should be visible. Tip on the spuds, an Etna of charred spuds, brittle, baked, withered. See the plate smoke.

Lug the plate to wherever you eat. Table, sofa, floor, study. The dogs will come too. Crush the spuds. Meld them with gravy. Eat. Give one dog the smeared plate, the other the gravy saucepan. Watch their tails. Ah, winter.

Hello again

I hadn't seen him for 35 years and of late I hadn't thought about him much so I didn't expect to meet him. And I certainly didn't expect to meet him in my hotel bathroom. Indeed I don't expect to meet anyone in my hotel bathroom because I haven't got a partner and hotels don't admit dogs.

They ought to, of course, and they probably would if I was Paris Hilton and Baz was portable. But Baz is about 35 kilos beyond portability, and I'm about the same number of kilos and rather a lot of biology beyond being mistaken for Ms Hilton.

Hotel bathrooms are strange places. There's a year's worth of towels and they're white. I don't know why. At home I use dark towels. One towel lasts me two months because I can't see anything wrong with it. With a white towel you can immediately see everything wrong with it.

There's also a little notice in the bathroom these days. It engages you in cosy eco-chat. 'Can you imagine,' it says, 'how many hotel towels are washed every day around the globe? This causes lots and lots of horrible pollution and kills all the cuddly creatures and destroys the planet. Unfortunately, NASA hasn't found us anywhere else to live yet, so if, treasured guest, with the generosity and eco-sensitivity for which you are rightly renowned, you could see your way to using a towel twice before biffing it, you will have made a huge contribution to the survival of the planet and there will be no more suffering anywhere ever again. And we'll have saved a few bob. Though of course, if you do choose to biff the towel after a single rub of your celebrated flesh, we'll wash it in the most ferocious detergents we can find, slaying beasties by the billion as we do so, and all in the abundant spirit of happiness with which we at the Treatubest Hotelcorp serve all our treasured guests.'

The word guest is a lie. Guests are invited, whereas you've bought your way into the room. But lies come standard in hotels. There's often one round the toilet seat. It's printed on a strip of paper and announces that this facility — and don't you just love that term? — has been sanitised for your protection. Call me an inveterate risk taker, but I've never felt threatened by toilets. I've been astonished by some and rendered nauseous by a few — including a cracker that consisted of . . . but you may be eating breakfast so I'll say only that the pigs were plump — but I have never felt in need of being protected from toilets. And I'm not being protected. I'm merely being reassured that, as one would hope, a maid on the minimum wage has had a go at the nastier stains with the hedgehog on a stick.

Hotels like to provide what they call the personal touch. These are generally about as personal as a letter from the IRD. The chocolate on the bed is an old trick, and in the bathroom there are unguents in little bottles. These bottles suggest that you and only you will ever use this bathroom. My mother nicks them. But most people leave them behind, whereupon they are refilled from the bulk vats in the backyard then returned to the bathroom to suggest that caring personal touch to the next unique and treasured guest.

One night in a hotel bathroom is enough to demolish any illusion of luxury. Indeed one shower is enough. Towels lie everywhere, the floor is awash because as you battled to master the shower controls you failed to notice that the shower curtain hung outside the bath, the toilet is emphatically desanitised, the sanitising strip is lying in a puddle because its lack of aerodynamic qualities meant that you missed the basket, the sodden bathmat is scrunched under the door, and scattered across the vanity unit are your own travel-weary accoutrements, the toothbrush with the wilting bristles, the pills and ointments that testify to your age and frailty, all the used and damp and half-squeezed and sorry stuff that is yours and yours alone.

What you've added, so quickly and thoughtlessly, is the true personal touch. You've replaced the commercial parody of perfection with the authentic mess of self.

But you haven't ruined the mirrors. Hotel bathrooms are full of mirrors, because hotels rooms are places of solipsism. Rendered undisturbable by a sign on the door handle, they permit protracted study of one's awful naked flesh. In the room I rented recently there were two sets of mirrors, one of which fronted a cabinet. I opened the cabinet to find disappointing nothing, left it open and returned to the mirror above the sink. It was then that I saw him. It was only a glimpse, but I recognised him immediately. I saw him in quarter profile and recognised the shape of the head, the nose, the recession of the chin, the bland features, the baldness, all captured momentarily in the cabinet mirror reflected in the main mirror. I jumped. I physically jumped. And he disappeared. For the first time since 1972, which was when he died, I'd seen my father.

Travel

As a young man I lusted after foreign lands. Today the lust has wilted to a gentle tug, but there are still places in the atlas whose mere names make me want to pack a bag.

The notion that travel equates to freedom is false. The one piece of luggage you always pack, but that is mentioned in no travel ads, is yourself. If you're timid or a miserable shit at home, you'll be timid or a miserable shit abroad.

From here to prostate

I was pretending to read a plastic picture card telling me how to jump out of the plane, but surreptitiously I was scanning the passengers coming down the aisle for the one who would sit next to me. I have a gift for attracting the seriously religious and mothers with psychotic infants. Somehow you always know who's going to sit beside you the moment you see them. Perhaps it's the dangling saliva.

She had to squeeze past me to get to the window seat. Aeroplane friendships always begin with your eyes about eight inches from the other's crotch, the sort of position it can take a normal friendship a good month to attain, if ever. Such instant proximity can break the ice, of course. It can also thicken it.

'These seats are made for anorexics,' she said. I could detect no hint of religion in the sentence, and if there was a psychotic infant then she had stowed it in the overhead locker, which was just fine by me. On Bennett Airlines, all children travel as freight.

Anyway, as opening comments go this one seemed to go pretty well. I decided to risk a flight's-worth of evangelism by an expansive gesture of friendship. I flicked an eyebrow and expelled a little air through one nostril. It's one of my more effective come-ons.

Two minutes later I had tucked the picture card back in that nifty little seat pocket and was ignoring the safety pantomime starring a bored stewardess and an implausible oxygen mask that is attached to nothing but which one is supposed to tug. There's no point in watching it. Just as I know that I like Guinness, have never grown up and can't stop smoking, so I know with equal certainty that in the event of an air accident I would exhibit without hesitation my talent for panic.

But this was not why I was ignoring the panto on this occasion. Rather my attention was held elsewhere, for beside me, I had discovered, was sitting a creature whom I had never thought about before but whom, if I had ever got round to thinking about her, I would have presumed not to exist.

Barbara, for that was her name — well, actually it wasn't; I can't quite remember her name but I think it had the same number of syllables — lived in Southland, which of course is nothing remarkable — several people have been doing it for years and don't seem much the worse for the experience — but the extraordinary thing is that Barbara, or rather 'Barbara', made her living down there where the nights are long and the grass longer, by selling, wait for it, vitamins.

I think I had better repeat that, without any of those interruptions which seem to be creeping into the sentences today — not that I mind them, of course, in fact I think they add a ring of authenticity, the stamp of a mind in action, don't you think? Anyway, Barbara, or rather 'Barbara', (you're with me? good) sold vitamins, which she pronounced vi-tamins whereas I was brought up to say vit-amins, not that it makes much difference I suppose, in Southland. Is that clearer now? Have you latched on to the full import of that statement?

Now, I'm no Ranulph Fiennes, but I have been to Southland. Last year. January. High summer. Gore. Sunday afternoon. It was raining. Hard.

The main street of Gore was wide and wet — and empty but for two elderly men on stationary old-fashioned bicycles about ten feet apart outside the Four Square Superstore which was, astonishingly, closed. Both elderly men were wearing brown overcoats and cycle clips. Neither elderly man was looking at the other elderly man. Both elderly men were using battered vegetable knives to slash at their wrists.

All of the above is true apart from the bit about the vegetable knives. They may have been chisels. It was hard to tell at that distance and unfortunately the photos didn't come out. I needed a flash.

Anyway, that's all I know of Southland. So when 'Barbara' said she sold vi-tamins down there I thought of the two elderly men and I thought ah-ha and said, eloquently, 'Oh.'

And as if that wasn't enough I added, 'So, how's business?'

'Booming,' said 'Barbara'.

I have never been one to fear repetition. If the word is right, use it as many times as you like. So I said, 'Oh' again.

'Barbara' looked me up and down. I could hardly begrudge her this look given my earlier intimacy with her crotch. She took in my thinning hair, and the other one that isn't thinning quite so badly. She took in my hammer toes. 'You need zinc,' she said.

We then had a witty little interchange about zinc. It went like this:

'Zinc?'
'Zinc.'
'Zinc?'
'Zinc.'
'Oh.'

Already half convinced I asked her why I needed zinc. 'Barbara' insisted that all men need zinc. It fixes everything.

'Everything?'

'From here to prostate.'

I immediately knew that I had got from this trip, if nothing else, the ideal title for every man's autobiography. I told her so.

'No,' said 'Barbara', 'from HAIR to prostate.'

'Oh,' I said, 'well, that's not bad either.'

She laughed. I laughed. We laughed all the way to Auckland. The flight took about ten minutes. She was a charming woman. But then she would have to be to sell vitamins in Gore.

Not that I'm a convert to vitamins, you understand. I will admit to having had, since my return, a nibble or two at a galvanised hinge on the laundry door, but that's only because there's nothing to lose. Soon hair will be a memory and the prostate prostrate. And then you jump out of the plane.

Moose-hunting by supermarket trolley

It's one of those Sundays. You know how it is. One of those Sundays when you can settle to nothing and the neighbours are playing the Bee Gees' Greatest Hits at full volume and the wasps of irritation in your skull say turn the telly on. So you do and there's a woman wearing a pair of athletic shorts that shouldn't be legal and she has come all the way from Latvia to New Zealand to throw the hammer. The hammer isn't a hammer, you understand, but more like one of those things used to fell mammoths from a safe distance, though it might as well be a hammer for all the good it does mankind, not that you particularly want to do mankind any good because mankind means huge women from Latvia, commentators who think hammer-throwing matters and people who like the Bee Gees.

So you zap the telly and pick up the paper only to discover that a supermarket chain has decided to make you pay a two-dollar bond on your trolley because they, poor dears, lose 200 trolleys a year and each one costs $350. At that price you immediately decide to become a trolley manufacturer and then equally immediately ditch the idea because it would lead to impossible conversations.

'Yes, that's right, yes trolleys, you know, for supermarkets . . . no, I don't expect you have . . . well, you sort of get some wire and sort of bend it . . . yes that's right, three good wheels and one spastic one . . . no, actually it *isn't* easy to make them stick together like that . . . ha ha, yes, mating, yes that's very funny . . . well, actually, about $350 each . . . well, it wouldn't be a very *good* second-hand car for $350, would it . . . yes, I know, well you can always take a basket.'

But what I really want to say is that the trolley bond will put paid to moose-hunting. Well, not exactly hunting, I suppose, more like moose-finding-by-chance. In Canada, Banff to be precise, on a skiing trip with Dave Collier way back in the days before mortgages and lady Latvians.

The après-ski at the Silver Dollar Bar and Grill has gone with a swing and about midnight we find a supermarket trolley in the street. Dave says get in, so I get in. Well, I've always been what mothers call broad in the beam, so there I am, wedged into the belly of this trolley with feet over the front and head up against the kiddy-seat and absolutely no chance of getting out without help and what with the ice on the street and Dave full of Labatts it's a bit like the two-man bob and in ten seconds we're up to thirty miles an hour. Suddenly I see this neon motel sign with a sort of silhouette in front of it and it looks like a gigantic head of a . . . 'Stop!' I scream and Dave digs the heels in and says, 'Why?' 'Look,' I say, 'moose.' And he says, 'Where?' and I say, 'There,' and he says, 'That's not a moose,' and I say, 'It is so,' though I don't think it is any more.

So Dave biffs a snowball at it and it turns its antlered head, bellows a sort of uniquely moosey bellow and comes charging up the street towards us.

Friendship's a great thing. Dave and I grew up together. We were inseparable. One rapidly approaching suburban moose, however, and we have discovered the joys of separability which is fine for Dave who's off up the street like a man being chased by a moose but less fine for me who has a beam wedged inextricably in the belly of a supermarket trolley. Hooves are thundering my way and I'm trying to lever myself out and wondering whether Canadian supermarket trolleys are crash-tested against two thousand pounds of moose flesh with horns and deciding they probably aren't and I am wrestling and struggling and the trolley is rocking and then ever so slowly it just topples over on its side. But my beam is still wedged so I curl like a caged foetus and pray like billyo and good old god or rather God makes the moose thunder past and head on up the street after Dave.

'Get him!' I scream, and then, quickly, 'Sorry, didn't mean it', because I don't want him or rather Him to change his mind and make the moose do a 180.

But now, I suppose, with $2 bonds on trolleys no one will leave them around any more, so yet another source of fun will dissolve in what is becoming a puritan world, but at least moose will be able to browse in peace.

Meanwhile gangs of horror-children will hang around in supermarket carparks with their skateboards and their hideous haircuts and when some poor pensioner wheels the groceries out to the Honda Civic, whack! it'll be a skateboard on the bonce and a horizontal pensioner and the kids will be off with the trolley, and all for two lousy bucks.

So I suppose the supermarket will have to hire carpark guards, and what better than a vast lady Latvian with a penchant for hammer-throwing? The urchins will evaporate, and if some itinerant moose happens to wander into the carpark she could let rip with the hammer and a great Latvian grunt and take its legs out from under it.

Dave got away, by the way. He always did.

▓ Aleppo

I used to teach him English. Now he's teaching me geography. In the traditional manner of the young he's gone travelling, having first bought one of those compulsory little money belt pouch things that keep passport and traveller's cheques conveniently close to the genitals so that everything can be defended at once when abroad turns nasty.

He's just sent me an e-mail from Aleppo. If, yesterday, you had stopped me in the street and asked me where Aleppo was, I would have been surprised, but I would have said Egypt. And I would have been wrong. I now know it's in Syria, although, to be frank, that doesn't help much. It invites an obvious second question, which is where Syria is. I think it may be in Egypt.

Everything else that I know of Aleppo I got from Shakespeare.

Early in *Macbeth* the first witch tells the story of a woman who is roasting chestnuts. The witch describes the woman as a rump-fed ronyon — and who hasn't met a few of those? Lyttelton seethes with them — but anyway the witch asks her for some chestnuts. The ronyon replies 'aroint, thee witch' which translates loosely as 'no'. It is not a wise reply.

The witch happens to know that the ronyon's husband is a mariner. He has recently sailed for Aleppo. The witch resolves to follow him — travelling rather ostentatiously by sieve. She promises that once she gets to Aleppo, 'I'll do, I'll do, and I'll do'.

What she'll do she doesn't specify but you sense that the ronyon may soon be selling chestnuts full time to supplement her widow's pension.

Anyway, my former pupil with the money belt pouch thing is in Aleppo and by all accounts he's having a wizard time. But then having a wizard time is what you do when travelling. Few people send postcards moaning that they are bored, lonely or frightened. Travel's good and brave and exhilarating. Travel means striding manfully towards the heroic horizon with one's money belt pouch thing swinging audaciously in the warm winds of hope.

And of course I envy the lad. How could one not envy him Aleppo? When you drop it into a conversation, Aleppo lands with so much more of a clang than, say, Ashburton.

Aleppo's such a squalid-romantic name. It sings of tall donkey-coloured buildings with a smallpox of bullet holes, narrow streets, fetid beggars, men with stumps, women with washing, flies, dogs, danger and all the other tourist attractions.

Time was when I'd have hauled my money belt pouch thing from the dusty cupboard and hi-hoed for Aleppo at the drop of an e-mail. In those days the horrible walls of habit hadn't grown so high that I couldn't peep over them and take a peek at all the other lovely places. Atlases made me salivate. Travel ads trembled my knees. What they depicted was Elsewhere, that glorious place where I wasn't. And off I would trot.

I didn't trot well. I made nothing happen. If things did happen it was because someone else made them happen, some quaint local with unquaint idiosyncrasies. He or she would do something unpredictable involving knives or drugs or budgerigars and I would find myself in a hole I didn't think I could clamber out of. I always did clamber out, of course, but even as I did so I would be mentally rehearsing the story I could tell when I got home. I still tell those stories. They're crackers. They make me laugh. They didn't make me laugh at the time.

But the real trouble was that whenever I got to the place I was trotting to I found it was no longer Elsewhere. I'd imported something to spoil it and that something was me. In direct consequence I spent most of my time being scared or bored or lonely or the whole trifecta and pining for the tall walls of habit.

I think it was a character in a Hardy poem who said that you can see everything there is to see from your own back doorstep. I know it was a character in a Graves poem who said that every ocean smells alike of tar. And I know now that to the citizens of Aleppo, paradise is Ashburton. Elsewhere is a universal myth.

Elsewhere is of a piece with yesterday and tomorrow. You never get there. It's one of the roast chestnuts that the rump-fed ronyon of life tempts you with but never hands over. So why is it that even now, the thought of the strangeness of Aleppo makes something in my stomach deliquesce? I think it may be just the sound of the place. Aleppo.

Cuchulain's children

No, no, it just won't do, this Irish stuff. It's got to stop.

Now I'm as fond of a pint of stout as the next man, so come St Patrick's Day the next man and I duly toddled down to the joke local Irish bar where the heirs to the warrior tradition of Cuchulain the Strong were wearing wigs of green tinsel. But at least they'd maintained the ancient Irish tradition of emigrating.

So many Paddies have hightailed it out of Ireland that only the Catholic church's sexual ethics have kept the place populated. Not that there's anything wrong with emigrating. I've done a fair swag of it myself but if you ever catch me boohooing for the land of my birth, kindly take a shillelagh to my softer parts then lash me to the mizzen of the first ship home.

The Irish have made boohooing into an art. Apart from people, their only export crop is nostalgia, as summed up by the character in a Hardy novel who 'sang sweet songs of his own dear country that he loved so much as never to have revisited it'. Because, of course, no sooner is Paddy O'Flaherty on the boat bound for Opportunity than he's humming 'Danny Boy', going misty-eyed at any mention of the Emerald Isle and acquiring a rackful of CDs by Daniel O'Bleeding Donnell.

Most of the Irish have emigrated for that most cogent of reasons, poverty. Too few spuds on the table for a family of 27 meant Liam took the first boat to New York where his love of fighting after the pub shut would lead him naturally into the police force. Once there he could start lying.

Liam and his mates the world over have woven not so much a tissue of lies about poor old Ireland as a heavy-duty tarpaulin. And it's a tarpaulin that the rest of the world, in the manner of a snake ingesting a goat, has swallowed.

Bung the word Irish in front of anything these days and it sells. Irish ballads, Irish tenors, and, most wonderful of all, traditional Irish dancing featuring a man in traditional sequined trousers and a line up of colleens in apt but invisible straitjackets, all of them heel-and-toeing it as if picking their way through an IRA bomb stash. The whole shebang is as authentically Irish as coq au vin.

Heritage, they call it, of a piece with the rich Irish literary tradition starring Jonathan Swift who spent three-quarters of his life in London, James Joyce who set up shop in either Paris or Zurich — I can't remember and don't care which, and neither did he, so long as it wasn't Dublin — and dreary Sam Beckett who did most of his waiting for O'Godot on the left bank of the Seine. Most recently we've had Frank McCourt. Son of a stout-sodden ne'er-do-well who spectacularly failed to keep his family of 50 in bread and pigsheads, dear old Frank headed across the Atlantic with understandable haste to write an account of his childhood with such lyrical intensity that every author envies him his deprivation. His tumbledown place of birth has become a shrine for semi-literate female tourists who've fallen in love with the heaving of Michael Flatley's chest or Val Doonican's cable-knit cardigan.

And then there are the Irish pubs. Oh spare us. To qualify as an Irish pub you've got to serve Guinness and play an over-loud CD of fiddle music. That's it. Plus a dozen green balloons on March 17th and a sturdy bag for lugging the loot to the bank. Irish pubs have sprung up wherever market research has revealed an untapped seam of bogus sentiment. That means everywhere. A former pupil of mine who's as Irish as a mob of hoggets has recently opened one in Sao Paulo. Hong Kong's got them like measles. The only place that hasn't got Irish pubs as the world knows them is Ireland.

I've been to Ireland. It's wet. The typical pub holds a wall-eyed son of the soil called Pete gobbing gloomily into a fire of the same name and wondering why he didn't join Dominic, Moirag et al on the first boat to Elsewhere, while the raddled barmaid breaks occasionally into a basso profundo rendition of 'One Day at a Time, Sweet Jesus' in the hope of sucking in a tourist. Meanwhile round the back of this scene of Irish authenticity lurks a bulldozer with the engine running on Euro tax dollars just waiting for the nod from Brussels to bowl the wreck of a pub and put up a tilt slab factory to assemble a thousand televisions a day so the tourist board can continue to beam images of old Ireland to every expatriate Paddy in the globe.

If you imagine we live in a secular age, freed from the superstitious burden of myth, just think Ireland.

Ooooh la bloody la

'I think,' gushed the woman on the radio in a manner that immediately caused me to doubt the accuracy of the verb, 'I think that France is such a wonderful sensory overload, don't you?'

'No,' I squealed, reaching for the volume control on the radio with a vigour that almost broke the thing off, 'no, I bloody well don't.'

How have the French done it? How have they hoodwinked the world?

Well, let's start where the French start, and where they go on, and where they also finish, which is with food. They are besotted with food, and by and large they cook well. But boy, are they smug about it. Smug and patronising and monomaniac. They are particularly boring about their regional delicacies — the terrine here, the sucking pig there, and, in the region of France where I used to live, the eau de vie de mirabelle. Eau de vie de mirabelle is a liqueur made by infusing the flavours from the small and bitter local plum, the mirabelle, into four-star petrol. The locals talked about it a lot more than they drank it. They also gave it away in tellingly large quantities.

The gushy woman on the radio no doubt finds France a sensory overload because they have outdoor markets where the women sniff melons, squeeze peaches, prod cheeses and generally go to enormous trouble to pass bacteria around. All of which is very picturesque in a touristy sort of way but for one thing it is not unique to France and for another thing I fail to see how it has contributed to the French image of romantic elegance.

For this I suspect we have to look at the language. French, they say, is the language of love. What they mean is that English is the language of love when spoken with a French accent. Why else should all French crooners — from Charles poloneck-sweater Aznavour to that ancient monsieur whose name I've forgotten but who used to knock 'em out with the highly suspect 'Zank heaven for leetle girls' — sing in English? When a Frenchman lays it on, rolling his r's, mispronouncing his th's and throwing the stress onto all ze wrong syllables, every English-speaking woman in a hundred-yard radius goes googly at the knee and subsides into a form of catatonia that disqualifies her from recognising that the average Frenchman is about as romantic as a diesel mechanic from Greymouth.

French itself is a heavily bastardised form of Latin, less mellifluous than Italian, less racy than Spanish and infinitely, but infinitely, less flexible than English. Hence the crusty Académie Française is so terrified of the superior language that for years it has forbidden its citizens, on pain of being pelted to death with pétanque balls, to say le weekend. The French, in an unusual display of wisdom, have ignored it.

There is no English Academy. Confident of its own resilience, English has cheerfully absorbed words from wherever it could get them and many have been French. And a remarkable number of these — chic, couture, suave — are associated with style rather than substance.

For somehow the land of berets, bicycles, onions, blue boiler suits, grey plaster houses with grey wooden shutters, straight roads, elm trees that may on reflection be poplars, too many poodles, throat-peeling cigarettes, feeble mopeds and thin beer into which they tip the nauseatingly sweet syrop de grenadine, has become a byword for style and fashion. And as for the notion that the women of France are supposed to be the most beautiful in the world, that stands up to the rigours of close inspection about as well as the notion that it is possible to play rugby against their menfolk without danger to one's testicles.

And then there's Paris. Paris, where fraudulent painters knock up daubs of Montmartre to flog to the tourist dupes and where the most famous building is a giant electricity pylon serving no practical purpose and which was erected in the late nineteenth century as a temporary bit of engineering show-offery. Constantly lauded as the most beautiful city of the world, the city of romance and all the rest of that guff, Paris, like every other European capital, has a fair collection of public buildings — emphatically excluding the Pompidou Centre — but some of the ugliest suburbs in the world, all high-rise sixties monstrosities and streets as mean as Miami.

Yet despite all this, despite the *Rainbow Warrior* and Moruroa Atoll, despite their embarrassing military and imperial record, despite the 2CV and the force-fed geese and the wines that aren't as good as ours, and despite in particular their extraordinary chauvinism — a word derived inevitably from a Frenchman, a Nicholas Chauvin who was ferociously patriotic and devoted in an unhealthy way to that bellicose dwarf Napoleon — France and the French retain a sort of mystique in the Anglo-Saxon mind. Off goes Peter Mayle to Provence to — God, I can hardly bring myself to type this — to do up a farmhouse, and his book sells a squillion copies.

The French are just people like everybody else. They have faults, they have virtues, they have huge numbers of myths associated with them and they have a popular fizzy drink called Pshitt.

Wrong room

Last week I stayed in a expensive hotel. Someone else was paying.

The woman at reception programmed a credit card and called it my key. She also gave me a sachet of ground coffee.

On the wall in the lift a picture of a couple in the hotel dining room. She was all blouse and breast. His jaw jutted. Each had a plate of prawns, a glass of white wine and a smile as wide as a bridge.

In the corridor, Muzak, deep carpet and a row of doors like closed eyes. Behind them, no doubt, happy couples preparing to dine. Maids of foreign birth towed carts of sheets and soap and cleaning fluids, and flattened themselves against the wall as I approached.

It didn't take long to open my door with the credit card but the lights in the room didn't work. Because the lights didn't work I couldn't read the telephone instructions. I dialled 1 and spoke to a humming sound. I dialled 9 and spoke to silence. I dialled 0 and spoke to reception.

No, she said in a professional tone that made me feel foolish, of course I wasn't foolish.

When I slipped the credit card into the slot by the door the lights revealed a single chocolate at the head of the bed. While I ate it I read the note from the manager. It wished me happiness and used my Christian name. In search of happiness I opened every cupboard then dialled 0.

No, she said, there wasn't an ashtray because it wasn't a smoking room, and no of course she didn't think me foolish. I agreed to change rooms but didn't mention that I'd eaten the chocolate.

My new room was identical except for an ozone-maker — a metal cube with dials, like the sort of machine that you are supposed to but don't attach to the electricity supply when you're using a hedge trimmer in the rain.

I had to fill the kettle in the bathroom. It fitted awkwardly under the tap. I mopped the floor with two white towels and left them there.

A hotel room is the bed. I took the coffee plunger to the bed, wrestled the pillows from the counterpane, stacked them and folded the top one to support my neck. The bed was aligned inescapably to the television. I flicked through fifteen channels then watched golf. The players wore the same sort of clothes as the jut-jawed man who dined. The caddies wore bibs, like maids.

I would have liked a snack from the mini-bar — peanuts, biscuits, chocolate — but was scared of the prices. At the golf it started raining. The caddies held umbrellas over the players but not over themselves. I pressed the top of the coffee plunger. Coffee spurted over the bedside table and the ozone-maker. I rolled off the bed and fetched a towel from the bathroom then sat on the side of the bed and drank the coffee.

Putting the ironing board up to iron my shirt for the evening was easy. Putting it down again was beyond me. Choosing not to dial 0 I left the ironing board standing.

The bathroom was all mirrors and unguents. Tiny bottles of body lotion and moisturising cream and conditioner and two cakes of pomegranate and honey soap.

Getting the temperature right in the shower took only a few minutes, then I conditioned my armpits and moisturised my crotch. I hadn't closed the shower door properly. I dropped another towel on the floor to soak. While I was drying myself I wiped the condensation from the enormous mirror and did Mr Muscle poses.

I dressed, edged past the ironing board and went out.

I woke in the morning to knocking. A maid, breakfast and a newspaper. I ate in bed, spilling peach juice on my chest and yoghurt on the pillow. I licked the yoghurt off but couldn't reach the peach juice with my tongue. The countless sections of the unfamiliar newspaper dispersed themselves about the bed. On the television, highlights of the golf.

I showered again, using the last of the thousand towels, dressed, gathered my things, made to leave, stopped and surveyed the room that had been home for some fourteen hours. Sodden towels in the bathroom, the bed a stained shambles, the pillows piled haphazardly, the counterpane twisted like a bowel, the breakfast tray lying at a precarious angle, newspaper scattered, the ashtray full, coffee stains on the ozone-maker, the ironing board standing sentinel. Though the place cost $170 a night and was crammed with luxury, it and I had never found a fit. My chin never jutted. I never sipped the white wine, never peeled the prawns of pleasure.

In the corridor the self-effacing maids were hovering, waiting for me to go, waiting to put things right.

The things people do

I guess every section of this book could come under this heading. Like every writer except J.K. Rowling, and possibly that pipe-smoking old bore Tolkein, I write about what people get up to. And what they get up to is often puzzling or self-deluding or vain or dishonest. I love several people, but I find it hard to love the human race. And that paradox underpins what I write, I think, and my fondness for dogs.

The ods roll over

As a child my main joy was watching the car's odometer. Of course, in those innocent pre-metric days we called it the milometer; back then we barely knew what an od was. Nevertheless, what I craved was that moment when the odometer numbers all rolled round together to produce a row of zeros.

Not daring to blink, I would follow the odometer's slow progress through the 990s. I would urge my father to drive faster, but he would decline on the grounds that top gear was for hooligans.

In the end, of course, it turned out like the weather forecast. Just as, however closely you listen to the weather forecast you always seem to miss the bit you want, so somehow I always seemed to miss the great odometer roll. One moment of distraction and 999.7 was suddenly 1000.1.

Immediately I would order my father to reverse. He would refuse, partly because he didn't believe in pandering to children, but mainly because he despised reverse. He called it the foreigners' gear.

Why do I mention all this? Partly to show modern youth that in my day we knew how to make our own fun, but more because it has something to do with the end of a year. Tonight at midnight the globe's odometer ticks over a notch and it matters.

Here in the port tonight those people who can wrench themselves away from The Moira Anderson Hogmanay Special will tour the pubs. There are several pubs here. In them will gather a cosmopolitan mix. There will be gold-toothed Russian trawlermen smelling of the fierce disinfectant used to kill cockroaches on board their awful ships. There will be Korean and Vietnamese, wharfies and rugmakers, émigré artists and Arthur the bee-keeper side by side in a seething mass.

A billion words will be shouted or slurred across tables awash with slops. Few of the words will be heard but that doesn't matter. It's the doing of it that will count, the being there.

I am told that when women share a house, their biorhythms gradually merge until eventually they find they are all pedalling their menstrual cycles in time with each other. So it is with the revellers at New Year's Eve in the port. As the evening wears on this ruck of humanity becomes like a school of fish. It develops an unconscious group will. Without anyone saying anything, all the revellers decide at more or less the same time to move to the next pub. One minute a bar will be bulging till its walls groan; the next it will be a wasteland of glasses, ashtrays and nobody. If you get out of phase with the mob you wonder if you've got the date wrong.

As midnight looms a crowd gathers at the corner of Oxford and London Streets. There is a sense in the air of something important, something ritualistic and significant. A ship's siren blasts the night. A cheer erupts, and the people join hands to sing 'Auld Lang Syne' with such tunefulness that every dog in town joins in.

Then it's hugs. Some hug only their lovers; others, like random octopuses, hug anyone within range; while a few sly youths hug the girls they've have spent the past year wanting to hug. And that is apt because New Year's Eve is a vent for feelings that spend the rest of the year deep in the burrows of reserve.

The mob drifts apart. Those who threw away their cigarettes at midnight nip back to the pub to replace them. Those who emerged from the rusting trawlers return to them singing. Those who came down from the hills stumble gently back up towards home. Halfway up the slope they may pause to catch breath, and perhaps, encouraged by the twinkle of the lights and the dark of the sea and the black presence of the hills, they will reflect on the passage of time, the year that has gone, the year that is to come.

For that, I think, is what this ritual of New Year's Eve is all about. It is a marker-post stuck down at random along the great amorphous road of time. It serves the same function as a birth or a marriage or a death. And like those occasions it arouses sentimentality.

For some that sentiment is the mawkishness of televisual Hogmanay; for others it's the euphoria of the hug; for me I'm afraid it's a grim little poem.

> *Life is mainly froth and bubble.*
> *Two things stand as stone:*
> *Kindness in another's trouble,*
> *Courage in your own.*

Every New Year's Eve this hideous doggerel rises unbidden to my mind. And every year, softened by beer, I resolve that henceforth I shall be kinder and more courageous. And having so resolved I meander the last few ods to home and grateful bed.

The resolution, of course, comes to nothing, but it's the thought that counts. Happy New Year.

Eating with experts

Today I woke to hear an expert — and I am terribly fond of experts — recounting on the radio the joys of the Mediterranean diet. I missed the first part of the interview so I did not hear which Mediterranean diet he was extolling. I wondered if perhaps he meant the Greek diet of octopus and goat cheese or the Libyan diet of dictatorship and poverty, or perhaps the Palestinian diet of rubber bullets. But I gathered, I think, that he meant a trendy Italian diet of olives, pasta, salads, Vespas, bambini, linguini and Catholicism. This diet, said the man, would lengthen our lives.

Our expert told us with gloom in his voice that the New Zealand diet is slow suicide. It gives us cancer, stills our fluttering hearts. All that fat, he said, it kills us.

Now I do not know if this expert was the same expert who told me last year that the Japanese diet of fish, rice and lightly braised kimonos was the one that would lengthen my life. He certainly had the same tone in his voice, that mix of zeal and lamentation. Or was he perhaps last week's expert who told me that chocolate would kill me? Or there again he may have been this week's expert who told me that chocolate was good for me, that indeed it would enhance both my shelf-life and my sex-life. Since I heard that news, of course, I've been shovelling down the Cadbury's and I can already tell you he's at least 50 per cent wrong. When I know about the other 50 per cent I'll let you know.

So perhaps he was the expert who wrote the magazine questionnaire which I dutifully completed in the dentist's waiting room only to find that I was an alcoholic, doomed to grow a liver like a cauliflower and to pop my cork within months. Or perhaps he was the expert who told me, to my great relief, that if I wanted to be as sprightly as a rat, the first thing I should do each morning was to gargle a couple of glasses of cabernet sauvignon.

There again he could have been closely related to the scientific expert who brought free radicals to my attention, those dramatic little independent entities espousing obscure political causes, which can, I believe, either kill me or render me immortal — I forget which but it is always the one or the other.

Or was he the man who goes around putting ticks on tins, or the one who spends his life usefully measuring the fat content of the pastry in meat pies? Or the woman who made millions from a book about cleaning your liver? Was he even the man who looked like a stringbean, who invented jogging and who keeled over at the age of fifty-five in mid-jog? Or perhaps he was the man who tells me that I have to drink 8 litres of water a day, or even the splendid chap who tells me that smoking fends off Alzheimer's, presumably by killing me before I can go doolally.

Well, he is all of these people and none of them. He is every dietary expert under the merry sun. He is also a busybody and a Jeremiah. I do not need him and nor, for a host of reasons, do you.

For a start, he is often giving us information that will be contradicted next week. As a child I remember being told, for example, that potatoes would make me fat.

But even if this propaganda were proveable fact, he would still only be telling me more or less what my body knows. If I drink too much I get a hangover. It is the body telling me to rein in the horses of licentiousness. I can choose, of course, to let the horses gallop, but the warning is there and the responsibility mine. Similarly, if I eat two scoops of chips and a shoal of deep-fried fish, and round it off with a box of Mars bars, I feel sick. Or if I eat nothing but hamburgers I grow constipated and weary. I may be fool enough to ignore those warnings, but that is my affair.

People have worried about dying since the first clock ticked, and a fat lot of good it has done them. Indeed it has done them harm. I am confident that the surest way to shorten one's life is to worry about how long it is going to be.

And if Italians live longer than New Zealanders — and I don't for one minute believe that they do — they do so because they snooze in the sun, dandle bambini, shovel linguini, take it easy, try to be happy and, most importantly of all, they worry as little as possible, and laugh as much as possible, especially at experts.

I believe in pigs

A pig's orgasm lasts for half an hour.

I learned this splendid nugget a couple of weeks ago and it has since become a fixture in my conversational repertoire. It sparks a lively response at any social event but is best reserved for formal dinner parties. It goes down well with loin of pork.

I learned about the pig from Pat, a music teacher who has never to my knowledge or suspicion been in a position to verify the truth of his assertion. But that doesn't stop me believing it. The nub of the matter is not that I think it is true, but that I want it to be true.

There is probably a word for this tendency of mine, but I suspect it is a Greek word and I'm afraid all Greek is Greek to me. The word I'm looking for isn't stupidity and it isn't credulousness. I want a word to describe something altogether more wilful which has been the mainstay of my intellectual life. I want a word to describe the tendency of human beings to prefer the excitingly improbable idea to the dull and more probable one.

Why is it, for example, that for thirty years or so I have believed that glass is a liquid? It looks and feels like a solid, it sounds like a solid when I tap it, when I tap it too hard it slices my flesh and yet I have told innumerable people that it is a liquid and for evidence I have pointed out that ancient windows are thicker at the bottom than at the top because, over the course of the centuries, the glass has slowly dripped. Obviously, I have never examined ancient windows to see if it is so, but someone whom I can no longer remember once told me it was so and it sounded exciting to me and so I decided it was so.

And while I am at it, why should I and so many other people have believed that powdered glass in coffee is a recognised method of murder? Powdered glass in coffee would settle as sludge at the bottom of the cup and the victim would have to spoon the murder weapon down his throat himself. And even if he did so the glass would pass harmlessly through his gut. Nevertheless for years I have believed the irrational exciting opposite of the truth.

Just as when people come across flattened wheat they presume not that wind has laid it low or that people or animals have trodden it down but that aliens have travelled hundreds of light years across the galaxy in order to crush a fraction of a cereal crop before going home. And how we all would like it to be true.

And why, when a friend is late for a meeting, do I always imagine that something disastrous has happened, that a car crash has left him mangled in a ditch? And if I am alone in a house at night why, when I hear a noise, do I assume that it is not a possum on the roof or a creak in the weatherboards but rather an intruder with a baseball bat and malice, or a ghost with the face of a skull, so that I withdraw whimpering beneath the blankets?

And why, when probability theory tells the plainest story of folly, do a million people troop to the Lotto shop every Saturday to hand over the money that they love in the strange conviction that they have been singled out?

And why do people who know that we live in a galaxy of cooling lumps of matter circling other cooling lumps of matter cling to the belief, the hope, that destiny is written in the heavens, that the orbit of the planets somehow impinges on the fate of each of us?

And why, when Elvis is dead, for which relief much thanks, should he reappear so frequently in the supermarkets of Tennessee?

Why should these and a thousand other superstitions, myths and fallacies so grasp our minds? For sure the wish is father to the thought but why should the wish exist? Why should we want the world to be more than it is, to offer greater delights, stranger truths, greater mysteries? Could it be that the miraculous truth of life is essentially a mundane miracle and we cannot accept that dust returns to dust, that the great random concatenation of chance and carbon and other stuff is ultimately barren, explicable and purposeless? Is it that our consciousness, that gift which is both boon and burden, cannot be satisfied by brutal fact, cannot accommodate our own mortality, cannot accept that what is, is and there's an end to it?

I'm afraid I do not know. The only thing I know for sure is why pigs appear always to be grinning.

Of chopping and sticking

It was not a successful evening. For a start I went grudgingly, because — well, you don't need the details. Let me just say that I went to say sorry. I had been in the wrong, of course, but that was all water under the bridge, or at least last night was meant to shove the water under the bridge and out into the great ocean of forgiveness. I planned, in short, to eat humble pie.

But I didn't eat humble pie. I ate Chinese. Chinese food does little for me. I have yet to find flavour in either noodles or rice. And then, of course, I got chopsticks.

Well now, I am as dextrous as the next man. I can tie my shoelaces, do up my flies and only on the very worst mornings do I confuse the activities. But I do not hold with chopsticks. Chopsticks are sticks. Sticks are bad cutlery.

Chopsticks do not chop and neither do they stick. If they were pointed you could at least spear the more substantial bits, but they aren't so you can't. And if a competition were held to discover the food least suited to consumption by chopsticks, rice would get the silver medal and noodles the gold.

We are supposed to be a tool-making species. Tool making is what has raised us into dominion over the beasts of the field and the birds of the air and the fishes of the sea. And when it comes to eating the beasts, birds and fishes, and in particular the smaller vegetables, the fork is a better tool than chopsticks. The spoon is a better tool than chopsticks. Indeed, virtually everything in your pockets is a better tool than chopsticks.

I do not mind other people using chopsticks. Though it may seem to me that those who are adept with chopsticks still use them mainly as shovels, and I find it impossible to imagine a worse design for a shovel, nevertheless, as I say, I have no quarrel with the users of chopsticks. Let them depart in peace.

Those I do have a quarrel with are those who expect me to use chopsticks. And these people are never those who were brought up with the things. Chinese restaurants are always delighted to fetch me my preferred weaponry.

No, the people who think it somehow right to use chopsticks to eat a dish that has been cut into little bits and laid on a bed of even littler bits, are people who were raised as I was raised with a silver-plated fork in the mouth. But when I call for a fork they look at each other in a mixture of shock and disdain and they tut. They consider me an oaf.

Now I do not deny oafdom. Oaf is a speciality of the house. But I fail to see why it should be considered a further black mark on my much marked escutcheon for me to wish to eat my food efficiently. It seems unreasonable. But reason, of course, doesn't come into it.

What does come into it is sycophancy, the belief that somehow one will ingratiate oneself with people from overseas by doing as they do. Wrong, of course. Restaurateurs of any breed don't give a fig how you eat their food. They give a fig only about whether you pay for it.

But the sycophants go further. By using chopsticks, they believe, one is leaving one's comfort zone and getting the authentic cultural experience.

Well phooey to that. For a start I like my comfort zone. I find it comfortable. But more significantly, I can think of no phrase more barren of meaning than authentic cultural experience. Authentic cultural experience means Disneyland. Authentic cultural experience means watching dances by grass-skirted people who, if you weren't paying them, would be wearing jeans and not dancing. Authentic cultural experience means bogus, artificial boredom.

All of which, of course, I didn't say. I was supposed to be behaving so I just bit my lip, grabbed a chopstick in each hand and spent a bitter evening scattering food. Hungry and angry make potent bedfellows. The water remains this side of the bridge and seems to have increased in volume.

Would you care to?

'Dancing,' she said, 'there will be dancing.'

'Oh good,' I said. 'Will there be country and western dancing led by a man with a stetson and a microphone whose ignorance of cattle-ranching is matched only by his ignorance of English, chanting bizarre instructions in an accent and a jargon that I can neither understand nor pardon to a group of people dressed in check shirts, bandannas, and embarrassment? I do hope so.

'Or failing that,' I said with a fervour that I found hard to hide, 'is there any chance of a throwback bash for the middle-aged, giving them a chance to fling their bald spots around to the songs of long-dead adolescents, songs whose lyrics have the emotional complexity of crockery but which the oldsters can remember to the last syllable, an achievement of which they don't seem in the least ashamed? What fun that will be. A couple of hours and the baby boomers will be telling spectacular lies about the swinging sixties that swung for everyone except them and then they will gather in grinning circles to perform an activity called the twist which will lead directly and promptly to a local citizens' petition to build an enlarged spinal unit. Groovy.

'But if not that, then perhaps you're running one of those lovely formal balls that recall a more gracious age in which the music is supplied by a spindleshank dance orchestra and the costumes by a museum? Those attending will have prepared for the event with a month of evening classes run by a haggard woman from Wainoni with a fake Hungarian accent and grey, wispy hair clenched into something called a bun — though if you sank your teeth into this bun they would bounce.

'And while the dancers lurch around the floor, the fortunate few who have managed to sit out this particular dance will be divided neatly by sex. The women will coo and melt and mutter how it takes them back to the days of elegance when courtship was civilised, men were gentlemen and groping was what you did for your teeth in the morning, while the men will say nothing at all because they've long since snuck out the fire exit, their hips a-bulge with flasks of relief. Is that the sort of dancing you have in mind?

'Or maybe you mean to stage a truly modern dance event involving a condemned warehouse, a couple of turntables, an illiterate DJ in laughable sunglasses, a skipload of illicit drugs and a pullulation of teenagers? The girls will be wearing short skirts of net curtain over the top of trousers, like a valance round the legs of a bed, while the boys will sport canvas cargo-pants whose crotch sits snugly at knee level.' (Such low-slung trousers may be a fashion statement, whatever that may mean, but they are not an athletic aid. A friend of mine was recently attacked by a group of youths in such trousers. They hit him a bit so he ran off, and though he had half their lung capacity, twice their years and three times their paunch, he got away with ease. He said it was like being chased by pygmies in shackles.)

'If,' I said, 'it is this sort of rave dancing that you have in mind, remember that it is not the music itself that matters but the level at which it is played, that indeed the volume and in particular the bass must be of such prodigious intensity that the noise is not heard but rather felt. And remember to truck in a container of narrow cans of caffeine and sugar concoctions known as energy drinks, so called because they have supplied energy in abundance to three hundred advertising agencies who have got into the profitable business of conning the young into buying them.

'Or maybe,' I said as a thought struck me, 'you are planning an evening of performance dancing, in which we watch either women of improbable fleshlessness tottering around the stage in a bid to inflict terminal damage to their toes while pretending to be swans in a fairy story put to music in 1860 by an unlamentedly dead Russian, or else, best of all, a programme of modern dance for us to watch in which men and women intertwine themselves inexplicably in a sort of space-suit pornography to music that sounds like a leaking outhouse. What larks,' I said.

'Actually,' she said, 'I was thinking of a disco.'

'Oh crikey,' I said, 'what more could I wish for? A chance for me to relive the humiliation of my teenage years, when everyone was supposed to like dancing and while it was all right for the girls who could jig pointlessly on the spot, it was firmly not all right for the boys, of whom two were gifted dancers while the rest of us were deeply and permanently incapable of any movement that didn't look self-conscious, contrived, demented or simply the quintessence of jerkdom.'

'You're not really into dancing, are you?' she said.

The squeals of children

The hills are alive with the squeals of children. I've got a cageful of the little darlings all pleading for forgiveness, having dared to approach my battlements last week in their capes and plastic teeth squeaking trick or treat in bogus American accents. Well, they got the trick and I got the treat and the dogs are still fetching in the stragglers. Not much warmth in those tinsel capes either, as the honeys are discovering these cool spring nights.

'Let us out, mister,' they whine as I curl up on the rococo sofa smug with whisky, 'we didn't mean no harm.'

Nor did I, as it happened, it just sort of turned out that way. Not that I haven't given them the chance of redemption. 'Tell me the historical and religious significance of Halloween,' I said, 'and all will be forgiven.' They shrugged what pass for shoulders.

Same thing happened to the Guy Fawkes mob last weekend. 'Penny for the guy,' they squeaked over the pramful of straw. Well, that was enough for me. Now they're all locked in the garage, howling like banshees while I toss an occasional cheap firework through the window. They'll be there till they give me a decent biographical summary of Mr Fawkes or at least an explanation of imperial currency. To give them a chance I even slid an encyclopaedia through the grating, but most of the little sods couldn't read a word, and the only one who could looked up Guy Fawkes under cutlery.

Nice to turn the tables on the tyranny of youth. Not that it's all their fault of course. About ten years old, most of them, ten years of advertising, television, video games and the Spice Girls, so it's hardly surprising they're as ignorant as suet. As for any sense of historical perspective or the reasons for ritual, you might as well go scraping round for poets in the Stock Exchange.

And did you listen to the outcry over Halloween? 'Oh gosh,' say the adults, 'it's just another ghastly American import.' Well pfui to that for a start. Mother's Day, Father's Day, where do they come from? 'Oh,' we say, 'but it's so commercial', we who do a third of our annual retail spending for the great religious bash of Christmas, which is a nice little import from the Middle East, that notorious bastion of peace and goodwill to all men. Add a wallop of paganism and Teutonic solstice-worship and a plastic Christmas tree and things that unfurl and go toot when you blow in them and then we have a real cultural event of symbolic significance. But the kiddies can't have one of their own. Oh no, Halloween is sending out all the wrong signals.

The wrong signals? Surely it's sending out all the right signals. Spend money, make the economy boom, chisel as much as you can out of the old, weak and housebound, by terror if necessary, con the populace into paying for shoddiness, surely these are better and more realistic lessons than they've had in school for many a long year. That's the society they're being groomed for and then we moan when they turn out like us.

No, if you want to do something about the little buggers turning out wrong you've got a couple of choices. One, of course, is to biff a brick through the telly, sell all shares in The Warehouse and go back to singing hymns round the piano with the servants and a roomful of family values.

The other way is my way and it's much more fun. Try beating the little darlings into submission. The cult of the child has gone on far too long. The quaint eighteenth-century idea that they're all little angels whose self-esteem has been devastated by the traumas of industrial society got well and truly exploded in the French Revolution and at roughly 50-year intervals ever since. But the whole of our current education system is founded on that mischievous little myth and look where it's got us: tides of ignorance seeping under the skirting boards. No, far better to presume that the tinies are born twisted and all need straightening out to some degree or other, which is a far older notion known as the fall of man and which makes a sight more sense when you're faced with the reality of a classroom full of the little loves.

Once bitten twice shy, so bite them. They don't come back. My Halloween next year will be as peaceful as All Saints Day. And there's an idea. All Saints Day — what a marketing opportunity. Think of the merchandising, think of the slogans. Those saints were good guys. They'll be a doddle to sell.

Hobbes at the trough

It was Thomas Hobbes who said that human behaviour was dictated by two opposite and more or less equal forces, one being fear and the other desire. Hobbes would have been intrigued by smorgasbords.

Smorgasbords were unheard of in my youth. The nearest we came was in books and films where the higher classes had breakfast buffets featuring silver chafing dishes like plump partridges under which lay eggs benedict and kedgeree. I didn't know what either of these were, but they came with servants and tennis on the lawn and horses and girls in muslin and were out of my league.

But the inventions of the upper class have a habit of filtering down through the ranks in debased form. Hence the smorgasbord. It appeared, I think, in the late seventies as a successor to the fondue which was as fine a way as any yet invented of inducing people to buy equipment for buggering food about. The closest modern rival is the barbecue.

Anyway, the smorgasbord seemed the gastronomic equivalent of a round-the-world air ticket with unlimited stopovers. You could live at a smorgasbord. It was consumerism rampant. 'All You Can Eat' is probably the best slogan any ad man ever concocted. Hobbes would have been impressed.

The word smorgasbord sounds like a hog with its snout in something viscous but, in the original Swedish, smorgasbord is simply a verb meaning to economise on waiters while giving an illusion of opulence.

The essence of a smorgasbord is con food. Con food is placed at the near end. It aims to fill you up before you get to the good stuff. Soup is the original and still the best con food, although it has been challenged in recent years by salad. Salad used to mean leaves but with the arrival of the smorgasbord it has broadened its repertoire. Now there's an array of bowls containing what appear at best to be leftovers and at worst jokes.

Cold pasta like the flesh of the dead, only stickier; rice and sultanas dotted with sweetcorn and microscopic shrimps; tomato, cucumber, olives and cubes of polystyrene cheese soused in the sort of oil that is supposed to do your heart good and turn you into a wrinkled centenarian Italian peasant.

Beside the salads stand hot trays of cheap vegetables and lumps buried in sauce. One of these is a chicken dish and another a fish dish — indistinguishable to the eye and, as it later proves, to the palate — but one of them is also dangerously vegetarian. There's bread too and a bowl of boiled eggs cut in half and something moulded with beetroot and gelatin and a mound of traditional salad, which means very dark lettuce and very pale tomato. The tomato tastes of water; the lettuce of bitter water.

All this stuff should be shunned. That it isn't is testimony to Hobbes. Desire dictates that, on the bird-in-the-hand principle, the food in front of you, regardless of its merits, is hard to resist. Meanwhile fear warns you of the possibility of arriving at the end of the smorgasbord with too little on your plate. So on it all goes: spuds, a dab of chicken stew, a disintegrating smidgin of fish, Greek cheese, something green to assuage guilt, giant brine-soaked mussels with frill string round them like toothless gums, a dollop of unidentified gunk and then the slow shuffle while the sod in front of you picks the shrimps out of the rice salad and everyone looks at everyone else's plate.

Finally you reach a perspiring chef wearing an alarmingly stained apron and a hat like a fluted Greek column. In front of him sit two recognisable hunks of flesh under a theatrical spotlight. This concluding flourish is designed to give the belated impression of a medieval spit roast, a feast and celebration, all bounty and beneficence. Ham or beef, he asks. Your plate is a tumulus of ill-assorted substances. Nothing goes with anything. The choice of meat is irrelevant. Desire to eat and fear of missing out have rendered the meal a disappointment before you start. The promise of everything has become the delivery of too much.

The chef bloke balances too little ham on top of your mound. It looks like a garnish. For a brief Oliver Twisty moment you keep holding your plate out, but the plate is full to the point of superabundance, you don't want to look greedy and besides the chef has turned his attention to the next victim. Trailing morsels of salad you bear your plate to your table. It is impossible to know where to start eating this heap. You stab the ham and the spuds scatter and everything squashes into everything else and Hobbes chuckles.

Mad as accountants

Have you heard them? Surely you've heard them. The people who claim to be nuts. They say it smugly. They announce it like a badge. They trumpet their lunacy. 'When I'm dancing, you know, I just go mad. Absolutely mad.' They pretend to be ashamed but they invite us to admire their disdain for convention, their rich courage. It is chic to be mad, they suggest, admirable to be outré, to step beyond the perimeter fence of sanity and dance to the light of the moon.

Then there are the self-styled artists, the writers, the potters, the sculptors, and especially the painters. The painters are particularly keen on their madness, and the women painters are the worst. It's as if their supposed madness stamped their visa to the country of creation. It validates their canvases. 'My family,' say the women painters with the arch smile implying that their family, oh dear, have got it right, 'all think I'm mad. And I suppose you have to be a little mad to want, you know, to want to paint, to need to paint, as desperately as I do. Yes, I suppose you could say I'm a little mad.'

They lie. The lie makes my teeth grind. I hate it more than I hate prunes. These people are not mad. They are as sane as accountants and a lot less honest.

Let's get this straight. The truly permanently mad don't know they're mad. Their madness is ghastly and useless. It offers no insight, no worth, no good. Only grief. Madness is disconcerting, wearing, scaring. Most of us will choose to keep our distance unless we've had the ill luck to love someone who has gone mad. Then we try to stand by them and suffer their madness with them and everything hurts for ever.

These days we don't say mad. We say mentally ill. And unusually for our softened inoffensive tongue, the change is right. Mad is ill in the head. And most people who are mentally ill are ill in episodes. The illness comes and goes. The awful cruelty of it lies in knowing that it will come again. The head doctors can't do much. They'll tell you so themselves.

For the rest of us, many will be briefly ill at some time in our lives, depression in adolescence or the menopause or whenever and we'll come right again quite soon under sweet old Dr Time. But none of it is pretty. Madness is never good or brave or pretty.

So why should art and romance have attached themselves to it? Why should those who are evidently well, brag of a tinge of ill health? Why should they want to?

Shakespeare has to cop a bit of blame here. It was he who wrote that 'the poet and the lover and the lunatic are of imagination all compact'. And I for one can remember a time when I believed him. I was a sighing youthful lover who fancied himself ethereal and spiritual but who was rather afraid of bodily contact. I thought it rich to be nuts. I thought it creative to be out of my tree. I cringe to think of it. My excuse is that I was young. I knew nothing. What's their excuse? What's the excuse of the dancers and the lady daubers?

Of course Shakespeare's lines aren't Shakespeare's lines. He wrote plays. His characters said the lines. Shakespeare himself, the poet who out-poets every poet since, was as sane as a bank balance. Of the few documents we have with his signature on, one's a will and another's a mortgage, neither of which suggests the madman frothing through the world of men with never a care for reality. He held shares in his theatres. He wrote for dosh. When he'd got enough dosh he snapped his pens and bought a house and took it easy.

None of the greats have been mad. They may have been drunks or fighters, but drunks and fighters are ten a penny. The drunken fighting writers who write well, write sober. Take bardic Dylan Thomas, the soak and ne'er-do-well, the idle sponger. He was as sane and sober a writer as you could hope to find the length of Serious Street. He wrote, lord love him, with a thesaurus. You can read the number references in the margins of his manuscripts. And only when the text was done and every page of the thesaurus scoured did he reach for the whisky to celebrate. No madman he, nor did he ever claim to be.

It is one of the myths of our society that genius and lunacy are twins. They are not twins. They are not of the same family. Those who boast of being touched in the head are untouched by anything but the blessing of ordinariness.

The big question

'Why?' I said, 'why?'

He looked at me as though I was single-celled. To be fair he was only the waiter, an underling hired to do the bidding of the boss. But the boss was away hitting his profits round a golf course.

It was not the first time I have fired the question. I have fired it in perhaps 20 restaurants over the years with varying degrees of wonder and vehemence. I have fired it so often because I have never received a credible answer. It is the question of the lone giant pepper mill.

I like restaurants. I didn't go into one till I was sixteen and I've barely been out of them since. Food doesn't interest me hugely but not cooking does and so does not washing up. And so does talking to people I like on neutral territory with a little grove of unplugged bottles to ease the gears of conversation.

For the non-cooking, non-washing up reasons all restaurants are good. But some are better. The best of the lot serve large quantities of recognisable food. The furniture is various, the plates and the prices are of human proportion and there's only one cook. And that cook's a woman.

The waiter tells you neither his name nor that he is going to look after you for the evening. He does not have a pony-tail and he does not tell jokes. He does not lie in ambush at the door like a pottle of lard. He does not simper after coats and jackets, nor does he address the customer in the third person and the conditional tense — Would sir care to . . . ? — because this sir wouldn't.

The good waiter is one you immediately forget. He does not forget you. He appears by telepathy the instant you need him and at all other times he is somewhere else doing what he's paid to do, which is waiting. If at the end of an evening I haven't noticed the waiter I tip him fatly.

As soon as you enter a restaurant, order a beer. The variety of beer doesn't matter because there are only two — brown and yellow — and they taste the same. The beer's a snout-wetter. Its purpose is to get you through the barren rigmarole of menu and wine list.

Of all the restaurant flummeries the wine list wins the prize.

But its florid prose goes unread. Wine is sold only by colour and price. Colour is easy. White is for lunch, red for dinner and rosé for the pretentious who pretend they like it. Price is just as easy. The dearest wines on the list are there only for entertainment. They shape the reader's mouth into a gasp. The cheapest are there as ballast.

It would be more honest and practical if wines were not named but numbered. If, say, five wines were available, No. 1 would be the comically expensive one and No. 5 would be the cheapo. And everyone would order number No. 4.

Then the menu. I have written before about the vaunting absurdity of menus but it hasn't done any good. Tiny meals continue to be described in monstrous paragraphs. Drizzling goes on, as does grain-feeding, vine-ripening and no end of nestling.

But in the end the are-we-having-starters debate has been delicately raised and settled, the wine's been unplugged, some food has landed, minds are beginning to mesh and all is set to fulfil the purpose of restaurants, which is to increase the sum of human happiness. Enter, with waiter attached, the lone giant pepper mill. And driven by fury, puzzlement and impotence I fire my unanswerable question. Why?

Why can I not be trusted to pepper my own food? Why can pepper not be treated as salt? Why is the pepper mill so vast? Why in Italian restaurants in particular is it the size of a totem pole, except in Italian restaurants that happen to be in Italy? Why is the waiter allowed to judge the size and location of the shower of pepper on my plate?

The answers I have received have been risible. I have been told that that's how it's done these days. I have been told with staggering redundancy that it is because some customers don't like pepper. I have even been told that it is a way for the waiter to bond with his customers. I left that restaurant unfed.

So when I fired the question last night I did so without hope. I was merely venting my fist-clenching exasperation. But then, last night, at long long last, I met with honesty and sense.

'Why,' I said, 'can you not just leave pepper mills on each table?'

'Because,' said the waiter, 'the punters nick them.'
The tip I left him was a metaphorical kiss.

How far away is the lizard?

I like getting older. It allows me to be crusty. I like being crusty. For example, I submit copy to newspapers containing such sentences as, 'The lizard stood two inches from my nose'. But when it appears in print the lizard has crept five centimetres away and no reader over the age of 35 has any idea whether the lizard was lounging on the horizon or close enough to kiss.

Or am I alone in having gained no grasp of metric distances? I still don't know, for instance, how far a kilometre is. I think of a kilometre as being over there a bit, not a long way away but sort of half to three-quarters of the distance to being a long way away. In fact I think of it as being half to three-quarters of a mile. And I do know how long a mile is. A mile is just enough distance to feel that you've had a good walk. A mile takes exactly a quarter of an hour to cover at a brisk pace, the pace of, say, an accountant leaving a clinic for sexually transmitted diseases.

We used to measure in yards and I still do. A yard is a stride. Blindfold me and I will pace you out a 22-yard cricket pitch to within a foot. A metre is a stride and a bit. Try to pace out a cricket pitch in metres and you'll strain your crotch.

How tall is a tall man? He is and always has been six foot tall. How long is a foot? The answer is obvious and it's got toes. How long is a metre? If I recall it is handily the distance travelled by light in a vacuum during 1/299,792,458 of a second. But I don't recall. I had to look it up.

I do better with metric weights. I know, for example, how many apples there are in a kilogram. There are three more apples than I want. What I want is a pound of apples. A pound sounds like a weight. A kilogram sounds like an exercise machine.

When the police tell me to be on the lookout for a man 1.83 metres tall and weighing 80 kilograms, I suspect everybody.

How much is a pint? It is the amount of beer I want at a time. How much is half a litre? It is a swindler's pint. How much is a litre?

It is a glass of beer that can be easily raised by a forklift truck or a German barmaid.

How long is an inch? It is exactly the length of the top joint of my thumb. I measure short things in inches because I always carry a thumb. How long is a centimetre? It is exactly the length of a maggot. I rarely carry a maggot. If I hear that something is 30 centimetres long I have to imagine a maggot train. Or else I turn the centimetres into inches by dividing by two and a half.

Fortunately I can divide by two and a half. And I can do it because I spent my infancy in classrooms where the sun beat through the high windows and lit squares on the walls, squares that stretched into rectangles as the afternoon lengthened, all unnoticed by me because I was working out the compound interest on a sum of 21 pounds, ten shillings and threepence halfpenny invested at 5½ per cent over seven years. I am not naturally given to arithmetic but such exercise gave me a mind that handles numbers with the ease of a gibbon in a gym.

And I loved the old money. It had substance. I loved its ancient quirks. Twelve pence to the shilling. Twenty shillings to the pound. Five pounds to the pub. The abbreviation for pounds, shillings and pence was LSD, a hallucinatory bit of notation based on Latin and taking the money back a couple of thousand years. Thomas Cook was paid in this money. And the old pound sign was all twirls and flourishes. To write it was to feel rich.

Metrication and decimalisation are irreversible. Thirty years ago the authorities threw out a few thousand years of accreted history for two good reasons. One was that everyone else was doing it. This is a sound principle of behaviour that has always been popular with lemmings. In human society it has been used over the centuries to justify everything from genocide to flared trousers.

But the second reason was and is irrefutable. That reason was trade. If you retained gallons and pints and feet and inches and pounds and ounces, how could you hope to trade with the rest of a world that operated in metric terms? Why, any economy run on such ancient oddities would wither and perish, just as the economy of, say, the United States of America has done.

You too

We've all heard it said that everyone has a bore in them, and the plain fact is that it's true. Everyone does have a bore in them. But it's no use just talking about it and putting it off till you've got a bit more time on your hands. There's only one difference between real professional bores and people who fancy that they might get round to boring some day, and that difference is that bores bore.

Bores don't waste time telling people how they are working hard on boring and any day now they'll burst onto the boring scene with a dazzle that will throw all other bores into invisibility. No sir, true bores just go right ahead and bore. To be sure, they don't get it right all the time but the only way to learn to bore is by boring.

That's the tough news and I thought I'd give it to you straight. The best thing you could do now is to put this book down, buttonhole someone and bore them. You'll make mistakes but you'll also have made a start.

Your first hurdle is your natural modesty. You've seen great bores in action and you've stood in stupefaction and wondered how anyone could be so boring. You may not have said so in so many words perhaps, but somewhere in the soundless reaches of the soul you have felt it. You could never be that boring.

Well, take a moment to reflect that the bore who so arouses your wonder was once a demure uncertain fawn not unlike yourself. Hard to believe, I know, but he once doubted his opinions, deferred to others, thought listening was a virtue and worried about what other people thought. Like you he was weak. Like you he had no fun at parties. But since that date he has gone on a journey of discovery and so can you. Each one of us, be he never so lowly, has a bore in him, and don't let anyone tell you otherwise.

And indeed that is perhaps the nub of it in one sentence: don't let anyone tell you otherwise. Indeed don't let anyone tell you anything.

When you first try to bore you will trawl your mind for something to be boring about and come up with an empty net. Don't despair. You are just fishing too deep. Go to the surface of your life. You need look no further than your children. They make perfect beginner's boring material. If you are childless, pets are just as good. I began my own career with dogs.

As a nervous beginner you will feel the need to arm yourself with facts — an early hero of mine could manage a full hour without digression on medium-density fibreboard — but as you grow into boringness you will find yourself discarding facts as a porcupine discards its quills. A bore does not have to know things. He only has to say things. Manner, in short, is greater than matter. Dogmatic certainty is everything and facts are nothing.

For example, I have no idea if a porcupine discards its quills but so long as I state it emphatically and allow no interruptions I can bore. If your technique is sound, people will shrink from trying to correct you, just as you shrink from correcting the bores you so admire.

From then on the joys are unlimited. You will become a connoisseur of boring. Remember always that a bore is a body as well as a voice. The good bore uses his body like a sheep dog. Even while he is boring he is quietly guiding his victim into a corner, nudging him by imperceptible shifts of the feet until he has him pinned against the fridge. Then he uses his arm like one of those barriers at army camps to block the only route of escape.

Eyes matter too. As a good bore you must always look straight at your victim. He feels obliged to meet your manic gaze and so cannot scour the room for help.

To begin with your victim may try to contribute to the conversation. 'Ah yes,' he'll say, 'that reminds me of . . .' Quash him instantly and hard. Reduce him to expressions of agreement only. If these are not forthcoming, insist on them. 'Am I right or am I right?' is a phrase that all bores master. It works unfailingly. You can sense your victim slump.

When his eyes finally fall to his feet and he swirls the dregs in his glass and watches himself dig the toe of his shoe into the carpet and swivel it about, you know you've got him. It's a lovely moment. Once you've found the joys of boring you'll see social functions in a whole new light. It is more blessed to give than to receive.

■ I shall

Yes of course I've made a New Year's resolution. I shall behave better at parties.

When I am going to a party in 2002 I shall not take the bottle of Fijian riesling that someone once brought to my party because someone once brought it to their party. And when I take the Fijian riesling I shall not carry it with my hand over the label, nor shall I go straight to the kitchen and hide it among the other bottles of Fijian riesling and look in the fridge for beer.

I shall not pretend to recognise people. When someone at a party says, 'Hello Joe, how lovely to see you again', I shall not say it is lovely to see them again. I shall say, 'What's your name?'

When people tell me their name I shall use it five times in the first five sentences so as not to forget it. When I forget it I shall not substitute the word 'mate'.

When I kiss a woman at a party I shall not let the woman dictate how we are going to kiss. I shall decide for myself whether it is to be the lips, the cheek or the full facial bypass. If it is the full facial bypass I shall not nibble the ear. If it is the lips I shall wait a full minute before wiping my mouth. When a man makes to hug me I shall go away.

If a conversation is boring I shall not say that I am just going to fetch a drink and then not come back. I shall say I am just going to the loo and then not come back. If I say I am just going to fetch a drink the bore can ask me to fetch him one too and we are back where we started.

I shall not escape bores by pretending to catch sight of someone I know on the far side of the room and saying, 'Excuse me a minute.' Nor shall I beckon a friend across, introduce the friend to the bore and then go away.

If a friend beckons me across to meet someone I shall go away. I shall go to the back doorstep to smoke and play with the dog.

I shall not spend long periods at parties sitting on the back doorstep smoking and playing with the dog. Nor shall I steal chicken vol-au-vents to feed the dog with. Nor shall I give it sips of Fijian riesling.

I shall always take a warm sweater to parties because it can get cold on the back doorstep. A cushion would be a good idea too. And some chicken vol-au-vents.

When the party begins at 8 o'clock I shall not go to the pub first for just a quick one. Nor shall I stay at home with a book until it is too late to go to the party and then ring up in the morning and say I've just looked in the diary and how sorry I am to have missed it and was it fun and we must do it again soon.

I shall never say we must do it again soon.

When someone at a party tells me something private and juicy I shall not tell it to the next person I talk to without first asking them if they can keep a secret. If they say no I shall not just go ahead and tell them anyway.

When people ask me if I can keep a secret I shall say no. They will just go ahead and tell me anyway.

I shall not stay right to the end of parties. When I stay right to the end of parties I shall not boast that I used to be reasonably good at gymnastics. When I boast that I used to be reasonably good at gymnastics I shall not offer to do a handstand. I shall always choose a well-carpeted bit of the house to do the handstand in.

When people at parties ask me if I'd be willing to help out with the bring-and-buy sale for the local kindergarten I shall say no. And when they ring up the next day to ask if I really meant it when I said yes, I shall not say, 'Of course I meant it.' I shall say, 'No, I didn't mean it.'

When they tell me the date of the bring-and-buy sale I shall not say, 'What a pity. I'll be out of town that day.' Nor shall I then go out of town that day in case someone rings from the bring-and-buy sale.

When the beer runs out at parties I shall not drink from left-over cans that are half full. I shall sieve them first to get the cigarette ends out.

I shall not dance.

Hope is dead

Shoot the astrologers. Burn the tarot cards. I'll give you a glimpse round time's corner myself.

No need even to cross my palm with low-denomination banknotes — though a little gin money is always welcome in this cruel weather. Behold, for nothing, courtesy of my generous disposition, the future.

But before you behold, beware. It is dangerous to know the future. All who've peeped at it — Oedipus, Faust and many another sadsack — have come to ends so sticky you could mend furniture with them. Better to turn the page now. Stay ignorant and happy.

If you choose to keep reading, the risk is yours. You've been warned. And if, on some distant morning, you wake to foam-rubber decor and electrodes on your temples, well, don't come bleating to me.

Soppy to the core, we imagine the future will be nice. The future means winning the jackpot of happiness. The future means chance encounters with beautiful strangers who immediately stop being strangers and take their clothes off. Experience tells a different story, of course, but we all prefer the fantasies of hope.

Well, hope is dead. Take my hand and I will show you the way the world is going.

I have a friend whom I'll call Adam. He works for the government. Adam has recently been posted to a Pacific Island. And there, despite the twanging ukuleles and the languorous lagoons and the soporific heat and the feathery palms and the phosphorescent fish, Adam chooses not to lounge on the beach sipping drinks with umbrellas in. He goes running. The lounging locals stare at Adam with the sort of detached amusement with which Elizabethans stared at the mad.

Wild dogs infest the island. They stare at Adam with a less detached amusement. Apparently these dogs live on crabs. And the dogs see Adam as a dietary supplement. Adam is understandably alarmed. Knowing I know something of dogs, Adam sought my advice.

I wrote Adam a substantial email. I told him of a Victorian vicar who always carried a coat and an umbrella. If a bad dog approached, the vicar draped the coat over the umbrella and shoved it at the dog. The dog seized the coat. This positioned the dog nicely for the vicar to swing his boot and collect the dog under the chin. Ungodly but effective.

I wrote plenty more such helpful stuff, including a cheerful description of a removal man I once saw bitten on the buttocks by a dog. Then I pressed 'send'. But the email did not reach Adam. The government sent it back to me.

For all I know, at this very moment and for want of my advice, Adam may be down on the sand beside the languorous lagoon being mauled to death by wild dogs, while the locals look on with detached amusement, strumming their ukuleles and taking care not to stab themselves in the eye with a drink umbrella. If so, blame the government. Or more specifically, blame MailMarshal.

Because MailMarshal intercepted my email to Adam, read it, went puce around the gills, and sent it back with a note attached. It was a curt note. No 'dear' at the start. No parting benison of love or kisses.

Here is what MailMarshal wrote:

> MailMarshal (an automated content monitoring gateway) has stopped the email for the following reason:
> It believes it may contain unacceptable language, or inappropriate material.
> Please remove any inappropriate language and send it again.
> Script Offensive Material Triggered
> Expression: (my OR your OR nice OR big OR the OR her OR his OR fat OR tight OR sweet OR great) FOLLOWED BY 'arse'

And there we have it. Behold tomorrow in all its unglory. Told off by a machine. A machine, furthermore, that is not subject to its own rules. I sent it a mild vulgarity. It sent me back a note so suggestive, so crammed with boggling sexual possibility, that I had to lie down and fan myself with a dog-eared copy of the *Norwegian Naturist*.

Once I'd recovered I set to work on MailMarshal. To find out where it drew its lines, I sent it screeds of emails. It accepted gluteus maximus. It accepted bum, buttocks, bottom, situpon, posterior, rectum and jacksie. But it turned down, well, let's not worry about what it turned down.

In a final provocative torrent I sent MailMarshal a note using every one of the offending words it sent me, and more than a few of my own, a note so rich that it would have shivered the timbers of my nautical great-uncle Dick. MailMarshal has yet to reply.

But it will. Machines persist. They know no better. MailMarshal will carry on long after the death of the prurient bureaucrat who programmed it. Indeed, long after Adam's bones have been bleached to the colour of the sand they may be lying on, long after Baghdad has been razed to rubble, long after, indeed, the human race has poisoned or bombed itself into holes in the ground, MailMarshal, son of MailMarshal, and a host of other 'content monitoring gateways' will be protecting us from naughty words, imposing arbitrary illiterate primness on words sent from friend to friend.

Automated censorship. You read it here first.

At the Dickens

I'd always wanted to get into motivational speaking but I owe the chance to my Auntie Debs. When she finally fell off the poop deck after a long and lucrative career in the fishing industry I was her sole heir. My brother got the cod.

But neither of us was interested in fishing. He sold his cod immediately and I palmed off my sole to a nice little man with a beard and a fork. We were rich. My brother was a born idler and took off for the land of milk and honey. But I stayed put.

For years, you see, I'd had my ear to the ground and my nose to the wind. As a result I had my eye on a struggling little motivational speakers' bureau in town. It was called the Dickens and had fallen on hard times.

On a breezy March morning I strode into the Dickens clutching my fishing cheque. I pushed open the battered door and found myself in a deep and fusty gloom. The place was scattered with dusty accoutrements. The Dickens was one bleak house.

As my pupils widened in the crepuscular office I made out a figure slumped over the only desk. I pulled out a gin bottle and he came to with a jerk. Pausing only to tell the jerk to beat it, I poured us both a stiff one and came straight to the point.

'Mr Dickens,' I said, 'I hear you got motivational speakers.'

He laughed a laugh so hollow that I tipped my slug of gin into it. 'Mate,' he said, 'I got more motivational speakers than you can shake a stick at.' He handed me a stick.

I shook it. And suddenly the dusty accoutrements took shape as human figures, shambling and derelict, score upon score of them. I tried to shake my stick at all of them but there were too many.

'How much for the lot?' I asked.

'Yours for a song.'

I gave him a Christmas carol and he was out the door of the Dickens before you could say knife.

'Knife,' said one of the shambling figures.

'Too late,' I said, 'he's gone. You're mine now. Now get out there and get motivating.'

'Ha,' said the shambling figure. 'You greenhorn. Any idea how many motivational speakers there are these days? The country's swarming with them. Ex-alcoholics, buggered triathletes, slimming champions, swimming champions, positive thinkers, stockmarket gurus — billions of us. And no one wants to hear us any more. People have seen through us. Everyone I know in the industry is trying to get out of it.'

Before you could say Jack Robinson I realised what I had to do. I buttonholed the shambling speaker. 'Name?' I barked.

'Jack Robinson,' he said.

'Jack,' I cried, 'we have nothing to fear but fear itself. I'm going to release your creative energies in a way that you wouldn't have dared to dream possible. Are you with me, Jack?'

'Whatever,' said Jack gloomily, 'but I never was into that positive thinking caper. I was the super-memory man. You know, twenty tapes for three easy payments of $99, guaranteed to help you recall everyone's name at a party.'

'Yeah, yeah,' I said, 'what happened to that racket?'

'Don't remember,' said Jack, 'but it's dead now, like everything else in this biz.'

'He's right,' came a voice, 'you don't have to be a rocket scientist to see it's all over, mate. They've rumbled us.'

'Name?'

'Kuzolski. Rocket scientist. Chief safety engineer on the Voyager mission.'

'The one they lost touch with?'

'No, the one that blew up 'cause of a cock-up by the chief safety engineer. When NASA gave me the elbow I thought I'd try the motivational speaking line. "'Your mistakes are your biggest asset' by the man who blew up the space probe." Thought it would be a nice comfy little number, you know, regular pay cheque, no responsibilities, all that stuff. And look at me now. Look at all of us.' He gestured to his fellow motivators, slumped in the shadows. 'We're dog tucker, mate, yesterday's men. No one's swallowing our baloney any more. Unleash your creative potential, be the CEO of your self, every idea's a good idea.' He chuckled. 'That particular idea was probably the worst of the lot.'

A murmur of assent scurried through the ranks.

'So,' I said, 'if motivation's a goner, where do we go from here?'

'Demotivation?' said one wag, from the echoing depths of his gloom.

'Precisely,' I bellowed. 'Got it in one.' I sensed eyes flicker into life and look up at me.

'It's time,' I said, 'to rediscover the wisdom of the ancients. Delude yourself is out. Know thyself's back in.'

I looked at my congregation of demotivated motivators. An old familiar light was burning in their eyes. One by one their careworn faces were shaking off their looks of rusty depression and shining like new roofing iron. They were galvanised.

'Now, put your little thinking caps on. I want ideas. I want catch-phrases. I want mottos.'

'How about,' said Jack, ' "Dare to be ordinary"?'

'Be alive. Work nine to five.'

'Orville Wright was wrong.'

'Stay at work. You're just a jerk.'

I've no need to go on. You're familiar with the story. How the Dickens Academy of Demotivation blew the whole motivational speaker racket out of the water. Made people happy to be who they were. Put all the team-building confidence courses into bankruptcy. To cut a long story short, I made a killing, cashed up at the peak of the market and flew out to join my bro in the land of milk and honey.

But things had turned sour for him. He'd come to a sticky end.

Warm, wet and threatless

I had a theory about the bathroom habits of the sexes, but I lacked evidence to support it. So I went to the trouble and expense of doing a survey. With full statistical rigour I surveyed everybody sitting at the bar.

The survey resoundingly proved my theory to be true: women prefer baths and men prefer showers. Or, to put it another way, my survey confirmed that men are more sensible than women, more hygienic, thrifty, musical and conscious of the dwindling of the earth's resources. I enjoyed typing that sentence. It will bring me death threats.

My theory may also explain why men are still in charge of most things. By the time a woman has run a bath, got the temperature right, soaked herself, soaped herself and played with her duck, a man has had a shower, put on a tie, gone to work and done at least half an hour of shouting. But what it doesn't explain is why women like baths so much.

The bath has a totemic quality. It often appears in television advertisements, containing a lot of bubbles and a woman stupefied with pleasure. That woman is not me.

Nevertheless I was brought up with a bath. I was dropped into it every second night along with my elder brother. And it was in that bath I learned that there is no sensation worse than water up the nostrils. It spells panic in capital letters. I was also suspicious of shampoo. It tasted bad and stung the eyes, so God alone knew what it was doing to my hair. Now I know that too. It was making my hair fall out.

When my brother decided he preferred to bath alone — a decision forced on him by the courses he chose at university — I had to run my own bath. I soon learned that the perfect temperature for a bath is the one it isn't at.

I also learned that the hand is a bad thermometer. Dangle it in a too-hot bath and it will tell you that it's not too hot, so you step in. Feet are better thermometers, but they are slow. You can stand there for several seconds while the too-hot message lumbers up the legs, circumnavigates the pelvis, dawdles up the spinal column and then emerges through the oesophagus as a yelp. You leap from the bath like a pole vaulter and find you've gained a pair of vermilion ankle socks.

So you cool the bath a little, before stepping back in. Then you grip the sides and lower your vulnerabilities towards the water in the manner of a tentative anglepoise lamp.

At this stage you hold your breath, so that at the moment of contact you can emit a series of little gasps like a chimp's orgasm. As you finally submerge your shoulders and the water sloshes lovingly onto the bathroom floor, you complete the chimp orgasm with a long satisfied 'aaaah'.

But then what? A chimp just says thanks, cleans itself up and goes about its business. But the bath-taker, well, what is there for him to do? Lie there stewing in his own dirt? Constantly and inaccurately adjust the taps with his toes in an effort to keep the temperature right? Read a book? I've no idea. You'll have to ask a woman.

The only bath I remember liking was after rugby. Someone else filled it and both teams got into it. If you were the fifth team playing on a muddy day, the bath looked like a tourist attraction in Rotorua. But unlike a tourist attraction in Rotorua, you could smoke, drink beer and boast to twenty-nine other men in it.

These days I rarely bath with twenty-nine men. The last person I bathed with was Jane Austen. I'd bought a house that came with a salmon pink spa-bath studded with water jets in what looked like amusing locations. Eager to try it I plucked Jane from the shelves and stripped off. To make the jets jet there was a small electric motor conveniently housed just below my right shoulder. When I pressed the button to start it my eyes vibrated. So did Jane Austen. Sadly the eyes and Jane vibrated at different speeds. I gave up, got out and have never had a bath since.

But every woman I know has. Though showers are better than baths for all purposes, up to and including sex and opera, women persist in taking baths.

Why is this so? Relentless in pursuit of truth I put the question to all the women in my bar survey. 'What exactly is it,' I said to her, 'that you like about baths? Is it that they offer a refuge from a spiky world, a cocooning warmth and privacy, an escape from the demands of children and men? Or is it that you are fundamentally a tactile being and a bath is like a million warm and threatless hands exploring you? Or is it something Freudian, a journey of nostalgia to the womb, a floating in the waters of security, a reversion to an amniotic world?'

'Yeah,' she said. So now you know.

Hapsburg staplers

'Everything's interesting,' I said.

'Everything?' she said.

'Everything,' I said. 'Lana Coc-Kroft, heavy metal, heavy petting, heavy water, diseased Peruvian conceptual artists, the lot.'

'Staplers,' she said.

'Well,' I said, 'perhaps not staplers, but Namibian cooking classes, phone-card collecting, Tahitian voting habits, the whole caboodle, every little bit of it is . . .'

'Staplers,' she said. 'You said that everything was interesting and everything includes staplers. So kindly explain why staplers are interesting. Come on. I'm waiting . . . No? I'm not surprised. Because staplers are just bureaucratic tools and bureaucracy is about as interesting as athlete's foot.'

'Which, interestingly,' I said, 'is most common among non-athletes.' But I might as well not have spoken.

'I mean,' she went on, 'what is bureaucracy but a doomed attempt to compartmentalise? Divide a random world into topics, assemble some pages on each topic, then clip them with the stapler and drop them into the file marked sussed. A futile business, doomed as the kakapo, but necessary to gratify the sort of tiny mind that cannot cope with lack of order. You can see it in the very way a man applies a staple, aligning the papers just so, angling the stapler at precisely 45°, then applying cautious pressure with the heel of his pudgy hand so that the scrap of metal passes through the wad without buckling and then neatly folds its arms on the other side, smug as the buddha under a tree, as if to say, that's done, that's dealt with. Next.

'And if, despite the man's precautions, the staple still insists on buckling and thus mars the perfect neatness of the whole, what does our deskbound functionary do but reach for his destapler, a baby pair of pincers designed specifically and solely for removing buckled staples without the risk of doing damage to the dirtless fingernails of Wellington? It's all so petty and depressing, so lacking in breadth, vision, risk. So come on, tell me why staplers are of the least interest to anyone at all except a shallow-minded, raincoat-wearing bureaucrat.'

'Well,' I said.

'And you are not allowed,' she said, 'to refer to the way boys at school insist on opening staplers out and using them as guns.'

'I wouldn't have dreamed of mentioning it,' I said.

'Because,' she said, 'that is merely typical of the primitive male psyche that seeks to turn everything into a weapon without regard to its purpose or to the waste of natural resources. Boys scatter staples as they scatter sperm. It's violence and profligacy without thought, the hallmark of the male. And while we're at it, do you know what is the biggest trading commodity today on this faltering little planet of ours? Do you imagine it's wheat or oil or fertiliser or something similar?'

'Staplers?' I ventured.

'It's armaments, boyo,' she said, pronouncing the word as if it were checkmate, 'armaments. And who commissions the armaments, designs the armaments, makes the armaments, sells the armaments, buys the armaments and presses the little buttons that fire the armaments? Answer me that, sonny.'

'Men?' I said.

'Men,' she said. 'Men who were once boys and who ripped the staplers off their female classmates who were constructively assembling projects on solar power and vegetarianism, and then turned the staplers into guns, thus inverting the biblical injunction to beat swords into stationery.'

'Ploughshares.'

'Exactly,' she said, 'and now that you've mentioned it, where do you think staplers come from, eh? I'll tell you where they come from.'

'Oh good,' I said.

'No,' she said, 'bad. Ever seen a stapler factory? Of course you haven't. The prosperous self-indulgent west doesn't make staplers any more, or anything else that's useful. We've forgotten how to make anything except armaments and geopolitical gaffes. We hand over all the humdrum manufacturing to what we're fond of calling the under-developed countries, where they employ six-year-olds with rickets.'

'I see,' I said.

'Oh no you don't,' she said. 'You barely see the start of it. That's just . . .'

'No clichés, please.'

'The tip of the iceberg,' she said. 'Because in the humble stapler you can see the twenty-first century unfolding and the fate of the dominant culture. The west has become bureaucracy-laden, and over-intricate. It's the classic symptom of an empire in decline. It happened to the Hapsburgs, to the Romans and, for all we know, to the Incas. They all became stapler freaks.

'Right this minute power is shifting unstoppably east and south to the hungry busy places, places like India, Indonesia and the hugely menacing China, places where they're not ashamed to get their hands dirty even if it means making silly little staplers for the effete societies that they are about to overtake and overwhelm and crush. So don't go around trying to tell me that staplers are uninteresting.'

'Sorry,' I said.

Let's make with the jam

Jet-skiers. I've thought about them. I really have. I've even tried, and I know it's unfashionable, to be fair. But I can see no way around my original conclusion. They should be arrested. They should be convicted. And then they should have their nostrils packed with raspberry jam and they should be strapped to the ground in an area popular with soldier ants.

At the toe-end of a hot day my dog often takes me to the beach. She likes it there. She can frolic in the cool water and she can piss on the sandcastles that the kiddiwinkies have made and then forgotten. When she pisses, the crenellations darken then melt. And she can bark at seagulls. They don't seem to mind being barked at. They just do a bit of effortless wheeling and mewing then settle twenty yards up the beach, which is simply too far for my ageing dog to bother to amble for another dose of barking pleasure.

I like the beach too but I don't bark at the gulls and I never piss on the sandcastles until after dark. What I like is the Wordsworthian stuff.

Wordsworth wrote a sonnet about an evening on the beach. He gave it an imaginative title. He called it 'Evening on the Beach'. Here's the start of it.

> It is a beauteous evening, calm and free;
> The holy time is quiet as a nun
> Breathless with adoration; the broad sun
> Is sinking down in its tranquillity.

The trouble with stuff like that is that you can't dislodge it. It enters your head at an early age and just sits there waiting. Thirty years later you pop down to the evening beach with the dog for a bit of pissing and communion, and the sea is calm and the air is warm and the sun is setting and the hills are darkening and a little flotilla of yachts is streaming across the bay, their sails as taut and sweet as pregnancies, and the ripples are susurrating on the sand and there's a great freight of peacefulness and you go, 'Oooh that's nice'.

And you try to decide exactly what it is that's nice about it, and your brain goes riffling through the memory banks as if they were some vast telephone directory. But instead of coming up with a startling new verbal arrangement that defines the relationship between the human and the sweetness of the great inane, the brain takes the easy route and comes up with Wordsworth. 'Holy time,' says the brain, 'quiet as a nun, and all that. There you go, that's that dealt with and pinned down. Anything else you want of me right now? No? Good, let's bugger off to the pub.' Which we did.

The following day the nor-wester blew and you could have grown rubber plants in my armpits, and the dog retired to the shade beneath the table on the deck, panting like a pump. But in the evening the wind abated and life was possible once more, and the dog and I went down to the seas again to the lonely sea and the sky, and all we asked was more of the same — sandcastles, gulls and nun-quiet. We got a jet-ski.

It was driven, astonishingly, by an adult. Less astonishingly he was a he. He drove in circles. In creative moments he drove in figures of eight. His jet-ski made a wake and then he drove excitingly over the wake. Physically he was going nowhere. Morally he was going backwards. He was reverting to infancy. He was a tot on a plastic tricycle making chugging noises. Here was movement for the sake of movement, power for the sake of power, noise for the sake of noise. Here was unthinking purposeless man driven by a grossly throaty engine and his own primordial testosterone.

The noise his contraption made had all the charm of a dental drill. The holy time was no longer quiet as a nun. The nuns were still breathless, but only because they were running away. And there, hot-footing it after them, was Wordsworth, his hands to his ears and the tails of his frock-coat streaming out behind him. And there was I, standing on the beach, cursing. Unlike the nuns, who are too nice, and Wordsworth who's too dead, I'd have happily hit the man. He had committed an act of theft. He had stolen the quiet, stolen the peace, plucked the necessary goodness from the evening and left only the bitter husk of anger.

Compare his contraption with the ancient silence of the yachts on the previous evening. On second thoughts, don't bother. The conclusions are too obvious. And anyway, now's not the time for thinking. I've done all that. Now's the time for action. Let's make with the nostrils and the raspberry jam. And a smear or two on the genitals might be amusing too.

▌Train me, please

How's your personal trainer? Do his silky shorts ripple? Is he oiled and chunky, as specified in the manual? Are his logo-encrusted training shoes still as bright as the day they were made by dollar-a-day peasants in Guandong? In short, is he well?

Oh, good. I am pleased. Though I can't say I'm surprised. Being well is what personal trainers do. One sees so few with stumps or dripping syphilitic sores.

Oh, thank you for asking. Yes, I'm delighted to say that my personal trainers are well too. They're outside at the moment, addressing bones. Jessie's a bit yellow in the tooth these days, but she and Baz still work their magic. They make me walk miles, every day of the week, come rain, wind or cricket on television. To be frank, I don't know quite what I'd do without them. Because one is so awfully weak, isn't one?

Hard to imagine it now but personal trainers were once exclusive to Hollywood stars. Stars depended on appearance. In a three-dimensional world stars were known in only two dimensions, so they just had to look good. But time and excess are always nipping at good looks. Stars knew the story of Johnny Weissmuller. Johnny Weissmuller was Tarzan. Tarzan was strong, but then Tarzan grew breasts. The vine on which Tarzan swung through the fake jungle had to be reinforced. In the end, as always, gravity won. When the last vine snapped, Tarzan landed with a fat splash in the swamp of obscurity and sank from view.

So the personal trainer was born. He lived on set in a caravan only slightly less plush than his owner's. His job was to haul the star from the silk sheets each morning and have him or her panting up Beverly Hills before the breakfast of peeled grapes and adulation.

Stars needed personal trainers because they were just too busy and too important to be able to do everything for themselves. But now, suddenly, personal trainers are as common as the cold. What can have happened?

Let's start, as always, with the language. How does a personal trainer differ from a mere trainer? Easy. The personal trainer is private property. He is uniquely yours, effectively a slave.

Only he isn't. These days a personal trainer may have 100 clients. But the language still implies otherwise. The word 'personal' carries a residual note of possession, of proprietary control. Over cocktails one casually mentions the personal trainer in the same way as one mentions the Porsche. He's an expensive accessory, a trophy, a Prada handbag with pecs. His very existence defines the life one leads, or the life one wants to be seen to be leading. He is exactly the sort of furniture that the magazines tell us we ought to be furnishing our lifestyles with. He is so zeitgeisty, so very chic and now.

He is also fresh flesh. Contemporary religious orthodoxy requires us to worship fresh flesh. Wisdom is nothing, looks are everything and looks belong to the young. The personal trainer is a totem of the times, a decorative fetish, and it is far easier to buy a fetish than to come to terms with ageing. The fetish may be thick as a shag-pile, and shallow as a puddle, but oh, just look at those abs.

Yet the more revealing word is 'trainer'. Once upon a time, only animals had trainers. Trainers taught seals to head beach balls and chimps to drink tea. The idea was to make them look amusingly like human beings. Human beings were the dominant species, uniquely autonomous.

We human beings needed trainers only in childhood. We were potty trained. Our first bike came with training wheels. We went to training school. But then we grew up. As adults we developed a will. Will is what makes us do what we might not instinctively do. It is will that makes us stand up to the bully who scares us. It is will that makes us persevere when a cause looks lost. It is will that keeps us calm when others panic. But it is always easier to cave in, to give up, to panic. Will is hard.

What could be more obvious, then, than to pay someone to embody our will for us? That someone is the personal trainer. He is our self-reliance externalised, our autonomy relinquished. He is an admission that we cannot do things for ourselves. When we feel we need determination, the personal trainer will provide. He will make us do what is good for us; make us clean our teeth, dry between our toes and go to bed early with cocoa. He is Mummy and Daddy. For a fee he will appear to care for us. We can take our guilt to him and he will shrive us and inspire us and praise us and he will scoop us up in his mighty forearms and he will carry us through the long nightmare of our lives, cared for and safe. He will not take us where we think we want to go, which is back to the body beautiful, but he will take us where we actually want to go, which is back to the kindergarten.

The things people believe

I have read somewhere that there's a belief gene that predisposes the owner to believe in such obvious nonsense as gods. I'm not convinced. Pretty well everybody in Teheran is Muslim and everyone in Salt Lake City Mormon. The cause has to be cultural indoctrination. And the sooner it withers the better. Belief gets people nowhere. If churches had had their way, life would still be ignorant, hungry and brief for everyone except priests. No church ever invented a washing machine.

And yet, at the most august universities in the Western world, it is still possible to study theology. I can think of no word more inherently self-contradictory or more fundamentally silly than theology. Ah well.

And it isn't just gods. Beliefs and superstitions abound. They dress up as thoughts, but underneath the finery there's nothing. Thought is the only thing that has ever got the human race anywhere.

Standing for nothing

I know my godson's name but he does not know mine. Shortly after he was born I sent him a present but he didn't write back so that was the end of that. But I have just learned that if his parents should perish in a car crash I will become responsible for my godson's moral education. Poor little darling. I wish his parents long and happy lives and I suggest they buy a Volvo.

My relationship with my godson resembles my relationship with God. Once or twice in times of stress I've tried to ring God but he hasn't answered the phone. I have spoken only to his secretary, Miss Time, an ancient spinster, all bosom and tweed. Miss Time always tells me that God's in a meeting and asks if she could be of help. I unburden myself to her and she offers unchanging advice. 'Wait,' she says, 'be patient. This too will pass.' She's right, of course, but it always takes a while for things to get better and by then I can't be bothered to write and thank her. In which respect, I suppose, I'm as ungrateful as my godson. But actually I prefer Miss Time to God. God's too definite for me. He's got strong opinions.

I once knew a school chaplain who wore short shorts and read short prayers. Children, he said, paid little attention to long prayers. I could have told him that they paid scant attention to any prayers, but I didn't because, well, I just didn't. Anyway, his favourite prayer ran thus: 'O Lord, let me stand for something lest I fall for anything. Amen.'

This prayer impressed me by its brevity, its memorability, its neat antithetical construction and its profound and unmatchable stupidity. It suggests that any opinion is better than no opinion. It suggests that having no opinion is dangerous. The truth of the world is precisely the opposite. Opinions are bad things.

By opinions I do not mean ideas, and I do not mean thought. An opinion is rarely born of thought. Instead it arrives fully formed in a head. Opinions are, as I have written elsewhere, almost always emotion in fancy dress. They can be inherited, or they can spring from fears or desires, but they are never right.

Yet look how ferociously, how indefatigably, people cling to their opinions in the face of a flood of evidence that those opinions are at best questionable, and more likely mere dump fodder.

Look at the intransigent folly of so much politics. Look at the nonsense that passes for political debate. Listen to the roaring when a political opponent slips. Hear the deep delighted belly laughs when Marian Hobbs gets confused. That isn't debate. That's merely a primal contest for power in which one side has caught a glimpse of an unprotected jugular. Yet if you want to take part in this contest you are required to join a team and in order to join a team you have to have a packaged set of opinions.

Where do those opinions come from? Are they arrived at by rational analysis? If so, and if reason is reason, how come they differ? But opinions are not reasonable.

We are emotional creatures in an irrational world. Anyone who holds opinions is wrong and dangerous. The European colonists of the nineteenth century were wrong and dangerous. Karl Marx was wrong and dangerous. George Speight is wrong and dangerous.

The only comfortable seat for a thinking human being is a fence. How is it, when we know so much about human nature from Shakespeare's plays, know more indeed than we could hope to garner from any other source, that we know so little about Shakespeare's opinions? The answer is that he doubted. He was a fence-sitter, an observer, a puppeteer who jigged his little figures about on stage and made them hold every opinion which was popular in the sixteenth century — and which, oddly enough, are the same opinions as are popular in the twenty-first — and he set his opinionated characters to play out their dramas of conflict and resolution, of crowns and thorns, of love and loss, of birth and death while he himself sat in among them smiling gently, tolerantly on their fierce little blindnesses. Shakespeare knew the primacy of emotion and the supreme virtue of doubt.

So if my buddy God should move in that mysterious way of his and drop a thunderbolt or a tree on the Volvo that belongs to my old friends Philip and Olivia and thereby squash them dead, then I shall indeed accept the duty of a godfather. And when I greet my grief-stricken godson at the airport, I shall straightway seize him by the ankles and shake him until all opinions tumble out of him. And I shall then endeavour to fill the gap with doubt.

And, as has always been the way of the world, and as will always be the way of the world, the boy won't listen to a word I say. Just like everybody else, he will have to nose his own way through Miss Time's assault course, sniffing an idea here, a theory there, moving on, and nudging, one hopes, ever closer to the throne of doubt. Meanwhile I shall be on my knees in the cathedral, praying 'O Lord, let him stand for nothing lest he should believe it'. Not, of course, that I shall expect my prayer to be answered.

And that's my opinion.

Deep in the dogs

It's Christmas. Raise the drawbridge, drop the portcullis, nail the letter box shut and draw the curtains. But it's no good. Christmas gets through. Only today an electronic Christmas card slid into my computer, starring a snowman and a sledge and a poem of greetings beside which Al Gore's concession speech seemed a model of sincerity.

The dogs and I flee daily to the hills for long meditative Scrooge-meets-Wordsworth walks. But then some fool in the pub tells me I shouldn't. Why, I say. Grass seeds, he says. Pfui, I say with emphasis on the f, but nevertheless I listen.

Apparently I'm endangering the dogs. Grass seeds can lodge between the pads of a dog's paw where all is dark and damp and composty and, having lodged there, they can sprout and wreak horrible damage. What sort of damage, I ask. Use your imagination, he says. Pfui, I say again, but while it's perfectly all right, indeed admirable, to say pfui to a bloke in the pub, you can't say pfui to the imagination. Well you can, but it's about as effective as saying 'stay' to my little black mongrel. Neither she nor my imagination ever attended obedience classes. Give my imagination a horror scene to play with and it's like a ferret in a chicken coop.

And so the mind conjures images of grass seeds lodging in paws and sprouting and sending shoots up the inside of my dogs' legs. The shoots follow the paths of the veins, drawing sustenance from the marrow, silent and insidious, blindly driving up towards the light, until suddenly they burst alien-like from the dogs' backs. The dogs yelp with a suffering I can alleviate only with a mower.

But I have told my imagination to sit and though it has continued to whine I have ignored it. Up the hills once more go the dogs and I for the joy that is in them. The warm wet spring has done wonders for the grass. It is more than dog deep. The dogs bound through it like furry dolphins. When they stand still they disappear. Meanwhile I sneeze along behind them through the wake of pollen.

My dogs have both been fixed and so lead an enviable existence from which the main source of expense and misery has been excised by a scalpel. I wish someone would spay the grass. Its reproductive weaponry is formidable. There are seeds like spears, and seeds like arrow-heads, and sticky seeds and seeds with hooks on and above all there are little bullet seeds with a pair of pointed ends. But the man in the pub was wrong about the seeds. The dogs are fine and dandy. It's me that is under attack. The seeds pierce my clothing, gather in trouser cuffs, stick in hair, mass in shoes and sink into socks. How they manage it I don't know but the bullet seeds in particular know how to burrow into socks like moles of malice. And, having burrowed, they scratch. They scratch wickedly and irresistibly. I weigh thirteen stone, and a seed weighs approximately nothing, but it brings me down. I sit, remove my shoe, remove my sock, remove the seed, replace the sock, replace the shoe, stand up and the seed's still there. When I get home I try washing the socks but seeds scoff at such feebleness. They're as persistent as Christmas.

And so it was yesterday that the seeds took me to Horrorville. Off to the shopping mall I drove where I found a convenient car park in little under an hour. Shunning the giant synthetic Christmas tree crowned with some sort of electrical bird that squawked as I passed, I sought out the shoe shop. I want, I said to the frazzled girl, a pair of shoes that are rugged enough to climb hills, that can be worn without socks and that do not collect grass seeds. She led me gently by the hand to a display of the sort of shoes that, in youth, one vowed never to buy. Ranged before me were a hundred pairs of the strappy brown sandals worn by chemists on holiday, disciples in nineteenth-century paintings and people who shouldn't wear shorts but do. 'There you go,' she said, 'Jesus boots.' I bought two pairs to run away from Christmas in.

The thyroid of Unks

I'm going to become a doctor.

This afternoon, you see, I was fool enough to pick up a ringing phone. I listened for a bit and then I said no.

'Sorry,' I said, 'I can't, not now, I'm busy.'

'Busy?'

'Busy,' I said, 'I'm going to bed.'

'It's two in the afternoon,' she said.

'And I'm going to bed.'

'Why?' she said.

'Because I like it,' I said, 'and because I can.'

'So when are you going to write this stuff?'

'Oh,' I said, 'sorry. I didn't quite grasp your meaning. You mean I should forgo the siesta that more enlightened societies consider a matter of national duty when the heat squats heavy on the hills and the dogs pant in the shade and when anyone in anything approaching a condition of sanity retreats into the deep cool of a shuttered bedroom, I should forgo, you say, that rich and luxurious pleasure and instead should sit sweating before a screen and a desk fan in order to write 500 words for you for some hideous brochure advertising an event which I would attend only with a ring through my nose, 500 words furthermore for which you are planning to pay me nothing but a flitting thank you. Have I got that right? Is that what you meant?'

'Yes,' she said.

'Fine,' I said. 'Okay. And then tomorrow when I am good for nothing because of a shortage of sleep I suppose I am to take sustenance from a few lightly grilled thank yous with a side salad of insincerity, tossing the remnants to the skeletal dogs. Is that what you rang to tell me?'

'I think you've got an underactive thyroid,' she said.

'A what?' I said so vigorously that the dogs retracted their tongues and lifted their heads in wonder at my expenditure of energy on a sweltering afternoon. 'A what?'

'An underactive thyroid,' she said, with the smug calm of someone who has read a whole magazine on her own without help and hardly mouthing the words at all as she read. 'It's quite common. Unks has got one.'

'Unks?'

'Unks. My uncle. It makes him tired in the afternoon and it makes him irritable and it makes him fat.'

'I'm not fat,' I said.

Silence.

'I'm not very fat,' I said.

'Fried food,' she said, 'beer. I bet you barely touch fruit from one end of a week to the other.'

'I find it hard to fry,' I said.

'Your antioxidants,' she said, 'where do you get them from? And think of the free radicals. You're a time bomb. The big C is lurking round the corner. You treat your body like a dog.'

'But I'm nice to my dogs,' I said. 'I let them sleep of an afternoon.'

She hung up. I lay down. But she had banished sleep. I could sense my thyroid snoozing. I could hear the slow clogging of cholesterol. I could feel the creaking of the arteries like hosepipes left out in the sun. I felt the dangers of a little knowledge bearing down on every side. And it was there in the hot discomfort of my enseamed bed that I decided to become a doctor.

It must be so easy now. No doctor needs to know a thing. Any patient worth his aspirin comes to the surgery with a headful of medical mysticism garnered from that fount of all hocus pocus, the Internet. All the doctor has to do is to agree. That wild yam cream, yes it's just the thing for those phyto-oestrogens. That selenium supplement, a bonzer idea. Zinc for the prostate, absolutely. Ginkgo, you can't go wrong. Your thyroid, as underactive as a dozing Spaniard.

Has there ever been a time when so many lay people have claimed some understanding of medicine? Has there ever been a time when so much simplistic nonsense has been spouted about health and so much credulous attention paid to it? Have we lost sight of the truth that the body is a massively complex entity and that most of our tinkering is little more than faith healing? And have we forgotten that the body is intrinsically robust, and that if we run around a bit and eat a bit and laugh a lot the body will see us out for an appropriate number of years more or less regardless of what we do to it? Have we ever been so hypochondriac?

I don't know, but I do know it's a good time to be a doctor. All I'll have to do is roll up for a couple of hours each morning to stamp my official approval on the diagnoses and the nostrums of my patients. And that will leave the afternoon free for something that actually does me good.

Girlie sox

Are you a sturdy independent, one who stands strong and rooted when the winds of fashion blow, one who disdains the mob, who proclaims 'no coward soul is mine', who stands for what he stands for and who rises above fad? Me too. And yet I've bought three pairs of girlie socks.

Girlie socks are the socks you wear when you pretend not to be wearing socks. Professional female tennis players have always worn girlie socks. And although professional female tennis players grow more muscular every year, and although they grunt like mastodons — or at least how I imagine mastodons would have grunted, which is effortlessly — they still, the tennis players that is and not the mastodons, wear girlie socks. At their girliest these socks have a pink bobble on the back to stop the sock shrivelling into the shoe.

My girlie socks do not have a pink bobble on the back. Nevertheless I cannot deny their girliness. Nor can I pretend they are an error. I drove to The Warehouse, strode through home appliances and stationery and reached menswear after a mere fifteen minutes. I studied the sock racks. I fingered and I pondered. For as long as I have been buying my own socks the result of this exercise has never varied. I have come away from the store with emphatically non-girlie socks. But not any more.

I can understand why female tennis players wear girlie socks. By being hidden in the shoe, girlie socks make legs look longer. Longer legs are sexier legs. What is harder to understand is why I should now wear them. My legs are as long as they need to be. Though they satisfactorily link my buttocks to my feet, my legs do not excite me and forty-five years of experience suggest that I would be unwise to expect them to excite others. Nevertheless I have now encased the southern ends of those legs in long-leg-making girlie socks.

Since I was seventeen I have played squash in the sort of white ankle socks that used-car salesmen in the eighties wore with slip-on shoes. I am pleased to report that the car salesmen have forsaken those socks, but I have persisted with them for squash. I have found them cheap and satisfactory.

They are made in some factory in Pakistan or Taiwan where the workers earn a dollar a day. I have never cared about these workers because I have never met them. If I did meet them I imagine that I would still not care.

I have worn a thousand pairs of their socks until the heel in each has withered from a cushion of fluff to a transparent but indestructible lattice of nylon. When a sock reaches that point I put it in a drawer. Five years later I come across it curled and grey like corpse skin, and I throw it away. But each sock has done its duty. Honest traditional ankle socks, convenient, cheap, serving their purpose, the dull foot soldiers in the hosiery war. But now I have forsaken them for girlie socks.

Money does not explain my change of heart. Girlie and non-girlie socks were the same price. Colour does not come into it either. White is white. A man with whom I used to play squash, now cruelly killed by cancer, used to play in unmatching fluorescent socks. But though I admired him and though he regularly beat me and laughed as he did so, I could never emulate him. I am a white sock man.

The only reason I can offer for my shift into girlie socks is, well, take down your photo album. Turn, if you are old enough, to the seventies. Stare at the flares and the hair and the chunky shoes and the cheesecloth shirt with the tear-drop collar. Or the hotpants or the maxi-skirt or the, well, you get the picture. Indeed you've got the picture. For once the camera, source of a million lies, doesn't lie.

To put it with cruel simplicity, I bought my girlie socks because they are the fashion and other men have started wearing them. And though I have openly scoffed at those men, and though I have rightly observed that girlie socks offer no advantages over ankle socks, nevertheless, gradually, regrettably, but inevitably, I have come to see my ankle socks as staid, as ugly, as the sporting equivalent of the knee-length walk socks of the holidaying bureaucrat.

Have you ever seen a million starlings coming in to roost at dusk? They wheel like a living cloud, darkening the sky, forming one minute a spinning upward vortex, the next a diving arrowhead, driven by God knows what imperative and all of them squealing. Listen closely to that squeal. 'No coward soul is mine,' proclaims each starling. 'I am a sturdy independent.'

Oi Popey-boy

I can't be bothered with interviewing people any more. Most of the people worth interviewing are dead.

But interviews abound. Interviews with pustular rock stars, installation artists, skeletal fashion models, subliterate Hollywood marionettes, quivering novelists with bad breath, footballers.

And the trouble is, of course, that everyone's so flattered to be interviewed that they imagine they must have some thoughts worth attending to and so they spend a day thinking a few up. Then they deliver same with such sonorous earnestness — 'Frankly I see my art works as a search for identity, creating a fusion from the different ways of seeing inherent in our cultural diversity' — that it's all I can do to keep my breakfast down.

Besides it's such a hassle organising an interview, ringing up, say, the Pope and trying to persuade him to nip down to the Volcano for a chat. And then when he does agree there's even more hassle about how to hide security guards behind the Bill Hammonds, what to feed the sniffer dogs, and the exact design of chalice that the Pope's going to swill his Monteith's from, so in the end I always sighingly agree to fly to Rome and to be ushered into the Papal presence as if it were some sort of marquee, a marquee thronged with chubby cardinals and other corporate executives of Him Upstairs. And given the lack of Monteith's and the abundance of circumambient cardinals with ears like tuning-forks, the Pope is always on his best behaviour and simply trots out the party line as laid out in the mission statement sent to all stakeholders a couple of thousand years ago.

So I've resolved to change all that. Henceforth I shall conduct all interviews, as many as three a day, in bed and alone. It's quicker, easier and it gets straight to the truth. Here, for example, is the complete and unedited transcript of the first interview of a series of one, conducted in bed with the Pope shortly after the alarm went off this morning at the crack of ten. It was all over by five past. Efficiency, see.

Me: Oi Popey-boy.

Pope (kneeling, fumbling for a ring to kiss, before I cuff him playfully away): Oh, Your Journalosity. May I say how honoured I am? And with regard to your bid for canonisation . . .

Me: Bid! Let's get this one straight for starters, my preachy pal. When I fancy canonisation I won't be doing any bidding. I'll be instructing. Canonisation, I'll say, and the gun will go off and that will be that. Capisch?

Pope: I'd prefer a flat white.

Me: Coming right up. Meanwhile I've got a short message and I want you to listen up good. You with me?

Pope: Being with you is a privilege, Your Columnness.

Me: Right. Good. Now stop it.

Pope: Stop what?

Me: It. All of it. This religious stuff. It won't do and you know it. It was okay once, laying down the moral law in a lawless time, trying to put an end to the tribal blood feuds and all that (though a glance at the Middle East doesn't suggest much in the way of success) but the point is it just won't wash any more.

Pope: Why are you picking on me?

Me: I'm not picking on you. I've got the rest of them lined up outside this bedroom door right this minute — archbishops, chief moderators, Archimandrites, televangelists, the lot. You just happened to be first because, well, I like you, Popey. I've said so in print before now and I don't retract a word of it, but nevertheless it's time to pull the plug.

Pope: But . . .

Me: But is not a word I'm fond of, Popey-boy. This isn't a discussion. This is an audience. So audiate away, my lad of the cloth, and audiate good. I want you to go forth and dismantle the whole shebang. Chasubles, rhythm methods, dog collars, waddling cardinals, the lot. Send it all down the same road as the sun-worship of the Aztecs. I'm not blaming you for all the empire building of the past, for the squillion heathen corpses slaughtered in the name of the boss, for siding with the rich against the poor and all the other ghastlies of yesterday, nor indeed for the retail monstrosity of Christmas, but I am saying that we need to ditch it all now. I mean it's no help when the head honcho of Bushbaby's own church comes out against the war on Iraq on the grounds of scriptural interpretation. Right answer but wrong method. Time to acknowledge, old son, and I know you won't take this the wrong way, the randomness of the world, the pointless atomic structure spinning in a void, and that if we're going to make a go of it we've got to accept there's no authority to fall back on and that it's up to us. All your lot do is cloud the issue. Think comic cosmic irony of purposelessness. Got it?

Pope: Yes.

Me: Good. Now dry your eyes and off you go. Just get out there and sack a few cardinals and you'll feel a whole lot better. Okay?

Pope: Thank you.

Me: A pleasure. Next! Ah, Ayatollah. Come in. Sit down. And listen up.

Lies to spare

Lies hold our world up. Take away the scaffolding of lies and things fall down. God, pornography, 100 per cent Pure New Zealand, deodorant, down they tumble. Rubble the lot. It's great fun.

Take mega-butch four-wheel-drive recreational vehicles. I wish you would. I can't see round them, past them or under them. Monstrous things, rolling off the automated assembly lines in Nagoya and Seoul, to infest the world. They're built of lies, lies from here to my Aunt Fanny. Lies from bull bar (Oh, those poor shunted bulls. You have to go miles these days to find an unshunted one) to tailgate.

Let's look at the tailgate. I often have to. It blocks my windscreen. It's got a spare wheel stuck on it.

Small cars haven't got a spare wheel stuck on them. Minis find space for their spare wheels somewhere inside. Mega-butches don't. Though their cabin space is measured in hectares, there's no room for the spare.

A lie, of course. There's room to spare for the spare. But the spare is hung on the back for a reason. It's hung there to tell fibs. 'Look at me,' bellows the spare, 'I am rugged practicality. My owners wear safari suits with sweat stains in the armpits. My owners know the world's awash with peril. My owners can cope.'

The dangling spare tyre implies that the moment one of the other tyres is picked off by a sniper, or holed by an assegai, or shredded by a landmine in the badland wastes of the supermarket car park, Mr or Mrs Safari-Armpit will leap from the cab, fall to their knees on the sun-bleached tarmac and make with the jack before you can say charging rhinoceros. They are rugged and practical people, men and women of action, terse, hard and with honest dirt beneath their fingernails. So says the spare.

But that isn't all it says. The spare tyre is shrouded in a tyre cover. That tyre cover prompts a question. That question is why?

The tyre cover can't be there to keep the tyre dry. Tyres don't mind getting wet.

And the tyre cover can't be there to protect the hands and clothing of Mr and Mrs Safari-Armpit. These are rugged people who care nothing for a smudge of dirt on the safari suit.

No, that tyre cover exists to send yet another lie out into the world to breed. The one I pootled along behind today told me a corker of a fib. And all in three words.

The first of these words was the name of the car-maker. Let's call it Carcorp. The other two words, in sequence, were 'likes' and 'nature'.

Carcorp likes nature. Well, isn't that just dandy.

Let's start with the first lie. Carcorp doesn't like nature. Carcorp doesn't like anything. It doesn't like cricket or pavlova or sex. It can't. It isn't a sentient being. It doesn't have feelings.

Carcorp is an organisation of lots of sentient beings, some of whom may like cricket, pavlova and sex, some of whom may even like them simultaneously, and some of whom may like none of them. But the only thing that binds these beings together is not what they like and dislike, but the making and selling of cars in order to earn dosh. Which is fine by me. I approve of cars. But not of fibs.

The purpose of saying 'Carcorp Likes Nature' is that we then think of Carcorp as a person, and a nice person at that. Carcorp is not going to publish a slogan such as 'Carcorp Kills Cats', even though it's a chunky, alliterative and memorable slogan. And a true one. Worldwide in the course of a normal day Carcorp probably runs over several tonnes of cats. But cat-slaughtering doesn't make Carcorp out to be a nice chap. No, Carcorp likes nature.

Nature here means cuddly things. It means soft grass and lapping waters and gentle herbivorous beasties that feed from our hands and look good on postcards.

If 'Carcorp Likes Nature' is true, then, by the rules of logic, the following statements must also be true. Carcorp likes blowflies. Carcorp likes warthogs. Carcorp likes death from exposure. Carcorp is particularly fond of that remarkable Amazonian parasite that a bloke told me about in the Volcano last week so it must be true. This parasite can swim up a stream of urine, take a grip, wriggle into the urethra and, well, you can imagine the rest, but I'd advise you not to.

Carcorp is lying. Spectacularly. Mr and Mrs Safari-Armpit buy Carcorp's cars because nature is nasty. Carcorp's cars shelter them from its brute indifference. Carcorp's cars ford rivers, scale scree, flatten saplings and pollute the world, while Mr and Mrs Safari-Armpit sit in air-conditioned comfort listening to Vivaldi.

None of this matters, of course. Carcorp's slogan is no worse than ads for toilet-tissue happiness or deodorant-driven sex, but it does seem to me to be a neat irony, that a company whose products are the brilliant inventions of scientific human reasoning should need to use emotional lies to sell them.

Glossy lala

I don't know whether it was an advertising stunt or an accident or a threat but someone left a pornographic magazine in my letter box. It's as glossy as a yacht and the weight of a paving slab. Rolled up it could be issued to the riot squad. But it's what's inside that's so devastating.

I am not easily shocked but I was shocked. I can only give thanks that I got to it before the local kiddiwinks did. If freedom of speech dictates that such stuff must be published it should at least be sold under brown paper covers and only to adults with a certificate signed by three psychologists testifying to the purchaser's imperturbable mental stability. The magazine in question is the Christmas issue of *House and Garden*.

The cover features a festive board — yes, that's the sort of language we're dealing with here — groaning — of course — under bowls of soup with swirls of cream in them, glasses of fresh-poured bubbly, lit green candles in a decorative candelabrum beneath a decorative chandelier and beside a decorative centrepiece of Christmas lilies and I don't know what else because I had to avert my eyes. In the background are chairs festooned with cushions, cushions so winsome that I felt the catch in the throat that warns of trouble to come.

I should never have read the text on the cover. I read the text on the cover. Here it is in full: 'Gorgeous table tops. Deck your halls. (I am not making this up.) Angels and tiaras. (No, really, I am not making this up.) Perfect puddings. Wrap it in an heirloom.'

And inside, well it was everything you could expect and worse. And where do I begin? I shall begin with the prurient glimpses into other people's houses. Either this stuff is all fictional, the people and the places they live in entirely knocked up for the purposes of selling magazines, or else there are two varieties of human beings, two varieties that have diverged so radically by the process of evolution that they can barely recognise each other, and I belong to the other variety. Here is a world where beds are made, pillows creaseless and 'in Wendy's wardrobe European shoes are lined up with military precision'. There's even a photograph of the wardrobe and the shoes, pair after pair of them, flimsy as tissue paper, barely capable of supporting the weight of their price tags.

It's a strange and horrible world to which they recruit them young. Tots design their own awful bedrooms. 'Six-year-old Iona has a green and cream toile wallpaper, matching curtains and upholstered slipper chair (slipper chair!) and an old French wooden bed. Georgia, almost twelve, . . . has a sophisticated tented ceiling.

(What's sophisticated about it is left unsaid. The word itself just stamps its own unarguable assertion. It's sophisticated because it's sophisticated.) Olivia, fourteen, relaxes on her "four-poster" achieved mainly with fabric.' It's all there in that last sentence. In *House-and-Garden* Land cloth is never cloth, nor is it even material. It is always fabric. And Olivia, poor thing, is not relaxing. She is posing for the camera on the 'four-poster' with a dog. Appearances suggest that if Fido were to leap onto the 'four-poster' at any time other than when the *House and Garden* photographer was present it would be sent forthwith to the dog shelter. And the moment the snap was taken, of course, the dog ran off in search of things to kill, eat or roll in and so, if she's got any sense, did Olivia.

Otherwise she's doomed to a life in which 'organic textures, flavours and fragrances set the scene for Christmas in a marquee. Coco husks sprinkled underfoot scent the air with chocolate. A bird bath and terracotta planters sprayed with copper act as centrepieces, encircled with bay leaves and cinnamon sticks and holding branches of twisted willow or reeds and dried orange slices.'

It's all there in sumptuous colour photography, the tableware arrayed around the copper-sprayed bird bath and the dried orange slices. The glasses and napery are set just so. No shots of the aftermath, of course, no candid snaps of stacked and sullied crockery, or of the live-in Filipina treasure with the chapped hands bent over the scullery sink, or of Uncle Trevor drunk as a moose in rut. No record either of the conversation that took place around the copper-sprayed bird bath over the cloying fragrance (no smells allowed in paradise) of the crushed coco husks. Imagine that conversation. On second thoughts, don't bother. Spare yourself. The conversation is irrelevant. It didn't happen. For this is lala-land.

Most telling of all, as you flick through the magazine it's impossible, at a glance, to distinguish the text from the ads. Both picture the perfect, the faultless, the moment before things happen, the moment of expectation, of order, of hope, of idealised material lust, of how things should be but aren't. It's porn.

Destiny's children

I'm looking at a picture of Brian Tamaki attending a rally. Mr Tamaki is the spiritual leader of an organisation called Destiny Church. Apparently Mr Tamaki led the rally on an extremely spiritual Harley Davidson motor bike, but sadly the bike is not pictured.

Mr Tamaki is wearing black trousers and a black shirt. Black clothing has a long and splendid spiritual history. Black shirts, for example, have always attracted the sort of people who are spiritually right and keen to mend the ways of the spiritually wrong.

Mr Tamaki is also wearing sunglasses. Sunglasses have a less extensive but still promising spiritual history. In recent years they have been favoured by such spiritual leaders as bouncers, gangsters and New Zealand First MPs. Mr Tamaki may be wishing to express his solidarity with these spiritual leaders, but I wouldn't be surprised if he were also, and typically, thinking of the ordinary people. For eyes are the windows of the soul, and Mr Tamaki's soul is of such sun-like radiance that a glimpse of it would damage any mortal retina.

If you look closely at the picture you can see that the man behind Mr Tamaki is fiddling with an earpiece in the best spiritual tradition of CIA bruisers. It is not clear who is talking into that earpiece but I expect it is God, issuing instructions for the rally held in his name.

The appearance of Mr Tamaki and friends, then, is spiritually promising. But, as any spiritual analyst will tell you, what matters is substance, and I am pleased to report that Mr Tamaki has a lot of substance. Aside from being a strongly built chap he is also a television evangelist. Television evangelists have a long history of spiritual and financial excellence. Admittedly that financial excellence has led some of them into the valley of sin where the prostitutes dwell, but then they've wept and asked for forgiveness and more money. I don't know if Mr Tamaki has done any weeping yet, but he's certainly asked for money. He tells his congregation that they should give money to Destiny churches, because that is what God wants.

According to its poorly spelt but deeply spiritual website, Destiny Church is a 'god-appointed apostolic ministry'. Of the two apostles or 'senior pastors' that God has appointed, one is Mr Tamaki. The other, by an extraordinary coincidence, is Mrs Tamaki. Families don't come any holier.

The rally at which the photo was taken was called to oppose the Civil Union Bill, the bill that will permit dangerous homosexuals to form quasi-marriages that will gnaw at the fabric of society.

God and Mr Tamaki are both opposed to such quasi-marriages. What God wants is always right. Mr Tamaki wants what God wants. Therefore Mr Tamaki is always right too. It's an impressive form of reasoning, known in the business as begging the question.

At the rally, Mr Tamaki's disciples carried placards bearing the legend 'Enough is Enough', which is an example of the same impressive reasoning. It can't be faulted. Enough is indeed enough, just as a circular argument is a circular argument, and a cult is a cult, and inflammatory fundamentalism is inflammatory fundamentalism.

Lots of children took part in the rally but some of them hadn't quite grasped the meaning of 'enough is enough'. When interviewed by a reporter, one child amusingly interpreted the message as meaning 'we're standing up against the bad people'. Children in black shirts have stood up against the bad people before and have proved jolly good at it.

But if some of the children were puzzled, fortunately the Maxim Institute was there to help them. The Maxim Institute kindly wrote a letter explaining to the children what they, the children, thought about the Civil Union Bill. Having found out what they thought, the children could then sign the letter and send it to the nasty government. It turned out, astonishingly, that what the children thought was exactly the same as what the Maxim Institute thought and what Destiny New Zealand thought.

Destiny New Zealand is the political wing of Destiny Church. Churches with political wings have a splendid spiritual record. They've made a lot of history happen. Much of that history has been bloody, but you can hardly blame the churches or the spiritual leaders for that. They've merely been doing God's bidding for the good of society. And if they've had to tickle up a few members of that society in order to impress upon them what a loving God wants of them, then so be it. Over the centuries there have been a wide variety of tickling sticks and they've proved jolly useful. Imagine the mess we'd be in now if it hadn't been for the rack, the thumbscrew, the stake, the gas-chambers, the suicide bombers and all the rest of those expressions of the divine will.

Destiny is a young organisation but it follows a formula that is as old as mankind. It takes its mandate from a mythological authority. It defies reason, brainwashes children and fleeces the weak. There ought to be words to describe a formula so banal yet so persistent and so effective, and there are. The kindest of those words is delusional. The most direct is evil.

Hi ho

Hi ho, hi ho (and I am bellowing that hi ho with exactly the same anticipatory exultation as in the dwarf song), I'm off to see a medium. Or, as I like to think of them, an average.

(Have you noticed, by the way, how the word average has changed its meaning? (Not that I care whether you've noticed or not. I've noticed and that's all that matters here.) Average no longer means what it means. If a cricket team has had an average season or a resort has had average weather, then you know that the team has come bottom of the league and the tourists have got wet. Average isn't middling any more. Average is bad. Because, in a hyperised world, we want super, we want extreme, we want more intensity, more excitement, more records broken, more adrenalin, more, bigger, better, whee whee, oooh oooh, hyperventilation, acceleration, g-force, beyond the limits, beyond the pale, superfast, superheated, supernatural, which brings us back to the medium.)

I wrote rude things about mediums in a newspaper column a while ago and this medium read my words (no, I am not going to ask why she reads a newspaper when her super-receptive ganglions are already bombarded by a mass of paranormal information to which we normal chaps and chappesses are not privy) and she thought oooh, what a silly and wrong and insulting thing for this nasty columnist to say, and, good on her, she picked up a pen and wrote me a letter (and no, I am not going to ask why she didn't just telepathise me, because the answer is obvious. She is perfectly capable of telepathising, of course, but I, with my untuned rice-pudding brain, am incapable of receiving the message. For I, to change the metaphor to something utterly contemporary and horrid, am a muggle, the reference being drawn from that epitome of twenty-first-century dummkopf culture, Harry Bloody Yawn Yawn Potter.). In the letter the medium insisted that I didn't know what I was talking about and that if I cared to meet her she would prove, yes prove, the truth of her trade. I would be converted. The blinkers of scepticism would tumble from my eyes and I would behold for the first time in all its glistening auroral beauty the thrilling horse paddock of the supernatural.

I wrote back.

'Dear Miss Medium,' (I wrote.) (Ooh what a lot of brackets I'm having today, reflecting, perhaps, the omni-directional fecundity of my giant throbbing brain.)

'Good. Thank you. Yes. Let's meet.

'Lotsalove (as you already knew)

Joe'

And so tomorrow she drives down from sunny Napier and I fly up from sunnier Lyttelton and we meet on the steps of Parliament at noon and I have no idea what she looks like but she will clearly sense by a thumb-twitch or two that I am I, although in case she's suffering from some sort of ethereal static I have promised to wear a jaunty Tyrolean hat (green, with feather). And not just to wear it. The hat is also a provisional packed lunch. For I have promised that if, as she has promised, she sends me back to Lyttelton convinced of the existence of spooky things and life after croaking and all the rest of the extraordinary range of the extraordinary, then I'll eat the hat.

(I shall also be taking, though not wearing, some cheese and pickle sandwiches.)

What will happen at our meeting? Well, self-evidently, she ought to know and I should be in the dark. But the truth, as it happens (ha ha), is the other way round. She hasn't got a clue how tomorrow will unfold. And I, the muggle, the rice-pudding brain, the unreceptive receptacle, Mr Dull-as-dirt, know exactly what will happen. Exactly.

We'll meet. We'll laugh. She'll make jesting reference to my hat and its imminent consumption, in response to which I shall be suave and charming — no novelty in any of that, of course. Then we shall go to some coffee joint and over a brace of flat whites she'll ask me questions. (She has, to be fair, already vouchsafed that she will ask me questions. What she hasn't told me is why. But I shall tell you. She will ask me questions because without my answers she will be as deeply in the dark as a worm in a compost heap.)

From my answers she will draw inferences about me and my family and my friends and my inside-leg measurement and my everything, and she will suggest those inferences to me, subtly, hoping for unconscious indications from me (a nod of the head, a smile, a widening or crinkling of the eyes) that she is on the right track. And I will be supposed to be astonished. It's an easy trick.

But what she doesn't know is that she will be on the wrong track. Utterly the wrong track. Because I will tell her fibs. And on the basis of those fibs she will get in touch with, say, a one-legged aunt of mine who never existed, and I will say, yes yes, that's Auntie Peg and thus I shall suck her in, utterly, just as she and her kind have been doing to the world for ever, and encouraged by my encouragement she will blunder ever deeper into the dark night of wrongness, and I shall remain the gleaming white knight of truth and honesty and rectitude and throbbing brackets. (I'm looking forward to it.)

Dear College of Cardinals

To: CollofCards@Vatican.com
CC: All World Leaders
Subject: Job Application

Dear College of Cardinals,
Forgive the email but I gather I've got to be quick. Besides, I don't trust the post. The only Italian postman I ever knew was not what one would call conscientious, being only too ready on a warm day to hear the call of the grappa and dump his sack in the Tiber.

Anyway, I'll come straight to the point. I want to be Pope.

I'm sure you're up to here with applications for the job, but before you toss this one into the furnace under St Peter's — and the heating system, by the way, is one of the first things I'd get fixed, by fiat if necessary (though not, for obvious reasons, by Fiat) — I'd just like to point out what makes my application different.

I haven't included a mug shot. That's because I'm flexible. I'm white, of course, but if, as the rumour goes, you're looking for a black bloke this time round, then I'm quite prepared to make with the Nugget. Nor will you catch me complaining that choosing a black bloke because he's black is every bit as racist as not choosing a black bloke because he's black. No, I'm happy to go along with whatever you say. I just want the job and will do what's necessary.

I'm not bothered about salary. So long as there's something dropping into a Vatican Bank Accumulator account every month, I'm not going to haggle about how many zeroes are dangling on the end of it. I realise too that there won't be any pension provision, this not being a job from which you retire, though if you want to throw in a termination clause on the grounds of senility, a gaga get-out as I believe it's known, then that's fine by me. In other words, you dictate the terms and I'll just sign on the dotted. Getting the picture now? I want this job.

Don't worry that I'm an unknown. Who'd heard of old John Paul when he was ministering to the vodka-sodden round the back of Warsaw Cathedral, eh? Precisely. As you and I know, fame comes with the job. And I want it. I like idolatry. Not that I'd call it idolatry, of course, that being fairly strictly verboten in your church (or rather, *our* church, if you see sense) but I was greatly struck by the recent funeral, queues visible from space, people coming down the steps towards the waxwork papa clamping a hankie to the eyes with one hand and toting a camera-phone above their heads with the other. That's good for business, my friends. It's the sort of stuff I intend to foster not only post-mortem, but pre. Performance popery will be my catch-cry. We're talking celebrity. John Paul set the ball rolling. I'll give it a bloody great shove. You'll love it. I'll have them signing up all over the globe. I'll cram the pews.

The theology I'll leave to you. Just tell me which bits of the Bible we're going to take literally and which bits we're going to deem metaphorical in order to avoid their nasty implications, and I'll do the rest. But could I suggest a pretty staunch unwavering style. Not too many u-turns on the basics. You know, birth control, abortion, creation, female clergy, homosexuality, all the old chestnuts. It's just that the main competition these days are those blokes in the desert, much given to fanaticism, and the only way to compete with fundamental stuff like that is to offer equally fundamental stuff. It gives the punters a life raft to cling to amid the shifting seas of tolerance and liberalism. Everyone pretends to want tolerance etc. but it requires work. What they really want is a set of rules, and then they can just get back to watching six thousand channels of scabrous trash from the great couch of indolence, secure in the knowledge that all the moral issues have been resolved once and for all by the representatives of him upstairs, in other words us.

Not having seen the books, I can't give you a detailed business plan, but I can tell you that I'll be shaking things up a bit. You lot have always been good at real estate, and that sale of indulgences stuff you used to do was a wheeze which might be worth another look, but otherwise, frankly, you're hopeless. I mean, how much did you get for the TV rights to the funeral? Exactly.

My model will be one of the Super 12 rugby franchises down this way, the Crusaders to be precise. (What a pity that title's been taken.) I'll exploit all available methods of marketing to build up a fan base: TV promos, collector cards, stirring music (that's something you've got a head start on) and so on. I want to see 'Don't cross the Papa' plastered across the back bumper of every clapped-out Volvo in Christendom.

What we need, you see, is unswerving loyalty to the cause, because you don't have to be Thomas Aquinas to see which way the global geese are flying. There's a showdown looming. East meets West. Islam meets Christianity. It'll be just like the glory days of a thousand or so years ago. And when it comes to a showdown, wishy-washy secularism just doesn't cut the mustard. What's needed is dogma plus a figurehead, someone the punters revere and believe in. And that, my clothy friends, should be me. Be bold.

I look forward to hearing from you.

In hope

Joe.

Not if, but when

'It's not if,' said a virologist, 'but when.' With that one simple sentence he condemned a nation to its fate. He strapped New Zealand to the railway track as the H5N1 Express bore down en route from Media to Public. The train had no brakes. The track had no points. The metal wheels had no pity. The result was horrible to behold. New Zealand suffered an appalling case of fear of bird flu.

Symptoms vary. According to phobologists, the most obvious sign that the disease has taken hold is a slight but measurable distension of the vocabulary. The words 'virus', 'mutate' and especially 'pandemic' stream from the victim's mouth, along with entire phrases such as 'cross the species barrier'. Such phrases are known to phobologists as 'lexical floaters'. Though they appear to be associated with intellectual substance, closer examination, even under an ordinary household magnifying glass, reveals that they are attached to no scientific knowledge whatsoever.

Phobologists are at pains to remind the public that lexical floaters are extraordinarily contagious and that once contracted they are terminal. Any amateur examination should be conducted in ear muffs.

The fear virus works, say experts, by attaching itself to pre-existing fear radicals, left over from past epidemics. Capable of lying dormant for years, these radicals respond instantly to gossip or newspaper articles. They are particularly sensitive to television images, especially if these show scientists in white coats filling test tubes from a multiple glass pipette like a horse comb. Energised by these images, fear radicals will attach themselves automatically to the nearest jargon.

Like all fear viruses, the fear-of-bird-flu virus also contains a memory-killer gene. It supplants and suppresses all memories of fear of SARS, Ebola, Y2K, fat, global warming, tsunami, crime, coffee, cholesterol, earthquakes, paedophilia, the sun, snakes, house price collapse, asteroids, terrorism, rising sea level, butter, spitting, dogs and tap water.

At the same time the virus attacks the part of the brain responsible for reasoning. The skill of drawing conclusions from historical evidence is entirely disabled. Without it the brain cannot discern that previous fears have come to nothing, or that fear of the unknown is usually worse than the unknown when it finally makes itself known.

The effects are immediate. Stockpiling is a common response, as is a sense that the human being is a doomed beast in a hostile world. This can lead to lassitude, depression and fatalism, or to a frantic burst of activity characterised by bunker building or even credit-card binging.

The most extreme symptom appears comical at first but requires immediate hospitalisation. Belief in and prayer to a supreme being who is benign and yet simultaneously responsible for bird flu, is so severe a case of mental inconsistency that it must be treated within moments of infection if the patient is to have any hope of recovery.

Leading phobologists are at odds over the efficacy of vaccines against fear of bird flu. The makers of one popular vaccine acknowledged that they were uncertain whether their product offered anything other than temporary relief. 'But in the midst of a pandemic such as this one,' said a spokesman for Scottish Distilleries, 'surely any relief is better than none. Our vaccine promises at least one evening free from the fear virus before the end of the world arrives the next morning. Ours is also an ideal vaccine to stockpile. It works in the same temporary way against all known fear viruses, and it improves with age.'

Phobologists and government bodies generally prefer a vaccine known as Tammy-CD. Governments have drawn on vast stockpiles of Tammy-CD to immunise front-line workers such as experts and newsreaders. The active agent in Tammy-CD is the upbeat music of Tammy Wynette, the Country and Implant star. Tammy-CD is believed to work by causing the brain to secrete massive quantities of cheap sentiment, thereby depriving the fear virus of attention and causing it to shrivel.

Experts are united, however, in condemning one common form of treatment. 'The serious news item,' said a leading phobologist, 'suggesting that there is no need to panic, that bird flu may well arrive but there's nothing much anyone can do to stop it and certainly no point in worrying about it before it arrives, and that it will probably prove less deadly than the motor cars that we love, is laughable. By denying the need for panic such an item only adds to that panic.' For evidence he directed reporters to a research paper in a recent issue of *Phobology Quarterly*, entitled 'The Pathology of Panic — or the Corporal Jones Syndrome'.

'In short,' he went on, 'it's too late. The fear of bird flu has now escaped into the general population and there is nothing to do but to let it run its course. Eventually it will peak and be replaced by another fear. Or, of course, by bird flu, which would be a relief.'

Funny and true

What a coup for cartooning. I have heard it suggested that a dozen cartoons, from Denmark of all places, may yet spark World War III. They won't, of course, because the leaders of Islam know they haven't got enough guns, but it's nice to know that the art of caricature still packs a kick.

The purpose of a cartoon is not to be funny. Being funny is the method. The purpose of a cartoon is to tell the truth. Truth is immediately recognisable and often funny.

The Muslim world has not found the cartoons funny. The ostensible reason is that Islam forbids pictures of Mohammed. But that reason doesn't stand up to scrutiny. Five minutes on the Internet and I had discovered several pictures of Mohammed. I am also reliably informed that you can buy a picture of Mohammed in the central market at Teheran. So, there must be something else that's upsetting the Islamic world to the point that they're firebombing embassies, marching down Queen Street and boycotting Danish yoghurt.

I have seen only two of the cartoons. The first depicts Mohammed with a bomb in his turban. It is not particularly witty. The point it is obviously making is that some people commit acts of murder in the name of the prophet. Equally obviously, that point is true.

The reaction of a few Muslims has been funnier than the cartoon. 'Slay those who insult Islam,' said one placard carried by a protester, thereby exquisitely reinforcing the point of the cartoon he is protesting against. He reminds me of the Christian fundamentalist who murdered an abortionist on the grounds that the abortionist committed murder.

The second cartoon is wittier. It depicts Mohammed emerging from Muslim heaven to apologise to a stream of dead suicide bombers for having run out of virgins. The reference is to the promise of 144 virgins to anyone who dies for the Islamic cause. (What attitude this implies to women, I shall ignore for the moment, though it does make me wonder what female suicide bombers get in the hereafter. A gross of Islamic Brad Pitts? A platinum burka?)

What has been ignored amid the eruption of belligerence, apology, and yoghurt-flinging is that the two cartoons invite two simple questions: First, does Islam condone suicide bombers? Does it approve of people blowing themselves up and killing the innocent? If so, then cartoons should be only the start of the mockery. Such a faith should be as universally condemned as Nazism. If not, if Islam does not approve of murder, then every imam and ayatollah should stand up and say so.

Second, is it a tenet of the Islamic faith that suicide bombers get a gross of virgins in heaven? If so, then once again the faith should be universally condemned. If not, then every imam and ayatollah should stand up and say so. And if they did, the hated cartoons would stop.

What has prevented these simple questions being asked is the usual argument about respect. It is our duty, the argument runs, to respect other people's beliefs. I, for one, have never had any idea why. Anything true can always withstand mockery. Copernicus's belief that the earth moved round the sun endured everything the Catholic Inquisition could throw at it. And the Inquisition didn't just print cartoons. It pulled out fingernails. It incinerated its enemies. But the truth endured.

Moreover, the rule about respecting other religions is selectively maintained. If a religion is small it is known as a cult, and a cult is fair game. But the established religions are all former cults. They just happened to get big. Their beliefs are every bit as wacky as the beliefs of little cults. Not questioning those beliefs is not an act of respect. It's merely not upsetting the status quo.

The Western belief that has sparked this controversy is the belief in freedom of speech. It's a belief I share, because history demonstrates that a free press is our best defence against tyranny. Every tyrant in history has muzzled the press.

Ostensibly our leaders share my belief, but when the heat came on they renounced it.

'I approve of freedom of the press,' said Helen Clark on television, 'but . . .'

'I approve of freedom of the press,' said Don Brash on television, 'but . . .'

In other words, both of them worried more about votes or exports than about the truth.

In doing so they echoed Hamdi Hassan, an Egyptian MP. 'Freedom of expression,' said Mr Hassan, 'does not mean people are free to insult prophets.'

I'm sorry, Mr Hassan, but that is precisely what it does mean. Freedom means freedom. And if a prophet is really a prophet he's not going to get upset.

The vast majority of the one and a half billion Muslims in this world are good and peaceable people. They don't blow themselves up. They don't hate the West. They are superb hosts. They love their children. They are closer to Mohammed than their leaders are. The same is true of Christians and Christ.

Each religion began with one man. Both men were apparently tolerant. Each man proposed a system of living, a code of social behaviour. After their deaths, however, those teachings became perverted. They became dressed in nonsensical theology. That theology ossified into a system for gaining and retaining power. It became, in other words, merely political. The grip of the Islamic authorities in Iran is indistinguishable from the grip of, say, the Catholic authorities in Spain and Ireland well into the twentieth century, or the grip of the Communist Party in the Soviet Union. Such a grip is a noxious thing.

And if a dozen cartoons can shake it, it's a vulnerable thing.

Reverend reasoning

Minutes of the AGM of the Intelligent Design Steering Committee, held somewhere on the intelligently designed planet earth.

Attendance: Those attending were the Reverend Peastem, the Very Reverend Drinklittle, the Astonishingly Reverend Archbishop Thimbledick and God.

Apologies: A handwritten apology for absence was received from G.W. Bosh (*sic*) and an apology in Latin from the late Pope (*sick*). Exactly the same apology was received from an unnamed source with the word Pope twinked out and replaced with the words 'Maxim Institute'. A telephone apology was received from The So-Reverend-It-Hurts Bishop Brian Tamaki who said he was there in spirit but was currently too busy ministering to his flock in the diocese of Tithe, Harley and Davidson.

Proceedings: The meeting opened with a prayer to which God listened intently and which he promised to answer just as soon as he'd answered the eight billion others that had landed simultaneously in his in-tray, most of which related to bird flu.

Minutes: The minutes of the previous meeting were read and approved. (*Mover, in a mysterious way: God. Seconder: God.*)

Point of order: The Reverend Peastem queried whether it was constitutionally permissible for the same person to move and second a motion, but God argued through the chair that he was in fact three persons. For evidence he quoted from the Bible, whereupon the chairman congratulated God on the reasoned nature of his argument. 'This is just the sort of deductive scientific method that we on the Intelligent Design Steering Committee seek to promote,' he said.

'Thank you,' said God, and asked for his gratitude to be recorded in the minutes.

'No, we thank you,' said the chairman and moved a motion that the committee thank God for intelligently designing everything. (*Seconder: Thimbledick.*) Peastem proposed that the motion be amended to thank God for intelligently designing 'everything except bird flu, oh, and perhaps leprosy, the Pakistan earthquake, Hurricane Wilma and genital warts' but the amendment did not find a seconder. The unamended motion was passed nem con. (*Abstention: God.*)

General Business: Only one agenda item had been tabled, the bid to have Intelligent Design included in the school science curriculum throughout the Western world. As chairman of the ad hoc subcommittee the Very Reverend Drinklittle reported that the campaign was proving successful because it had been intelligently designed. (*Laughter*) He attributed the momentum of the campaign to three specific causes, the first of which was branding. Changing the name from Creationism to Intelligent Design had completely altered its image in the public mind. It was now seen as a scientific theory rather than a wishful belief. (*Coughing*) The second principal driver of success was funding. The extraordinary sums contributed by American business interests to support the campaign and also to establish propaganda bodies amusingly known as think-tanks had enabled the campaign to achieve unprecedented market penetration. 'In conclusion,' said the Very Reverend, 'it is the opinion of the ad hoc subcommittee that within ten years the average child will emerge from school unable to distinguish scientific method from a hamburger, and will consider both to be examples of Intelligent Design.' (*Applause, cheers, general acclamation, stamping of feet and an impromptu chorus of 'I'm no kin to the monkey, the monkey's no kin to me' enthusiastically conducted by Thimbledick with the femur of a chimpanzee.*)

The chairman congratulated Drinklittle on his subcommittee's success but reminded him that he had mentioned three contributing causes and wondered whether perhaps he might enlighten the assembly as to the nature of the third. In reply the Very Reverend merely looked towards God, bowed his head and said, 'Thank you.' (*Acclamation, blushes from God etc.*)

'Without your help,' said the Astonishingly Reverend, 'we

would never have been able to stem the advancing tide of thought. Branding and money are all very well, but if we hadn't created you in our image, you would never have been able to create us in yours. (*Chorus of 'Great reasoning, Rev', 'Yeeha' and other expressions of religious awe.*) And if we hadn't intelligently designed you so that you could have intelligently designed us, we would never have felt justified in considering ourselves superior to the beasts of the field and the dogs of the kennel, nor would we have felt entitled to eternal life and all the rest of the fringe benefits that come from being your loved and intelligently designed children.

'Thanks to you, our current funding, and a multi-media advertising blitz scheduled for the spring, there is every reason to hope that the devil Darwin and his heretical dependence on observation and repeatable controlled experiments, will be beaten back to the superstitious jungle where it belongs and the Western world can advance on the sort of theocracy that the Middle East has had the good sense to maintain all along. And then we can have a real cracker of a war.'

There being no other business the meeting closed at 8.41pm with the traditional chorus: 'All things bright and beautiful' sang the happy steering committee,

> All creatures great and small
> All things wise and wonderful
> The Lord God intelligently designed them all.

('Except,' added Peastem *sotto voce*, 'for bird flu, leprosy, the Pakistan earthquake, Hurricane Wilma and genital warts' but such was the general delight that nobody heard him.)

Little Miss Moss

Some dame rang, name of Moss. Said she'd never used a private dick before but she was worried about her kid. Was there somewhere discreet we could meet?

'The Ankle,' I said. '7.30,' and hung up.

My clients like The Ankle. It's a low-down joint. No cameras, no questions, no risk of being spotted with a dick.

I got there early, wrapped myself round a tooth mug of rye and ordered snails for the dame. I never met a dame yet who ain't impressed by snails.

She was five corny minutes late. 'The name's Dick,' I said, taking her coat. It stank of money. I can live with that stink. 'But they call me Private. Tell me about this little angel of yours.'

'Oh, Private,' she said, 'it's my Kate. I'm so worried about her.'

'What's she do, your Kate?'

'She puts clothes on and takes them off.'

Wouldn't be the first dame to do that, I thought. 'Yeah,' I said out loud, 'but what's she do for a crust?'

'Just that,' said the Moss. 'She earns millions.'

I sucked air through my teeth and laced it with rye. 'Nice work if you can get it,' I said. 'So what's the beef?'

'Oh, Private, haven't you heard? She's been accused of taking . . . boohoo.'

I never heard of anyone taking boohoo before but I seen plenty dames cry. Only thing to do is look away till it blows over. Some of them like a good blub, same as some jerks like washing the car of a Sunday. While I waited I picked up a paper. It was three days old and wearing ketchup. The Ankle has seen better times.

This Kate Moss broad was all over the front page. But broad ain't the word for her. She was six meals short of a decent curve. The modern look, I guess, but her story was as old as the Bible. Blonde makes good, gets sad and starts shoving chemistry up her hooter. I gave the tonsils another rinse.

Over the far side of the tablecloth things seem to have quietened down. I offered the dame a slug of rye but she said she'd stick with the snails.

'It's the end,' she sniffed. 'Burberry's gone. Chanel'll be next, then Next, then . . .'

'Slow down, Missus,' I said, 'you lost me at the first turn-off. Burberry? Are we talking fruit?'

'We're talking modelling millions and now it's all gone just because of a little . . .'

'Capisch,' I said. 'And now Kate's hoovering up the Special K.'

'If only,' said the Moss. 'But Kate's never been one for breakfast.'

'I ain't talking breakfast, Mrs. This Special K's a whole different stack of pancakes. Ketamine. That's horse dope to you.'

'Horse dope?'

'Yeah, they jab it into Dobbin and he rolls over like an Italian tank. Can't see the fun in it myself, but hey, it takes all sorts.'

'But can you help me, Private? Can you steer my little girl off the drug-strewn road to ruin and back onto the highway to riches and the *Vogue* front page?'

'Easy on the metaphors, lady,' I said. 'Leave the fancy stuff to me. In fact, leave everything to me, why don't you.'

I didn't want to get her hopes up but an idea was sprouting in the back of my mind like a rubber plant. It was a crap simile but a cracking idea. It was the horse stuff that did it. My mind was going like the clappers and those clappers had rung a bell.

Half an hour later I'd shifted the Moss and was on the phone to New Zealand. I got some bint with a weird accent.

'Crowe, Fox and Bull,' she said.

'Hey listen, sister, if I'd wanted the farmyard I'd have rung Old McDonald. I want the guys behind this Oxy-shot business, you know what I mean.'

'Mr Crowe and Mr Fox are currently unavailable.'

'Okay, sister, just gimme the bull.'

'Very well, sir. At Oxy-shot we are proud to have employed NASA technology to create a liquefied hydrox compound supersaturated with stabilised diatomic oxygen molecules guaranteed to enhance wellbeing and boost vital oxygen supply. For a mere $200 a litre . . .'

'Yeah yeah, sister, so you're selling holy water.'

'Oh, Mr Dick, how did you see through us? Oh, this is terrible. Mr Crowe and Mr Fox will be furious. The whole business will . . .'

'Spare me the sob-along, sister,' I said. 'I ain't here to pour cold water on your cold water. Far as I'm concerned in this life, you do what you can get away with. What I wanna know is how you're gonna plug this Oxy-shot stuff. You with me? If not, listen up and listen up good.'

You know the rest. How Kate Moss became the face of Oxy-shot. Soon as I told her it was horse dope with no calories she went for it. Only too happy to guzzle the stuff in front of the camera. Sales went north like Apollo 16. Everyone wanted in on it. Oxy-shot for oxymorons. Kate got as skinny as a boy with breasts. My wallet went the other way. I even bought into the company. Crowe, Fox, Bull and Dick. It's got a kinda ring to it.

In the deep midsummer

Sing heigh ho and recreational sex, it's that time of the year again. The time when firkin-gutted old men delve into the wardrobe that smells of dandruff and disappointment, to haul out the crimson uniform made of genuine 100 per cent nylonette. A quick sniff of the fabric confirms that a year's neglect has bleached the more bitter overnotes from the armpits, then on it slips, over the wrinkled dugs and the swollen belly and the shrivelled loins and the varicose veins and the gleaming shinbones. Add a hat like a windsock and half a metre or so of guaranteed flame-retardant draylon beard and it's yo ho ho time all over again. For the children, you understand.

It just wouldn't do to disappoint the little sweethearts who, with their rubber limbs, unblemished skin and self-whitening teeth, are innocence made flesh, their loving little souls beaming like the rising sun from their XXOS eye-sockets, and all of them gaga for a bit of wonder.

And for the best yo ho ho this year, why not take them to the profoundly traditional and spiritual Carols by Candlelight, held in the Wellington sports stadium? The stadium is named after a bank whose employees have risen in protest against instructions from the boardroom to press crippling quantities of Asian credit on already impoverished mums and dads so that they can shower Xbox consoles on their offspring to educate them in the necessary ways of the world, but who cares about all that? 'Tis the season to be jolly in the spirit of Shoppingmas, when all is joy and Chinese-made tinsel. The novelty bait at this year's Carols by Candlelight is that Santa is going to arrive by flying fox, just as he did all those years ago in Bethlehem. 'Oh, please, Mummy, can we go, can we, please, please, pretty please?'

Twenty thousand roll up. But they have to wait. Santa will be the climax. First comes the spiritual fumbling, the undressing of Christmas, as it were, before the final eruption. Carols. Ah lovely. Good King Wenceslas trudging through the snow (that we haven't got), 'Deck the Halls with Boughs of Holly' (that we also haven't got), the plangency of 'Silent Night' — ah Bach, ah beauty — and then, 'Look Mummy, look up there. Is it Baby Jesus? Is it, oh-my-God, Santa?'

But it isn't Baby Jesus. It isn't Santa. It's better than that. Up on the platform high above all mortal beings, up there where hope and dreams dwell, a mere spit from the portals of heaven itself, stand the Immortals, the true spiritual entities of today, the Cartoon Characters. Behold in the nimbus of the follow-spot, the blessed family of the Flinstones, and the angel that is called Shrek. Down the long wire they come, unthinkably real, and the children are sore with spiritual delight. 'Oh, Mummy, that was *wonderful*.'

A pause, a drum-roll and suddenly it's Santa time. On the lofty ramparts he stands, poised to swoop, his harness barely visible beneath the swathe of synthetics. Yo ho ho and here he comes, descending from the skies, the ancient god of acquisition coming to earth. 'Oh look, Mummy, look, oh look, oh . . . dear.' For something has happened.

Santa's stuck. The god is dangling, his descent from on high impeded, stalled, his gleaming shinbones kicking weakly in the spotlight of misfortune, his costume ruched about his hips, his progress halted a hundred feet up in the sky. It's his beard. His beard is caught in a pulley. The flame-retardant draylon simply refuses to give. And before the fire brigade can scramble, the kids are scrambling, gathering right underneath jolly old Santa as his face turns the colour of his costume.

The innocents, the darlings, the tinies, the future of the teeming globe, tomorrow's busy economic units, are milling beneath Santa by the hundred, peering up and pointing at the suspended deity, who is silhouetted against the early evening sky as in a medieval painting of the ascension. The kiddies have an unimpeded view of the divine undergarments, Chinese-made and plugged by that alternative Pantheon, the All Blacks.

Santa is effectively lynched, swinging impotent above the crowd of innocence, a gift from the sky that the sky has had second thoughts about, and the kiddies' dismay is so intense that they squeal and laugh and point at his discomfiture and every last one of them hauls out his photo-enabled cellular telephone bought with the credit urged on his heavily-mortgaged parents by the very foreign bank in whose temple they have congregated, and snaps the godhead in distress. The children are ecstatic with schadenfreude. Oh, the sweeties.

The time will come, of course, when they will learn to mask their delight in the misfortune of others, when they will sit in front of the pornography that is the television news and learn to tut and to pretend to be appalled, but for now they are radiant with honesty and make no effort to dissemble their delight.

Ah, Christmas. May you all have a merry one.

Circumbloodychristmas

A Christmas piece is obligatory for a columnist, just as circumcision is for a Jewish child. The difference between me and a Jewish child, however, is that I weigh 13 stone, which in metric terms translates as a lot more resistance. So if some bearded rabbi were to try sneaking up on my mid-section like a surgical anti-Santa with the blessed secateurs and a bloodstained copy of the Torah, he'd find himself having to cope with a patient flailing his arms like one of those flappy things in the last bit of the carwash. At the same time I'd be delivering such stout opinions on the anachronistic absurdity of tribal traditions that the rabbi would be trying to block his ears with one hand while hitching up his skirts with the other, the better to sprint for the A & E department of the Hospital of the Holy Foreskin in search of someone to minister to his bruising.

But anyway, happy festive yuletide nativity situation to you and all your — no, it's no good. I just can't mean any of the vicarish poop that gets wheeled out at this time of the year to make us feel gooey about ourselves in defiance of the facts, any more than I can mail off a stack of cards to people I haven't seen in the last 12 months in the hope that they might remember me when they visit the lawyer in January to record the annual fluctuation of their affections in the right-hand column of their wills. 'Peace on earth' it says inside those cards, printed lest we've forgotten the universal formula, 'and goodwill to all men', the first half of which is a laughable denial of reality and sure to become even more laughable as the planet gets drier, hotter and more populous, and the second half of which I don't feel, have never felt and have no desire to feel.

But at least Christmas is a fine time for a laugh. The whole festival is drenched in ironies so stupendous that it's a wonder Riccarton Mall isn't carpeted with shoppers writhing on their backs like so many flipped turtles, clutching their stomachs, laughing themselves all the way unto pain and bellowing, 'No, stop it, I can't take any more, this is just *too* funny.'

For all I know that may actually be how things are at Riccarton Mall, but I've no plans to find out, having done my Christmas shopping in one hit and ten minutes a couple of weeks ago with the aid of a biochemistry student who works in Ballantynes over the summer. She was magnificently cheerful and efficient and had a far better idea of what my elderly mother might want by way of a present, or rather multiple expensive presents, than I have ever had or am likely to have. All that was required of me was to sign the gift card and to punch my identity into the Eftpos gizmo. And I was even tempted to get Miss Biochemistry to perform the first of these duties on my behalf, since the parcel that will fly around the world will be so beautifully tissue-plumped, paper-wrapped and ribbon-tied that my mother, who is no fool, will not so much smell a rat as see, with 20–20 precision, an entire commercial rattery complete with twitching nostrils. But that, of course, is appropriate for Christmas, hypocrisy being the name of the seasonal game.

Even as I type this, the caretaker of a B52 will be hosing out a bomb-bay in preparation for cramming it with several hundred pallets of plump, dead, hormone-laden, Kentucky turkeys to be flown to the troops scattered about that epicentre of all things

Christmassy, the Middle East. And if the shaven-headed ones in camouflage gear are really lucky they may even get a flying visit from his holiness the president, thereby sending them into ecstasies of religious fervour to carry them through the next three months of being shot at by understandably upset fundamentalists with different fundamentals.

Meanwhile Christmas in the West reverts gradually to what it started as, which is a pagan binge. Every year gurgling baby Jesus slithers a bit further down the pop charts, while Santa, an invention of Coca-Cola Corp, is installed ever more firmly at No. 1. But none of that matters. What matters is that Christmas is a splendid example of human culture. Not culture in the sense of sitting through a performance of *Swan Lake* because somehow the boredom and stifled giggles will make one a better person, nor culture in the sense of pointing a camcorder at natives dancing in traditional costume that they wear only when they have camcorders pointed at them. No, this is true culture in the sense that it is something people do unselfconsciously without quite knowing why, something that makes no sense, something whose origins are lost in time, something that carries a sticky residue of yesterdays, and something that it is an act of heresy to be rude about. In other words, there's not much to distinguish Christmas from circumcision, so take your pick and have a good one.

Political and social stuff

Political life may be enjoyable for the participants but from the outside it looks grim. The truth is rarely spoken. Language is used as a smokescreen. Parliaments resemble boarding schools. And the sniff of power makes people do strange dishonest things. It's a depressing business. But it's also an essential one. No human society has ever found a satisfactory way of governing itself. Democracy is obviously the best we've got, but what an awful show it puts on stage. It's perpetually comic, but with a dangerous hidden edge. Like armed clowning.

P.C. Sturrock

On the morning when both my dogs were simultaneously, spectacularly and indeed voluminously sick in the car, police buttocks shone from the front page of my newspaper. And all this at a time when the police were marching in search of a pay rise. It would have been easy to conclude that the world was coming to an end.

Now, there are several points that need to be made here, but first, for reasons that should become clear, I need to introduce you to a boy with whom I went to school.

This boy had all the charm of dog-sick. He wore shorts in the fifth form. Nobody else did. It was agreed among the schoolboys of England that to wear shorts beyond the age of twelve was a sign of effeminacy, lunacy or both, which was exactly why this boy did it. He longed for people to say, 'You are wearing shorts, which means you are an effeminate lunatic,' because then he could kill them.

He terrified me, and even now I hesitate to name him. But perhaps at forty it is time for me to take my spindly courage in both hands. His name (come closer now; I am typing softly) was Sturrock.

Sturrock's greatest pleasure was Bawden. Bawden was a skinny child who never once called Sturrock an effeminate lunatic. Nevertheless, Sturrock regularly used to cram him into sports lockers the size of nesting boxes. On more creative days he would casually tie Bawden's limbs into a knot and place him on top of a cupboard like an ornament. When the ornament squealed Sturrock grinned.

At the end of the fifth form Sturrock decided there was little fun left in stirring the rubble of Bawden's psyche and he left school in search of fresh woods and pastures new. Driven no doubt by the wish to continue beating people up without being punished for it, Sturrock applied to join the police force.

Now, I do not know whether Sturrock became a copper, but for the sake of Great Britain I hope he didn't. Sturrock was not the sort of human being who took kindly to being asked the time.

Which brings us to the question of what sort of human beings police officers should be. The answer to that is extraordinary people. Armed only with the right to use the minimum force required to uphold the law, they are required to walk towards situations that instinct tells them to run away from.

They are required to accept insults but not bribes, to do as they are bid whether or not they agree with the instruction, to treat people whom they do not like in exactly the same way as they treat people whom they do like, and as a matter of routine to deal with the sordid and the sad, the brutal and the bloody. At rugby matches they must stand with their backs to the game.

In other words, they are required to behave unnaturally. They are paid to embody our better selves, to represent our civic conscience, the side of us that knows the way things ought to happen, to enforce the laws which we have elected people to Parliament to make. Having a police force is like paying someone to make us keep our New Year resolutions. They are not paid much to do it, and it cannot be much fun.

And then, behold, on the front page of the paper, a photograph of policemen having a lot of fun. In order to raise funds for their Dragon Boat team they are stripping off mock uniforms to the delight of a sizeable crowd.

The obvious point is that the police officers concerned were off duty. At work a police officer is required to be as rational as Mr Spock. Off duty he is allowed to have red blood in his veins; he is allowed to love and to laugh and to drink and to be wrong. And if he wants to remove his clothes in a night-club for a laugh, I am not at all surprised. It might help him tomorrow when he has to deal with someone who prefers removing the clothes from other people and then raping them.

Without the police the world would be an unfair place. If tonight the police all folded their tents and crept out of town, looting would begin within the hour, John Citizen would buy a gun tomorrow morning, the suburban vigilantes would be formed by afternoon tea and by lunchtime on Friday there would be anarchy. You and I, dear reader, could be dead.

In most countries of the world, the police are corrupt. Here, on the whole, they are not. No doubt the New Zealand police force contains the odd Sturrock but by and large the police act as they should; they guard the system by which we have chosen to govern ourselves.

In sum, then, the fuss over the strip show is wrong-headed and the fuss over pay is important. The police should be paid what they want and then some. The profession of policing should be so attractive that good and talented people queue to enter it.

Then when Sturrock emigrates to come looking for me and decides to do a little policing while he is here to keep his hand in, the recruiting officer can show him the door. With any luck Sturrock will kick it, whereupon he will be arrested.

Meanwhile, if you are seeking a Subaru Omega in good running order and fragrance is not a consideration, I might be able to help.

Ringing the world

I once rang Fidel Castro. It was at the fag end of a party, not a teenage party with snogging on the staircase, but a middle-aged party, with daggers in the sauvignon. But now it was late and the few remaining party-goers were barely going at all. They slumped on sofas with the dregs of drinks.

To cheer things up, I offered to phone the world.

'Name someone,' I said, 'anyone you like, and I'll get them on the line in three calls.'

It's a good boast. I have made it several times. People swallow the hook.

'Go on,' I said, 'anyone at all, famous as you like.'

'Elvis,' said a woman.

'Castro,' said a man.

'Give me the phone,' I said.

International directory enquiries gave me the number of some governmental office in Havana. I rang it and asked for el presidente. He was not available. He was at his country residence. Amazingly they gave me the number.

Castro intrigues me. He's the coelocanth of the Caribbean, the beast who should be fossil. The Berlin Wall has been made into souvenirs, the Kremlin has tottered and fallen like a shot elephant, but Castro goes on going on.

Castro no doubt sees himself as independent but he was merely a child of his time. The seasons of thought and feeling govern how we all grow and Castro flowered into power when all was communism and revolution. But having flowered and enjoyed flowering, Castro refused to wilt. He kept his combat fatigues and his ancient mariner beard and he stopped the political clock.

Castro's Cuba sits at the doorstep of America and reminds that country of otherness. America distrusts otherness. America tells us that Castro's bad because he doesn't let his people grow fat. He has banned them from the shopping mall of Western capitalism.

I have not been to Cuba so I don't know what I should think of Castro. I don't know if he runs a secret police. I don't know if he tortures his foes. I don't know if his people love him or fear him, though I suspect they do both. I am sure that someone will write to tell me what to think but I suspect that things are not as simple as they seem and that he's neither good nor bad.

But I do know that he's mad. The evidence came this week when Castro collapsed while giving a speech. He had been speaking for a mere two hours. Apparently there was an hour or two more to come.

Any politico who speaks for two hours is mad. Megalomania has maddened him. Power has distorted his picture. He thinks too well of himself. He is plump with hubris.

Castro was speaking outdoors to a crowd of I don't know who. While he stood and spoke they sat and fanned themselves. But then his voice crumpled like paper and he fell against the lectern. The cameras panned away but the people carried on staring. They were staring at Ozymandias.

> My name is Ozymandias, king of kings.
> Look on my works, ye mighty, and despair.

Castro's works are Cuba and his own status. But his audience would have seen that though his status is unassailable, his body is not. The enzymes of decay are busy in it. And suddenly those enzymes had made their first statement. We have been patient, said the enzymes, but look, we have been working. We will win. Bear with us. Prepare to lose thy leader.

It was a remarkable moment, a point of pivot. On a short clip of official film, pride met frailty, vanity said hello to the worms.

Castro will not go willingly or soon. He has so much to lose he dare not lose it. He is his office. And sure enough, within minutes of collapsing he was back on the podium intent on finishing the great bore. But his audience had seen a different finish. They had seen that for Castro, as for Ozymandias, the lone and level sands stretch far away.

When at that party I rang Castro's country residence I said I was a dignitary from Nueva Zelandia and that I would like to speak to the great revolutionary papa on a matter of some urgency. The secretary told me to esperar un momento and in the crackling of the tinny international line I felt unwonted excitement.

For though I had often boasted that I could locate anyone in three phone calls, the best I had done was the switchboard of the hotel at which Sophia Loren was staying. And now I was about to speak to international power.

The secretary returned. She was sorry. The revolutionary leader was having a nap. It was, she said, a warm afternoon.

'Gracias,' I said, and left the great leader swinging gently in his hammock.

The man was a pornographist

I wish I'd been the student who stood in Tiananmen Square and stopped the tank. It was all so right. The place, the time, the elevated camera angle, the way the tank manoeuvred to avoid him like some sort of lumbering Dalek, yes it would have been lovely. I wouldn't have wanted it permanently, of course. The idea of a life in Beijing trying to come to terms with bicycles and chopsticks is quite unthinkable, but how sweet to have been flashed around the world as a lone exemplar of heroism, to be wept over and venerated by an army of liberals in the West with their cheap Chinese-made underwear, their raffia place mats and their soft-boiled politics.

I know a woman who was teaching in Beijing at the time and living in a flat the size of a wok about half a mile from Tiananmen Square. By some bizarre bureaucratic oversight her state-sponsored flat had been furnished with a telephone. One morning the woman's husband called from Cambridgeshire, England to ask her how she was coping with the massacre, and she said what massacre, and he said the one down the road, and she said oh and at that moment a trio of her students came crashing into the flat with cheap underwear held to their skulls to stem the bleeding and she said oh *that* massacre.

Of course there's lots to say about that, tedious stuff about global villages and instant communication, but by far the most important question is what was her husband doing watching CNN in the middle of the day when he could have been playing golf or buying place mats or whatever it is that husbands do when their wives are away.

Of course he'll reply that he was watching CNN *because* his wife was away and trouble was obviously brewing in Beijing like that inexcusable tea they favour over there, but I'm afraid that won't wash at all. If he was worried he should have gone to China with her or chained her by the leg to the vacuum cleaner back in misty Cambridgeshire.

No, I'm afraid the man was a pornographist. All CNN watchers are. Nevertheless on the pyramid of wickedness they sit somewhere near the basement. The pinnacle is reserved for those heroes of contemporary journalism, the foreign correspondents, standing there as smug as Oscar-winners in their flak jackets in front of a hillside on which decorative puffs of smoke appear from time to time as the local heathens battle it out in the traditional manner with remaindered Cold War armaments. Then it's back to the hotel with the camera crew for a snort of manly brandy and a three-course lunch before planning tomorrow's raid on vicarious danger to titillate the zillions in the distant suburbs of Safetyville.

There's a splendid scene in some novel by Tom Wolfe in which a news room bemoans the shortage of good street violence in today's bulletin and sends a couple of cameras out to make things happen. It takes about ten minutes to start a riot among the grievance-loaded dispossessed, all of them hankering for the chance to lob a few stones at society's uniformed prefects. Perfectly legitimate fun, of course, but if it hadn't been for the cameras they'd have quietly lain around the back alleys being hopeless as usual.

And there's no need to shoot more footage of kids throwing stones in the Middle East because there's miles of that stuff in the vault already and nothing's changed. Nor have the comments of the watchers in suburbia who all wonder what the stone-chuckers' mothers are up to allowing their urchins to wander the streets with pockets full of bits of ruin to biff at the riot squad. Well, that's an easy one. Thanks to CNN, BBC, ABC and all the other vultures it's now perfectly easy for the said mothers to stay at home with the telly on and keep an eye on their offspring.

Meanwhile the urchins are having a lovely time, whether they're in Belfast, Seoul or Gaza, playing the local version of cricket with equipment supplied by mother earth. In my teenage years I'd have loved it too. Nothing gave me greater joy than throwing things. The school let me biff the javelin, discus and shot, all of them former weapons of war — though I do wonder quite how effective the shot was — and our aim on sports day was always to try and hit an inattentive official, but how much more fun it would have been if we'd been doing it for real and we'd known that the world was watching instead of a mob of bored teachers with clipboards who were pining for the pub.

Anyway, most of the places that were fighting when I was a kid are still fighting today — perhaps because they like it — and CNN's made lots of money out of them and us.

Because he is a man

Oh, it's so tedious and wrong. A judge or two has had a peek or two at a dirty picture or two. And so, say some, they shouldn't be judges.

Every male has his own private porn studio. It's called his head. At peak production shortly after puberty it can churn out a dozen reels a day of startlingly original material. It needs no prompt. It gets no encouragement. Indeed it gets the opposite of encouragement. It gets a pasting from every moral pulpit in the land. Each man is taught to hide it. Each man is taught to feel shame. And yet the studio carries on in blithe disregard, pumping out its steaming torrent of images.

It does not corrupt its owner. It is its owner. Man is a lust-racked beast. We can and do pretend this is not true. It is true.

In later life the dream factory becomes less fertile. It still rolls out the films but it cribs more of its ideas from screen and print. And there is and always has been a wealth of material to help it.

We have pornography in Latin and in Greek. We have the Karma Sutra and the nudes that Titian painted to titillate the Pope. Porn is as old as writing, as old, indeed, as drawings on the walls of caves.

Today it is an industry. In the United States the porn industry is bigger than the car industry. The internet is crammed with porn. It is so because men want it. It is not good that it is so. It is simply so.

I may have met a man who has never riffled through a skin mag or watched a blue movie or dwelt on images that stir him, but if I have I don't know who he is. And I do know that I have met thousands, and I am one of them, who have in their time done all of these things. And we are not bad men. We are men.

'All men are rapists,' screamed the strident women some 30 years ago and they were mad. Very few men are rapists. A randy man can also be a kind man. A lusty man can be good. A man can surf the internet for porn and also be a judge, a fine and honest, wise and decent judge.

A judge has a job to do. To say he cannot do that job because he is randy is to talk startling nonsense. It is to say he cannot do the job because he is a man.

Men are capable of self-knowledge. Men are capable of knowing what is good and what is right while still being men. Their lust does not blind them. If it blinded them then all men would indeed be rapists. But we have will and judgment and reason and sympathy. Without will or judgment or reason or sympathy there would be no courts of law, no civil society, things that men through history, men subject to lust, have forged.

Lurking behind all this is the presumption that people in authority should be androids, unstirred by the emotions that beset the rest of us. With this presumption comes a hideous delight in exposing their frailty. We pillory the judges, princes, kings and courtiers for having red blood in their veins, for being just like us. We pelt them with the sour tomatoes of hypocrisy. It is, I think, the least appealing feature of that animal called man.

Women know men are randy. And they want men to be randy. Women strive to attract men. They may pretend otherwise, but behind all diets, all make-up, all pretty clothes, lurks an evolutionary urge to be sexy. But women also want men to be trustworthy and to restrain themselves and not to make unwelcome advances. It is tough for men. Come here, say the women, and keep your distance. It is the endless dance of the mating game. Porn says only come here.

We live in a sex-driven world. Strip clubs litter the land. Increasingly the strippers are male. *Ladies Night* drew huge crowds. Because it happened in the theatre, that bastion of middle-class propriety, countless women went to watch it with an almost easy conscience. Were any of our female judges among them? And if they were, do they differ one jot from their porn-surfing counterparts?

Yes they do, because they attended *Ladies Night* in their own free time, whereas at least one of the male judges surfed for porn while at work. He used the court computer. He committed a crime, in other words, comparable with filching office stationery. He should be punished as all of us should be punished who have filched office stationery. Let him who is without sin cast the first roll of Sellotape.

Jules

Joseph Bennett, you stand before me . . .

Julian, m'lud. My Christian name's not Joseph. It's Julian.

But . . .

I know, m'lud. Both my friends call me Joe, but it's not my given name. I adopted it as a teenager.

Is that so?

It is, m'lud. Adolescence is a tough time, as I am sure m'lud will recall if he tosses his mind back a century or so. And it is made even tougher by being called Julian. At school, m'lud, they called me

Jules. I yearned to be hard, m'lud. It is hard to be hard when one is called Jules. No one expects a Jules to be able to make a tackle on the rugby field.

And could you make a tackle?

No, m'lud. That was the problem. I had something wrong with my back.

You're not going to make that joke about there being a big yellow streak down it.

Not now, m'lud, no. But I was a cowardly rugby player.

So the perceived effeminate connotations of your given name drove you to change that name to the seemingly tougher Joe, even though the effeminate connotations were, in truth, bang on. In short, you were and you remain a slack-wristed non-tackling nancy boy.

Precisely, m'lud.

I can't say you surprise me. Anyway, Julian Bennett, you stand before me today charged with mockery of politicians and a refusal to treat seriously the business of the recent electoral campaign. How do you plead?

Guilty, m'lud.

What? Come, come. Show some spine, for once. Put up your legal dukes.

I plead guilty to the charge, m'lud.

And to the additional charges of superficiality, levity, trivialisation and taking cheap shots?

Absolutely, m'lud, guilty as charged.

What, none of the customary liberal claptrap about freedom of speech, et bloody cetera?

None of that, m'lud.

So you're happy to be sentenced for reducing political debate to the level of a circus sideshow, for displaying, indeed, as little attention to serious and complicated matters of policy as the politicians did during the campaign?

I am, m'lud.

On the grounds, I presume, that you consider it apt and fitting to describe a superficial and clownish political performance in superficial and clownish terms.

Your words, m'lud.

Don't grovel, Jules.

Sorry, m'lud.

And so you imply that all elections, whether held in the agora of ancient Athens or in 100 per cent pure New Zealand, are essentially mood-driven and irrational popularity contests, and that both politicians and electorate expect it to be that way whatever they may say to the contrary?

I imply nothing, m'lud. You infer it.

Don't get clever, Jules. Are you also suggesting that the hard-won privilege of democracy, of power to the people, one person one vote, the peaceful submission to the will of the majority, is a notion so grand that we don't live up to it? That most people vote in a particular way because they have always voted that way, or because they feel some emotional warmth towards a candidate, or because they think there may be something in it for them?

I am suggesting nothing, m'lud. I have pleaded guilty.

Your guilt is for me to judge. Are you furthermore suggesting that because those in pursuit of power pander to that superficiality with their slogans and their airbrushed photographs, and that because they hire what I believe are called 'public relations consultants' in order to present themselves as bait to the fishy masses, you are justified in attacking them on precisely those superficial terms?

You said it, m'lud, not I.

And I suppose that underneath your petty bolshevism lurks the shop-worn belief that those who seek power are unlikely to be the people who should have it, and that the corrupting nature of power is as true today as it ever was, as illustrated by the current prime minister increasingly referring to herself in the third person, as 'The Prime Minister'.

I have pleaded guilty, m'lud.

And you're not going to try and weasel out of it with some trite nonsense about there being more truth in an ounce of comedy than in a hundredweight of seriousness?

I am not, m'lud. I am a convert to the metric system.

Enough. I have tired of you. I sentence you to publicise the name on your birth certificate. And may the Lord have mercy on your soul.

Food, fun and a tickle behind the ear

Most human beings are docile. They mean no harm and prefer to be left in peace. You and I are likely to get through life without suffering more than a few minor assaults from human beings on our persons or our property. Though there is good reason to be vigilant, there is no reason to be paranoid.

But, as happens every couple of years, events have occurred to inflame paranoia, and the media have cheerfully fanned that flame into a conflagration. It is time to douse it with the hosepipe of reason.

In the process I am not going to gloss over the truth that most attacks on human beings are committed by human beings. Nor am I going to deny that the proportion of viciousness in the human population is higher than in species such as dogs. But I am going to try to restore a sense of proportion.

As anyone who has ever lived with a human being will tell you, by and large they want the same things as you want — food, fun, a tickle behind the ear and as much sex as possible. Millions of human beings, in every part of the globe, offer love and loyalty to their companions and go to their graves having committed no greater sin than gluttony, selfishness or listening to Britney Spears.

That said, it must be noted that the human being is merely a parcel of instincts. Though the parcel comes wrapped in brown paper and string that we call civilisation, as every postman knows, paper can tear and string can fray. And when that happens the instincts poke out and we can get hurt. So it is sensible to understand the beast as well as we can if we are to defend ourselves against him.

The first thing to observe is that the human being is a pack animal. When he joins a pack he becomes a less tractable creature than when he is alone. For evidence one has only to consider parliament, or the crowd at a Britney Spears concert.

The larger the pack the greater the danger. Sometimes a huge pack can form under the leadership of a bellicose lunatic. Such a pack is known as a nation state. The leader rouses the pack by telling them lies and getting them to sing songs full of abstract nouns such as glory, honour and duty. The pack then sets off in formation to attack another pack. These days they send aeroplanes halfway round the planet to drop bombs. The condition is called war, it has recurred throughout human history, and there's not much you can do about it. But at least you get good warning when it's happening.

The human being suffers from delusions. Although few now believe in God — an amusing concept in which human beings created a supreme being in their own image and then insisted it had happened the other way round — most still suffer the hangover from that belief, an inflated sense of their own importance. Torturers, child pornographers, even Britney Spears fans, all take it for granted that they belong to a superior species.

It is true that the human being has a peculiar form of intelligence that has enabled him to make tools. From this has sprung his remarkable expansion across the globe. But at the same time the average human being has never made a tool in his life. The great tools were invented by a few talented and peaceable individuals. The rest of the species has been happy to use those tools and to take the credit by association.

Despite their intelligence, human beings are hard to train. I spent twenty years as a trainer and I'm still not sure how it's done. Nor do I know why a few human beings go bad. The one sure thing is that the damage is done young. It may even occur in the womb. At any rate, by the time a trainer gets to them, it is often too late. And although we no longer destroy vicious human beings, we still rarely cure them.

The other sure thing is that laws don't stop the vicious. They stop only the human beings who don't need stopping. More laws won't prevent more attacks, because human beings who attack already ignore the existing laws. The law can only react.

Some people have argued that control officers should be allowed to enter properties and seize vicious human beings before they attack. The idea is a tempting one, because it is not hard to spot the vicious. At the same time such a law would set a perilous precedent.

So we are left with the problem of how to defend ourselves from attack. A stout stick is useful, but the sort of weapons that would really do the job are illegal except in America. Personally I always carry a loaded Walkman. At the first sign of aggression I turn the volume knob to maximum and press 'play'. It is remarkable to see the instant deterrent effect of *Britney Spears' Greatest Hits*. But perhaps the simplest way, and by far the most pleasant, to defend yourself against the highly unlikely danger of attack by a human being is to get a dog.

Is there anybody there?

When I heard that the government had raised the excise tax on light spirits and fortified wines in order to separate the young from the stomach-pumps, I knew immediately that the story was beyond my scope. It called for someone who knew what was what with adolescence, so I rang Enid Blyton.

Her housekeeper informed me that the mistress had been a bit quiet these thirty-five years on account of an attack of jolly old death but if I cared to leave a message . . . I rang off. I knew what I had to do.

It was the work of a minute to scatter Scrabble pieces on the side table, place a wine glass upside down in their midst and drape the lot in a suitably eerie ambience. Enid's finger might be skeletal but I was confident it remained on the pulse of youth affairs and capable of tapping out a moral yarn that would say all that needed saying on the matter.

Within seconds the ouija glass was skidding like a boy racer. And here are the skid marks.

The Famous Five Go Binge-Drinking
By a shade purporting to be that of Ms Blyton

'I say, George,' said Dick, 'it's Saturday night. Let's go out and get completely . . . oh damn it.'

'Dick,' exclaimed George, 'what's the matter?'

'Dash it and golly,' said Dick sucking his finger. 'I've stabbed myself with the darning needle.'

'You silly thing, Dick,' said Anne reprovingly. 'But if you will go trying to lower the crotch of your skateboard trousers without wearing a thimble, what do you expect? Here, give them to me. Now just sit yourself down and George will get you a sherry.'

'Here you are, Dick,' said George. 'That'll put hairs on your chest.'

'Sherry's antiseptic, isn't it?' said Dick, plunging his finger into the glass and swirling it around so that blood mingled with the sun-soaked sweetness. But George was looking at Dick with horror.

'What's the matter, George?' said Dick. 'There's plenty more where that came from.'

'No Dick, there isn't. That's the last of the amontillado and the Dubonnet gave out last week.'

'Well, waste not want not,' said Dick, knocking back the crimson glass in a single swig. 'Whew, that's what I call a Bloody Mary. But don't worry George, I'll take Timmy the dog for a drive down to the bottle store in my $20,000 saloon car with the boombox that gave Julian renal damage, and we'll just flash the fake ID you bought in the Square and . . .'

'But Dick,' exclaimed George, 'you silly ass. Haven't you been listening to the radiogram? The grown-up government has just increased the tax on the fortified wines that we've been getting so jolly blotto on every night.'

'Nonsense,' exclaimed Dick. 'They can't. Everyone knows that we're below the legal drinking age. The government can't tax illegal drinking. They'd be taxing crime. And that amounts to living off immoral earnings.'

'O Dick,' said Julian, 'if your liver holds out you really ought to think about being a lawyer when you grow up. You're so frightfully clever. But all the same it's true what George says.'

'Well, I think this needs investigating,' said Dick. 'Is anybody up for an adventure?'

'You bet we are,' said everybody except for Timmy the dog who just barked, so Dick, Julian, George and Anne put on their having-an-adventure clothes and Timmy the dog put on the muzzle that the grown-up government required him to wear when outdoors and the Famous Five set off to Parliament.

'We may need this,' said Dick, brandishing half a dozen sticks of gelignite.

'Oh what fun,' said Julian.

As they bicycled into town they passed a long queue of traffic all heading towards Wellington airport. 'Who are all these people?' asked George.

'Well,' said Julian, 'some of them are old people who like a sherry of an evening, others are winemakers and the rest are smokers or dog-owners. They're all emigrating because . . .'

'Shh,' said Dick, 'we're here.' Before them stood the grey walls of Parliament. 'Come on,' said Dick and before they knew it they were in a shrubbery outside a window. By standing on tip toe they could see into a room where a group of very serious grown-ups were sitting round a table. On the table stood a model of a yacht with the names of several companies on the hull including a brewery.

'So,' said a waspish little man in spectacles, 'the increased excise tax will fund the bowsprit and the bailing bucket, but as for . . .' and then he stopped because Timmy the dog had ripped off his muzzle, seized the bundle of high explosives, leapt through the window, tied up all the grown-ups, lit the fuse, paused to widdle on the yacht and jumped back out of the window into the waiting arms of Dick.

'Run,' screamed Julian. And they all ran like billyo and dived through the door of The Backbencher as the blast rattled the windows.

'Well done everybody,' said Dick. 'And especially you, Timmy. This calls for sherry all round.'

'Woof woof,' said Timmy the dog.

De mortuis nihil nisi Latin

Well, there I was, all set with something to say about Yasser Arafat at last, and then he ups and dies on me, and *de mortuis*, as they say, *nihil nisi bonum*. Only they don't say, of course, because it's Latin.

I've got stacks of Latin floating around in my skull as a result of having it shouted into me by a man with vestigial malaria. Periodically the disease would cause him to collapse on the classroom floor in a sort of tropical sweat. It happened for the first time when we were in the third form and we duly panicked, sprinting to the staffroom for an adult and a mop. He tried pulling the same stunt three years later but by then we were sixteen and hairy and so super cool that we just sat around smoking cigarettes, playing poker and waiting for the bell, whereupon we left him on the floor for the next class to discover.

That story may be a tad exaggerated, but that's because it's a story and people have been exaggerating stories since they first put pen to papyrus. Take Homer, for example, as renowned a Latin poet as they come. He told monstrous porkies. Are we really supposed to believe that the Trojans went 'Ooh look, a wooden horse. How thoughtful of our eternal enemies the Greeks. Let's immediately haul it inside the city walls. Bound to come in useful some day.'? Precisely.

Meanwhile you can all put your pens down. No need after all to write the letter pointing out that Homer wrote in Greek. It was a trap, see, my own little Trojan horse.

Furthermore it was a trap with a purpose, conceived to illustrate the theme of today's little homily which I have just discovered and which isn't old beak-nosed Arafat after all. My theme is rather that the main use of learning is one-upmanship.

Take the Latin tag I rolled out in the first sentence. I'm perfectly capable of doing the same notion in English ('be nice to stiffs' does it neatly) but by whacking it out in a language as dead as Yasser I'm holding up a banner saying I'm frightfully educated. If you happen to be frightfully educated as well you're invited to join my smug little club.

But that doesn't mean we're friends. Because when a paragraph or two later I made an error about Homer, when, in short, I nodded (another classical allusion there. If you got it, give yourself a biscuit) what did you feel? Sympathy for poor benighted Joe? A fervent wish that everyone in this muddled world were as well educated as you? A lament for the decline of classical learning? Not a bit of it. If you're anything like me you felt the sort of bloodlust that my dingbat dog feels when he spots a possum in a bush. It's the chance to kill. Dingbat has developed the tactic of climbing the bank above the bush and then leaping onto the branches in order to dislodge the possum whereupon he kills it with relish and brings me the corpse, which suggests that he may not be entirely dingbat after all. But the point is that it's his equivalent of writing to the editor but much more fun. In other words, you and I and dingbat are all out there for one reason, which is to win. And good on us all, say I.

The Catholic church spotted the daunting show-off value of Latin from the beginning. By continuing to intone *in nomine* this and *in spiritu* that they kept the educationally deprived peasants in awestruck tithe-paying subjection for the best part of 2000 years.

It's not just Latin of course. Consider quiz nights in pubs. I love them. They're just about the only reward I get for suffering through seven years of high school accruing nuggets like the date of Shakey's birth (1564) and his inside leg measurement in millimetres (ditto). All the history, geography, physics, algebra that I absorbed but never found a use for comes into its own at last. Up goes my hand and with it my self-esteem. Ooh, look at me, I know stuff.

In other words most so-called education is simply the tedious acquisition of a grab-bag of nuggets that we then spend the rest of our days longing for the chance to trot out.

But it's too late for old Yasser, I'm afraid, not that he isn't better off out of it, having spent the last few years living among rubble provided at enormous expense by Israel and with the only compensation being that he was an extremely long way from his dingbat wife.

And too late for my little commentary on him as well, not that it was really worth it anyway. All I had to say about him, apart from his having kept a hundred smug foreign correspondents in business for forty indistinguishable years, was that whenever I saw his face on the telly he reminded of an Australian netball coach. But *de mortuis nihil nisi bonum* so I'd better not say that.

I, speechwriter

I, principal speech-writer to the President of the United States of America, do solemnly swear to write a doozy of a speech for President Bush's — and gee, yeah, I'm as astonished as you are — second inauguration.

When coaching the president in the delivery of this speech, I do solemnly swear to try to stop him grinning like a schoolboy at being re-elected, though I am not confident of success. I shall also encourage him to clench his eyebrows during the serious bits of the speech and to stress the important words.

The most important word for him to stress is liberty (*applause*), which I do solemnly swear to use more than thirty times during the speech, partly because it always spurs applause (*applause*) but mainly because everyone approves of it without being able to define it. If I tire of the word liberty (*applause*) I shall substitute the synonym freedom (*applause*), though I shall not use the word synonym because of potential presidential pronunciation problems. Nor for the same reason shall I use the phrase 'potential presidential pronunciation problems'.

I shall exploit standard rhetorical devices such as the triple construction, the aim of which is not to create a reasoned argument, nor yet to pile evidence on evidence, but simply to sound climactic. A quality that the periodic sentence, of which I shall also make use, reserving as it does its principal word or phrase, most commonly the verb, right to the end of the sentence, sometimes at the risk of mangling the syntax and baffling the audience (*bafflement*), shares.

I further pledge to coin illogical extended metaphors, such as 'the fire that America has lit in the minds of men'. Of this fire I shall say that 'it warms those who feel its power; it burns those who fight its progress; and one day this untamed fire of freedom will reach the darkest corners of our world'. But what this selective fire will do when it reaches those darkest corners, I shall not say. I hope it doesn't burn them down as fires tend to do.

In the course of the speech I shall make great use of the abstract noun courage because it sometimes induces applause (*silence*). But not always. Nevertheless courage combines with freedom (*applause*) to echo 'the land of the free and the home of the brave' and thus arouse patriotic fervour. Patriotic fervour achieves the first aim of an inaugural speech, which is to numb the power of reason.

The same is true of God (*reverential awe*). Therefore I do also solemnly swear to cram the speech with references to God (*reverential awe*). Not only will they induce a feeling of reverential awe but they will also align the president with the war leaders of history, all of whom from Julius Caesar to Osama bin Laden (*opposite of reverential awe*) have used references to God (*reverential awe*) or gods (*puzzlement*) to encourage their troops.

By these means I shall rewrite the truth of the conflict in Iraq. Rather than portraying it as a self-interested act of invasion, my words will make it seem a selfless act of liberation. And I do solemnly swear not to mention the lies about terrorist links and weapons of mass destruction that the president used to justify the self-interested act of invasion. Those lies are now history and I mean to ignore history.

Except, of course, when history is useful, for I intend to quote from the very historical Abraham Lincoln. This quotation will make the president look learned, will link him with an older and wiser president, and will provide me with another chance for a triple construction. It will also allow me to use the word freedom (*applause*) again.

According to old Abe, 'Those who deny freedom to others deserve it not for themselves, and, under the rule of a just god, cannot long retain it.'

But I shall not pursue these words to their logical conclusion because I do solemnly swear it would screw up the speech. For rather a lot of freedom-denying tyrants — Kim Il Jong, Mao Zedong, Joseph Stalin, Saddam Hussein (*opposite of applause*) and many another — have retained power for rather a long time. Indeed the first three on my list all managed to die in office. The only reasonable conclusion to draw is that there is no just God (*reverential shock*). At the same time it appears that the current president has adopted for himself the role of that just God.

Playing God is not a good look for a devout president so I do solemnly swear to leave the Abe-quote dangling. An inaugural speech does not exist to reach logical conclusions. It exists to appeal to the 90 per cent of Americans who believe in God. With any luck it will also blur the distinction between that God, the President of the United States, and American self-interest (*applause*).

After the speech I do solemnly swear to sink a lot of cocktails at each of the nine inauguration balls. And the reference to balls reminds me that it is time for the standard peroration. May God bless you and may he watch over the United States of America a bit more carefully than he did on the 11th of September 2001 despite constant reminders from every inaugural speech since 1776 that this was his number one priority (*thunderous and sustained applause*).

For we are young and free

In the same week as the premier of New South Wales has taken steps to encourage Australian patriotism, Shane Warne, the well-known Australian cricketer, has agreed to take part in an episode of *Neighbours*, the well-known Australian drivel. What writer could resist the opportunity to submit a script for the show? Here's mine:

Establishing scene: a beach in the typically Australian town of Girt-by-Sea where typically Australian things are going on. Bush tucker is simmering in a billy on the Harvey Norman barbecue. A mass brawl on the beach is degenerating into a game of Aussie Rules. Surfers pass by en route to Paradise. They ignore a man in a safari suit shouting at crocodiles with bogus enthusiasm. At the high-tide mark, a Lebanese man lies groaning, a 40-ounce bottle of Bundaberg protruding at a decorative angle from his skull. Wholesome Australian girls in bikinis are using him as a beach volleyball net.

Cut to the inside of Matilda's condominium on Billabong Avenue. The doorbell rings. Matilda leaves off frying an emu's egg and waltzes to the door.

Shane Warne is standing on the step. His hair is gelled like a hedgehog. He is holding a toboggan in one hand and a CD case in the other. Matilda waltzes two steps backwards with surprise, and one sideways.

Shane: Australians all, let us rejoice, for we are young and free.

Matilda: Mr Warne, what a lovely surprise. Been sledging, I see. But what brings you to the set of *Neighbours* where something dramatic happens in every episode, normally illustrating a point of contemporary concern such as racial tension or abortion or Aids, played for cheap emotion by a cast of young people who have been chosen for their sexiness rather than any ability to act?

Shane: Are you Matilda, headmistress of Girt-By-Sea Primary School?

Matilda: That's me, Mr Warne.

Shane: Well, in my capacity as Toohey's Light Patriotism Ambassador for the state of New South Wales, I bring you this. (*He hands her a CD in a green and gold case, etched with an exquisite image of original Australians in traditional tribal costume queuing at a liquor store.*) It's a recording of the national anthem which, by order of the state premier, you are to play at every Girt-By-Sea school assembly from now on, preferably with the children standing and singing along in joyful strains with one hand over their hearts and the other not up their noses.

Matilda: Crickey Dick, Mr Warne, our land may abound in nature's gifts of beauty rich and rare, such as red-back spiders, cane toads and chlamydia-riddled koalas, but don't you think we're getting a bit too much like the America of the South Pacific? Half our armed forces are in Iraq, we're becoming obese, we erect trade barriers on spurious grounds, and we export increasing numbers of tourists who have to shout to be heard above their clothes. So isn't a daily pledge of allegiance in schools just another step down Imitation-Yankee Avenue? Are you trying to come the raw prawn with me, Mr Warne, or some other equally incomprehensible local idiom?

Shane: How's that?

Matilda: Not out, but look who's coming.

Enter several pairs of Speedos and miniature bikinis occupied by young Australian neighbours, leading a life of perpetual sunshine and complex coupling arrangements in order to titillate a global audience living in Speedo-and-bikini-less climes.

Shane stops a boy with blue hair.

Shane: What's your name, son?

Boy: Reddy.

Shane: Well, Reddy, are you a proud young Australian?

Reddy: Fair dinkum, Shane.

Shane: Good boy. And are you aware that, according to the premier of New South Wales, 'the national anthem is about community spirit, being a proud Australian and recognising our shared national identity'? And are you furthermore aware that from now on your schooling will include units on 'Australian Values'? And are you even furtherermore aware that our noble premier has defined these Australian values as family values, community harmony, national identity and other deeply meaningful abstract nouns? We've golden soil and wealth for toil and . . .

Matilda: Sorry to interrupt, Mr Warne — and I do deeply admire your efforts in the recent Ashes series, so tragically lost despite your venomous leg-breaks — but isn't this brain-washing? Isn't it the sort of platitudinous blather used throughout the ages to bolster the people in power, to induce uncritical allegiance, and ultimately to turn the young into potential war-fodder?

Shane: No.

Matilda: That's okay then. Right, kids, all together now, 'In joyful strains then let us sing' . . . oh no, look, a bush fire. We're all going to die. Run for it, young Australians, but don't stop singing.

Cut to credits, and nauseating theme music etc.

White brain, black body

John joined the dogs and me on a late-night walk. A gibbous moon cast shadows like scissored black paper.

'Nice gibbous moon,' I said, on the principle that there's no point in knowing words if you don't flaunt them.

'Gibbous?' said John, which was the correct response.

Feeling the delicious glow of condescension, I began a definition of gibbous but John wasn't listening.

'See that star there,' he said, pointing, 'the reddish one?'

'Yes,' I lied.

'It's called Daktari.'

'Daktari,' I said, scattering exclamation marks like an asteroid shower. 'They've named a star after Dakbloodytari.'

Readers under the age of thirty-five may stop reading now. Go on, off you go to the pop-music reviews, both of you. It's time for middle-aged nostalgia.

Way back in the 1960s when the world was still in primary school, *Daktari* was a television programme set in Africa. It featured white men who wore safari suits and black men who didn't. The black men didn't because they were children of nature and the sun was a blessing on their lean taut flesh. Hard to imagine it now, of course, but back in those days of innocence and the Vietnam War, people thought the sun was a good thing.

Daktari was a vet and the principal white man. The safari suit spared the viewer the sight of Daktari's sloppy belly, but it also emphasised the important bit of Daktari, which was the bit sticking out the top of the safari suit. Daktari might not have had a lean taut body but he did have a white man's head. What he did with that head made him the bwana.

Black men used their heads differently. They used their mouths for grinning and they used their eyes for steering through the bush as they ran from wherever it was that they'd discovered a crisis to wherever it was that Daktari lay swinging in his hammock. When they got there they used their mouths to shout.

'Daktari, Daktari,' they shouted, 'come quickly. There is a crisis over here so please put down the gin, climb off the hammock and into your safari suit and don't forget to bring that throbbing brain of yours to solve the problem, because, sadly, we're only Africans, massa, and though our bodies may be lean and taut, and our teeth perhaps a shade whiter than yours, when it comes down to it we're just tribal meatheads.'

'On my way,' said Daktari, leaping into his Land Rover without spilling his gin. The Land Rover was a motorised safari suit. It was also the only way Daktari could keep up with Africans.

If Daktari got lost in the Land Rover he just called on a black man to sniff the ground or spot a broken twig or to take a compass bearing with the entrails of a snake and then he was off once more towards the problem that he would solve with his enormous white brain.

The only help Daktari got came not from his decorative female assistants, nor yet from the grinning black boys, but from animals. His two top animals were Clarence the cross-eyed lion and Judy the gibbering chimp.

There was a well-worn bit of footage that showed Judy gibbering and jumping up and down in a state of agitation. This footage was spliced into the programme whenever there was danger in the camp. The danger was always poachers. And clever Judy always spotted them first.

I have since heard that Judy had to have her teeth removed because she kept biting the cast. Perhaps it was at the dentist's that they shot the footage of her in a state of agitation. If so, neither fact was well publicised at the time. Everybody loved Judy.

Everyone loved Clarence even more. Clarence had his own cross-eyed point-of-view camera. It showed everything in blurry stereo. Clarence frightened poachers, but actually he wouldn't hurt a fly, perhaps because he could see two of them.

The animals were devoted to Daktari, or, in Clarence's case, to the Daktari twins. Daktari in turn was devoted to Clarence and Judy. But he was also devoted to all the wild animals in Africa who constantly needed his help to get by.

How the animals of Africa had got by for a trillion years before Daktari rolled up in his safari suit was a mystery. Presumably Clarence's forebears kept picking the wrong prey out of two and starved to death horribly, while Judy retained her teeth but got poached, then boiled or fried.

Daktari was a programme for children. And I loved it. At eight years old I never missed an episode. What I didn't notice at the time was that *Daktari* was sentimental, patronising, white supremacist propaganda. It portrayed Africa as a giant game park populated by nice animals and child-like humans, a place that needed to be saved from itself. Is it a coincidence that this also happens to be the view of Africa that has been adopted by the adult Western world throughout my lifetime with disastrous consequences? I'm not sure that it is. The stories we tell to children are potent things.

'I'm astonished,' I said to John, 'they named a star after *Daktari*. It was sentimental, patronising, white . . .'

'Not Daktari,' said John, 'Antares.'

'Oh,' I said. And we walked on in silence beneath the gibbous moon.

Dung time

There comes a time, doesn't there? A time to cease caring, to stop shivering in the garret of integrity and to start prospering in the mansion of success. A time to forsake sliced bread and instant coffee and to head down the highway towards the lobster thermidor and a beaded bottle of Krug. For me that time is now. I'm turning 50. My knees ache, my bladder's shrunk and my eyes are shot. To hell with writing for the few who are still prepared to ingest something more complex and of less immediate practical value than the pay-and-display notice in the car park at the mall. Those literate few have all become embittered by their growing isolation from the nose-led brain-dead Lotto-dreaming herd. They biff peanuts and pay the same. So it's adios to the literati and buenos dias to the moneyed mass. I am going to write a TV show. And what a cracking idea I've got. It'll pin them to the sofa like a javelin through the thorax. It's a cop show. And it will bring me Krug by the crate.

I'm going to invent a detective. He will be known by a single name. I haven't settled on that name yet, but it will be consonantal, chunky, allusive. A name like Kojak or Morse or Frost or Rebus or Cracker or Dung. Yes, Dung. I like Dung. It has everything necessary.

It is emphatic, chiming, ironic. It acts in counterpoint to the nature of Dung's work. Because Dung is batting for the angels. He cares. He cares for the weak and the ordinary. And he cares above all for the dead. For Dung is the murder man.

He has to be the murder man. Everyone loves a murder. It effortlessly stays at number one in the pop charts of fictional crime. It can't be dislodged. It gives a front-page cortical thrill to every punter. It never loses its power to delight. It's our greatest fear brought out from the murk of disavowal to have a chalk line drawn around it. Its environs are peopled by kneeling cops in plastic overalls. But not by Dung. Dung never kneels. Dung never scours a carpet for bloodstains. Dung merely ducks under the cordon of plastic tape, contaminates the crime scene just as much as he wishes, and stands there thinking. Despite all the advances in forensic science, Dung uses only a brain. He's a human being and he's a good thing. How terribly reassuring.

Not that Dung is without faults. He may be irascible, or shy, or abrupt. His private life is a mess. Indeed the cases he takes on often reflect some aspect of that private life — his fretting for his wayward daughter, perhaps, or his battles with his ex.

Dung also has idiosyncrasies. They are his stamp. He may stutter or collect Dresden figurines or keep pigs or suck lollipops or listen to classical music or take cocaine like old Sherlock. And like old Sherlock he may have a sidekick. The purpose of the sidekick will be to underline Dung's incomparable brain power, his dogged devotion to the hunch, his disregard of the rules. The sidekick will be a low-wattage functionary beside whom Dung glows like a comet.

But the ball and chain round the leg of the crusading Dung is his boss. That boss wears a uniform. He has been promoted beyond his talent. He is wedded to the rules. He has undeserved power over Dung. And he exercises it. He threatens Dung with dismissal. He takes him off the case. The audience on the Harvey Norman sofa writhes with the injustice of it. It confirms their world view that the authorities are all rule-bound mediocrities who have achieved their positions of eminence by slurping sycophancy. The audience identifies with Dung. Honest, rugged, downtrodden Dung.

But Dung refuses to be trodden down. Dung risks his career and his health, because the killer is still killing. The murders are implausibly motivated, but the common thread will be revealed to Dung as in a vision and he will follow that thread to the ends of the earth where at last he will collar the perpetrator.

The perpetrator will confess, will clarify the final puzzle in Dung's mind, and will be led to his fate through streets made safe once more by Dung. And in a quiet coda to the whole, Dung will return to his muddled private life where for once a small resolution will have been achieved, a wayward daughter back in the fold, an ex appeased, a loose end tidied, only for the whole to unravel again next week.

Formulaic? Of course it's formulaic. Formulas become formulas because they work. They play on us simpletons as on a stringed instrument. They make us feel the feelings that we like to feel. They make us believe the nonsense that we like to believe. They make us hope that hope is justified, that we're all right and that the world's all right. And they make writers rich. The time has come.

Gotcha

What a coup for our electronics research department. Or rather what a coup it would have been if the tape hadn't been stolen and broadcast by half of the world's media before this column could prove legal ownership.

I refer, of course, to the conversation captured by our most recent invention, the VIP-activated microphone. This device, which our boffins have been working on for several years, contains a switch triggered by the voice prints of designated VIPs. It had its first field trial at the G8 summit in St Petersburg and what a triumph it proved. As you all know by now, it recorded an off-the-record dialogue between the Most Powerful Person on the Planet and an unidentified lackey.

I don't have the transcript to hand but from memory it ran along the following lines:

Most Powerful Person on the Planet: Yo Blair.

Lackey: Oh most definitely, Your Excellency, and may I just say what a privilege it is to be addressed with such intimacy by the Most Powerful Person on the Planet who makes the birds to sing and the sun to rise? Do I have your gracious permission to breathe a little of the oxygen in this room or would you prefer me to go outside and fetch my own?

MPPotP: Whatever. But what about this Middle East shit? It's about time they stopped doing this shit, eh?

Lackey: O, your globosity, never have I heard such a perceptive analysis of an intransigent political situation. And as leader of a sovereign country I would like to stress that I exist solely to do your bidding. Could I further add that I admire the way you are eating that bread roll with your mouth open?

MPPotP: Whatever.

Lackey: Absolutely, your wondrousness. And now, in order to cleanse my tongue of Texan boot polish, I shall depart your glorious presence, turning off this strangely functioning microphone as I . . .

Well, we didn't make any money out of that, more's the pity, but we did learn our lesson. Since then we've nailed the patent office, and issued injunctions through every legal system from Albania to Zimbabwe. Henceforth every off-the-record conversation captured by our device will become our intellectual property in perpetuity under malfeasance and in fealty nunc vol. The text will be publishable only under sub-licence and we won't be issuing any sub-licences. In other words, this column has become Scoop City.

To give you a taste of what's in store, here's a snippet of dialogue captured last week by a microphone of ours in the White House. One of the speakers is an unbelievably important representative of a global power. The other is an unidentified American in a short skirt.

Unidentified American in a Short Skirt: Yo, Winston.

Unbelievably Important Representative of a Global Power: Just wait your turn, will you. Never have I seen anything so rude or arrogant in all my life. You journalists are just . . .

UAiaSS: Yo, Winston, it's me, Condi.

UIRoaGP: I don't care who you are. I'm an important person about to have an important meeting with a person of almost as much importance as myself. I've been invited here to explain how to quash international terrorism, pacify the Middle East and solve global warming, but you just barge in and . . .

UAiaSS: I haven't got long, Winston.

UIRoaGP: Don't touch me. Don't you know that I'm inviolable?

UAiaSS: I didn't touch you.

UIRoaGP: Ah Condoleezza, it's you. Why didn't you say so? May I just say what a pleasure it has been to make room for you in my heavy schedule of important meetings? But I must apologise for the behaviour of the New Zealand press corps, who've had it in for me since my career in politics began. They dog me. They harass me. They call me an opportunist hypocrite. They turn the baubles of office to dust.

UAiaSS: Let's get down to . . .

UIRoaGP: I ask you, Condi, is a man to be blamed for his past? Am I to blame for my unblemished record of failure? Am I to blame for my repeated use of cheap populist rhetoric to get myself elected? These reptiles just won't let go. Even now when I am here, in the United States, staying in a very nice hotel as a reward for my decades of endeavour on behalf of my own advancement, they insist on asking questions, questions that eat into the amount of time that I could be in the limelight. Oh, they phrase those questions to look as though they were addressed to you lot on the subject of a free trade deal or military alliances, but any fool can see that they are aimed at me, me, me. Yet when I lash out, they call me paranoid. Paranoid, I ask you. O Condi, do you think I'm paranoid? Or are you perhaps a journalist dressed up to look like Condoleezza?

UAiaSS: Time's up.

UIRoaGP: O Condi, don't leave me now. I've got no friends. Where are you going?

UAiaSS: Lebanon, turning off this strangely functioning microphone as I . . .

See? Expect more. Our microphones are everywhere.

Can't hear you

It was the occasion of the Grand Council and the delegates flocked from all over the globe. With the council chairmanship revolving by alphabetical order, this was the year of the frog.

The frog was welcomed to the dais by the outgoing chairman the fox, who gave the frog a playful nip as he handed over the gavel.

It was generally agreed that the fox had been an ineffectual chairman. Despite plans of unprecedented cunning, he had failed to solve the problem of the security council, whose five permanent members all had unlimited power of veto. Three of the members had never exercised that veto, and the lion had done so only once, to quash a motion that would have permitted antelope to evolve poison fangs.

The fifth member of the council, however, had proved obstructive and over the years had vetoed all but a handful of motions, including numerous efforts to limit his powers of veto.

But this year there was hope of great things. A sense of change was in the air and the delegates buzzed with expectation as they took their seats around the colossal table.

'I declare the Grand Council officially open,' said chairman frog. 'We will now observe a minute's silence to remember those delegates who for the first time are no longer with us. Please stand to the extent you are able to do so, and bow your heads. If you are headless, please bow a part of the anatomy to which reproductive organs are not attached.

'The extinction list this year is a lengthy one. We ask you to remember the golden-tongued honey eater of Indonesia, the Ethiopian spiral fly, all members of the Euchoinidae family, the Alaskan ratfish, the South American leaf lizard whose diet consisted exclusively of members of the Euchoinidae family, the . . . '

'Sand,' bellowed a voice. 'Where's my sand? I'm entitled to sand.'

All eyes turned to the speaker. Chairman frog sighed, nodded, and flunkeys came running with a large tray of sand. The delegate for the species *Homo sapiens* smiled with relief and buried his head in it.

Chairman frog continued his litany of extinctions. At the mention of each name he gestured dumbly to an empty chair around the council table. For the first time the empty chairs outnumbered the occupied ones. Even the monkeys were silent.

'Thank you,' said the frog, who had begun to sweat noticeably. 'I now move on to the first item of the agenda. It concerns the viral infection that is rapidly reducing the global population and diversity of toads, newts and, um, frogs.'

'Never,' exclaimed delegate homo sapiens, raising his head from the sand, 'never in all my time at this council have I heard such flagrant barrow pushing by a chairman. It is so amphibiocentric as to be laughable. Is this a serious forum or what? I veto the motion.'

Chairman frog wiped his forehead with a cloth, shivered, sighed and looked down at the order paper, but before he could speak delegate homo sapiens was back on his feet.

'Delegate whale,' he exclaimed, 'how lovely to see you. You're looking so cute. I just want you to know that my membership, with the odd national exception, has become extremely fond of you over the last few years. Absolutely delighted to see you here in such obvious rude health. Carry on, chairman frog,' and so saying homo sapiens plunged back into the sand.

'The next item affects us all,' said the chairman, directing his words unmistakably in the direction of the sand tray. 'It concerns imminent global breakdown, the collapse of intricate and interdependent ecosystems, the irrevocable heating of the planet, all of which are indisputably caused by the greed, folly and wilful disregard of fact by . . . '

'Can't hear you,' shouted homo sapiens happily from beneath the sand, 'can't hear you.'

'Order!' gasped chairman frog, his skin turning an unpleasant shade of grey.

'Oh, all right,' said homo sapiens, emerging from the sand spluttering with exasperation. 'I am under no obligation to justify my members' actions to this or any other gathering but listen up and listen up good. Just you look at yourselves. You too are rapacious. You too are ruthless. You too strive only to reproduce. You too do all in your power to win. But we're winning. If there are long-term consequences to our triumph, well so be it. We may be gifted with a tad more foresight than you are but if you think we're going to learn from our errors have a look at our history and think again. Nature is nature and we're no better than you are. So suck on that.'

But no one was listening. Every sensory organ in the hall had turned towards the dais. Chairman frog had collapsed. An aide rushed to his side, felt his pulse. The aide looked up at the assembly and the assembly looked at the aide.

'The chairman has croaked,' said the aide.

'Well, that's that then,' said delegate homo sapiens cheerfully, rising from his seat and dusting the sand from his features. 'See you all next year. Well, some of you, anyway. Toodle-oo.'

All you need to know

CONGRATULATIONS!!!! By applying to become an expert in international terrorism you've put yourself on the highway to success. Countless graduates of the School of Expertise have gone on to lucrative careers. Several occupy university chairs. And with the proliferation of media outlets, the demand for expertise is growing by the day, especially in your chosen field of international terrorism. Master the basics of this course and you'll never need to spend another evening off-camera. Your three easy payments of $49.95, and one slightly trickier one of $99.95, will prove the best investment of your life.

The first principle to grasp is the nature of expertise. At some schools you'll be told that an expert is merely anyone who calls himself an expert. Here at the School of Expertise, however, as befits the leader in the field, we have a more stringent definition. For us an expert is anyone whom someone else consults as an expert. In other words, an expert is only an expert when he becomes an acknowledged expert.

But we do concur with other authorities that an expert doesn't need to know much about his area of expertise. All he needs to know is how to be acknowledged as an expert. In other words, knowledge is dispensable, acknowledgement isn't.

This distinction is perhaps easiest to grasp in the context of your chosen field of study, because, to be frank, there isn't much to know about international terrorism. Terrorists in one form or another have been with us since men stopped hunting and went to live in cities, and you'll be pleased to know they won't be going away any time soon. Your gravy train will just keep on chugging.

Most terrorists are blokes. Most of them are young. All of them have got a grudge. They cleave to some sort of absolutist political or religious hogwash, which excuses them from the need to think. They're not in the business of thinking. They're in the business of blowing things up. They hate authority, and they like notoriety. Essentially they're adolescents. And that's about it. It's all pretty obvious stuff that anyone could arrive at after 30 seconds' thought, but 30 seconds' thought is as rare as the giant panda on this lovely little planet of ours, so don't worry. And anyway, as we have already said, expertise is not a business of knowing stuff.

Indeed, now that you know most of what there is to know about terrorists, forget it. Your job is not to dispel the clouds of ignorance. Your job is to add to them.

You have to understand why experts are in demand. The reasons are not rational, but emotional. People are afraid of terrorism. Though people are infinitely more likely to be killed by the car in their garage, or by the stepladder in their garage, or indeed by the hamster in their garage, than they are by terrorists, they remain afraid of terrorists. And people always want to learn more about things they're afraid of. You must add fuel to that fear.

For this you must master an elementary vocabulary. Terrorists must never belong to groups. Groups are innocuous. Terrorists must belong to shadowy organisations or paramilitary units or, best of all, cells. Cells sound nasty. They imply something vaguely biological or punitive or both. Sleeper cells are better still. They remind people of cancer, or even of the film *Alien*. They suggest that terrorism could erupt at any moment in any Acacia Avenue. That's good for business.

You must never refer to terrorists ringing each other up. Instead they have sophisticated communications systems. Nor is a leader of terrorists ever a leader of terrorists, or a chief, or a commander, or even the principal dingbat. He is and must always be the mastermind.

And he must never be in front of things, or to one side of them. His place is behind things. He is behind the campaign, behind the plot, behind the car bomb. Quite what sort of mastery of mind is required to strap gelignite to a Toyota Hilux will never be asked. People just enjoy picturing an arch terrorist who's a cross between Professor Moriarty and something with a beard that runs a planet in *Star Trek*. It makes them feel they're taking part in their own real-life Bond film.

And that's that. If you want to aim for the rarefied atmosphere of higher education and a professorial chair then you should probably mug up some stuff about the Baader-Meinhof Gang, or the Red Brigade, or any of the other former terrorist outfits indistinguishable from the current crop but now forgotten. Frankly, however, there's more money in the populist stuff, low-brow television and mass circulation newspapers. And one last hint — there's no u in Al Qaeda. God knows why.

Right, you're all set. Get out there and make money, Mr Expert. See you on the telly. And do let us know how you get on. We love to hear from our graduates.

Sprawled and gurgling

I was patronising a supermarket on Friday when it patronised me back. It spoke to me. In the vegetable section, if you don't mind, and I did. I was in vegetables only fleetingly, en route from bananas via bacon to beer, but it was long enough for the supermarket to have a little chat.

I am not intimate with this supermarket. I know one of its butchers — David, nice guy — well enough to sometimes get a trolleyful of chuck bones at a bargain price to keep the dogs grinning like gibbons (Do gibbons grin? They should. Whooping through trees is a fine life. And gibbons never have to shop.) but otherwise the supermarket and I are not close. Yet it spoke to me directly, as God is supposed to if one is holy.

I am not holy. Nor am I so vain as to presume that the supermarket spoke to me alone. It was addressing the public, via, believe it or not, its public address system. Only it didn't call us the public.

It called us shoppers, as if this were our primary function, what we were put on this earth to do. Shoppers don't whoop or grin or do jungle stunts. In the exciting 21st century they merely shop, grim-faced, solitary, intent, acquisitive, lurching from disappointment to disappointment. But the supermarket wasn't going to acknowledge any of that. It spoke to us with breezy synthetic cheeriness. 'Good morning, shoppers,' it said. Its voice was the authentic voice of the age, the jolly-uncle voice of commercial mendacity.

Only this was a jolly-auntie voice. I recognised it. I've seen its owner on television ads, wearing I'm-healthy clothes, dismounting a bicycle as if mid-triathlon and then launching into an encomium for supposedly healthy food. She's a dietician, or perhaps a nutritionist, in either case a busybody, and an actor so stilted, so wooden, that one wonders sometimes whether the whole business of breathing is worth going on with. But jolly auntie will go on, for she is swimming with the tide of the times. She is the well-rewarded mouthpiece for whatever fad is currently supposed to make us live for ever — bacterial yoghurt, needless 'supplements', dangerous quantities of bottled water and in particular 'five servings or more' of magically reviving fruit and veg. (Can you think of a nastier word than servings? Yes, so can I, and I said it, but they won't print it.)

Here in the supermarket she was reciting her usual litany, book one, chapter one of the Health Bible. The recipe for a good life. Follow the five or more commandments and you shall be blessed. (The commandments will change next week, of course, but after a brief befuddlement, you'll forget and obediently follow the new prescription, or feel vaguely guilty if you don't.)

So far so bad. But then worse, far worse. 'If you've already got it sorted,' said the disembodied voice, 'well done.'

'What?' I bellowed to the plastic boxes of tomatoes, the onions in nets, the bags of spuds with nutritional info printed so very helpfully on their flanks. 'What?'

'Sorted' was bad enough, an illiterate nod to contemporary street language, intended to convey a sort of matey, colloquial voguishness, and quite without meaning. But the real source of my bellow was the 'well done'. I was being congratulated,

congratulated for my presumed obedience to the diktats of those who would like to run my life for me.

We shoppers have got used to being dishonestly congratulated, but it has been mainly through the medium of print. 'Congratulations on choosing Prittinix,' it says on the instructions for care (care!) on a pair of underpants. 'By purchasing this garment, you have . . . ' But to be congratulated verbally by a supermarket loudspeaker was going a step further, injecting fake congratulation a little deeper under the skin. (While we're at it, consider the words 'purchasing this garment'. Who are they trying to kid? The answer is you. They are trying to impress on you the poshness and significance of your paltry shopping.)

Anyway, I was there mid-morning, and the supermarket was busy with old people. So Miss Five or More was also addressing 85-year-olds who have never touched a bottle of sports water, who have never ingested a single spoonful of bacterially active yoghurt, or anything else that is currently plugged as a life-extender, and yet who've managed to get to 85. Their every breath gave the lie to Miss Five or More's words.

But that's not all. Listen to those words again. 'If you've got it sorted, well done.' Whose voice is that? Where does its tone derive from? Exactly. It's Mummy. 'Oh look, you've eaten up all your lovely veggie-weggies. Who's a clever girl, then? Who's Mummy's little darling?' In other words, the 85-year-olds and I were being addressed as if we were two and a half. And being patted on the head for being good.

For that is where commerce wants us, just as all religions do and all authorities, not whooping through the trees in gibbonish autonomy, but sprawled on our backs in the pram, dependent, suggestible, obedient, frightened and yearning for praise.

Brand life

With the Beckhams heading for LA there is already talk of a reality TV series about their home life in the great tradition of the Osbournes. The opening show is titled *Posh Saves the Middle East*.

Posh'n'Becks are in the study of their modest Beverly Hills mansion, studying. He is bent over the stills of a recent fashion shoot, and she is attending to a map of downtown LA, circling the more expensive stores with a marker pen.

Becks: Snot the money.

Posh: Of course it isn't, David.

Becks: I just love this country. What's that noise?

Posh: It's the doorbell, darling. I had it rigged up to sound like a cash register. But don't get up. Our Mexican maid, whose $8 a month salary we can just about afford now that you're earning approximately $200 for every minute spent awake, will answer it.

Mexican maid: Ees big man at door but ee no speak good Engleesh.

Posh: How mysterious. Show him in, Maria Pilar. He may provide the opportunity to make a satirical point at the expense of shallow Los Angeles culture. Ah, Governor Schwarzenegger.

Governor Schwarzenegger: Ja.

Posh: I expect you've called to congratulate David on his contract with a local football team in the hope that he will enhance the image of what America considers to be a minor sport because it doesn't have enough breaks in play to accommodate the networks' need for advertising, or the spectators' need to buy lethal super-sized fizzy drinks and hotdogs made out of offal and earlobes.

Governor Schwarzenegger: Ja.

Posh: Well, that's very sweet of you. Your support is appreciated. While you're here, allow me to observe that this room right now is accommodating the whole of contemporary masculinity. There you stand at one end of the spectrum, the very definition of the warrior hero with biceps, triceps and quadriceps all striving to burst open the seams of your impeccably tailored clothes and feast on the sunlight like reptiles hatching. Meanwhile, at the other end of the masculinity spectrum stands my pretty husband, the epitome of boy-band cute, whose impish grin sets every teenage female heart a-thump. In other words, here are the archetypes of achieved manhood and adolescent beauty, Ulysses and Narcissus. If the two of you were ever to combine your talents, the earnings potential would be unlimited, appealing as you do to pre-linguistic emotional urges that are as durable as superstition.

Governor Schwarzenegger: Ja.

Becks: What's that noise?

Posh: It's the doorbell again, David. I wonder what other seminal American figure could be coming to visit us. Perhaps it's our new and exciting friend Mr A-list Cruise with his new and exciting wife.

Becks: Who does he play for?

Posh: Oh David. I've told you before. Tom's a theologian. He belongs to the Church of Scientology, which is a very profitable religion resembling *Star Trek* but without the intellectual rigour.

Mexican maid: Ees little man at door but ee no speak good Engleesh.

Posh: Sounds just like Tom. Show him in. Golly gosh! Mr President, how nice of you to visit our humble Beverly Hills mansion.

President Bush: It is a great humble to meet you both. They tell me that you are very talented and famous.

Becks: My wife shops and I play football.

President Bush: Soccer.

Becks: There's no need. She can shop as much as she likes.

President Bush: Of course. Now, I understand that this football of yours is real popular in the Middle East.

Posh: Yes indeed, Mr President. David sells more clothing in the Persian Gulf than he does anywhere other than in the preposterously devotional society of Japan. So half the thugs biffing mortars at your armoured personnel carriers are wearing England football shirts bearing David's name.

President Bush: Good. You see, I was wondering whether David had given any thought to becoming President of Iraq. Might calm them down a bit. The salary's huge and comes with the chance to get in on the ground floor of numerous munitions contracts.

Posh: Sorry, Mr President, but no can do. David's here for a reason. LA is the capital of brands. It was the birthplace of modern commercial imagery. It acted as maternity ward to the film stars and the cartoon characters that are instantly recognised around the planet. My husband's sporting life may be all but over, but his brand life is only beginning. He's here to find out whether his cuteness can cut it against the best in the business. Can his image sell more cars, phones, razor blades and fizzy drinks than, say, the image of racially mixed, hygienic decency that is Tiger Woods? That's the true test of athletic prowess these days. So thanks, Mr President, but no thanks.

Becks: Snot the money.
President Bush: Ah well, but aw shucks.
Posh: What about Governor Schwarzenegger here?
President Bush: Why didn't I think of that? Want the job, Arnie? I'll give you 20,000 extra troops to play with.
Governor Schwarzenegger: Ja.

You can say things like

The phone in your kitchen is dead. The phone in the study is dead. The internet's dead, the email's dead and the fairy lights on the modem are flashing in a configuration you have never seen before. You are cut off. Cut off from solipsistic illiterate bloggers, three-rupee-a-day call centres, phishing, boundless porn, videos of swinging Saddam, the tat-circulating, misery-enhancing auctions of TradeMe (Why the me? Am I what I buy and sell?), Viagra vendors, Nigerian scamsters and importunate telephone survey-takers who want you to rate your experience of puppy-branded double-ply pre-moistened easy-tear toilet tissue on a scale of one to five where five means thrilled to bits by it, can't get enough of it, the apogee of consumer gratification, and one means your finger went through it.

Because your phone line is ruptured, none of these can reach you. What do you do? Obvious, really. A short jig, a long dog walk and then a seat in the shade with a lean novel by Edward St Aubyn and a fat tumbler by Gordon's. But I didn't. I used my cellphone to ring Telecom. So it was all my fault.

I knew what I'd get. An automated voice would ask me to choose from 17 options, none of which bore the least resemblance to my problem, and most of which would encourage me to buy something.

Eventually, after an interlude of fist-whitening music, I would reach some soul in purgatory whose capacity for independent speech had been restricted by company protocol to seven expressions, and who, if faced with anything other than a simple request, was obliged to pass me on to the district supervisor with a nasal infection and a magazine-directed devotion to his career.

Career. Is there a worse word than career? Yes there is. There is career planning. As someone Jewish once said with the sort of wisdom that we no longer have time for, 'If you want to make God laugh, tell him your plans.' But the corporate age has got rid of truth like that. No longer may we giggle and shrug at what happens to happen. Now we must plan, set goals, be focused, career-driven, achievement-orientated, and then we shall be happy. Well, doubleply toilet tissue to that.

But Telecom surprised me. The voice that answered the phone was automated as expected, but it didn't offer me options. Instead it addressed me as an equal. This machine wanted to chat with me. 'Welcome to Telecom,' it said, and its voice was authentic margarinead fake. 'To help me direct you to the right place, please tell me what you're calling about. You can say a few words or just ask a question. So, what can I help you with today?'

At this point, of course, correct procedure was to detach my dead phone from the wall, decorate it with obscenities, drench it in essence de skunk and post it first class COD to Theresa Gattung, but I am a timid beast, and anyway I wanted my phone mended.

'My phone,' I said, 'is as dead as Anna Nicole Smith. Not this phone, obviously. This is my cellphone which I never use except to ring you to say that my other phone is, as I've already explained, dead.'

'I'm sorry,' said the machine, 'I didn't catch that. Are you asking about call plans to Australia?'

'No I'm bloody well not,' I said, 'I'm trying to tell your electronic circuits that my phone is defunct.'

'I'm sorry,' it said, 'I didn't catch that. Please explain what you are calling about. You can say things like, "What's my balance?" or "Buying a cellphone".'

At which point I issued some instructions of my own. 'Don't,' I said, 'talk to me in the first person. Don't pretend to be what you're not. Don't jolly me along. Don't try and suck me into your horrible world. Just go and tell your inventors or programmers or whatever they call themselves that, though I am confident Telecom has a customer service manual as thick as a brick and a director of customer services with a salary resembling my phone number, the business of serving customers is as simple as bread. People want to talk to people. So tell your bosses it is time to forgo some of their enormous profits and to disappoint some of their rapacious shareholders and to employ 500 English-speaking people of decent intelligence on decent salaries to answer their phones, rather than to simulate with a recorded robot the sort of attention that they obviously realise I want but are too grasping to supply. For this, honeybun, is the way the world ends, not with a bang, which would at least be fun, but with a breathing thinking autonomous adult, in other words me, being told what I can or cannot say by a bloody machine.'

'I'm sorry,' said the machine, and I am not making a word of this up, 'I didn't catch that. Let's try this a different way. If you are enquiring about broadband, press 1. If you are enquiring about . . .'

It was almost a relief.

Catabingo

Aren't things jolly? So jolly it may even be worth hanging around to see how they turn out, in which case I suppose I ought to give up smoking. I don't like smoking, of course, but I even more don't like the people who want me to stop and the thought of giving them satisfaction is enough to keep me at it. Besides, I take an ironic pleasure in the taxes I pay to the hypocritical authorities in exchange for my smokes. They ought to be paying me and everyone else to smoke because of the colossal sums that we won't be claiming in pensions and because of the rest homes that won't have to be built to house us in our wallpaper-gazing, television-watching, 1961-remembering, community-singing dotage. So I'll keep smoking.

But if I didn't, if I took up clean air, vegetables and whichever forms of lightly boiled yoghurt and fish oil are currently in favour with the faddists who consider mortality to be unfair, I would open a book. Not a booky sort of book, you understand, but a betty sort of book. And I'd set up for business in the rest home of my choice, accepting punts from smokers' widows who are long on money but short on the vitality to enjoy it. I'll give them Cataclysm Bingo.

All they've got to do is sit back and watch the telly and tick the things off one by one as they happen. It'll give them an interest, see, by making them assiduous students of current affairs. And here, off the top of my head, research undone, is a list of the sort of thing the widows will be punting on.

1. Middle East meltdown. Admittedly the Middle East has never satisfactorily melted up, but the widows won't quibble about that. Extra points will be available for nailing the precise cause of the cataclysm. See 2, 3 and 7.

2. Iraq. Good old Cowboy George finally admits that Iraq is a rerun of Vietnam and that the Yankees will never be seen as liberating angels because they never were liberating angels. He claims victory and pulls the troops out whereupon everyone else pours the troops in. Biblical grudges are finally worked out in Baghdad with every Arab faction bunging its missiles at every other faction, while the Israelis lob in a mortar every now and then just to keep the pot boiling and in the certain knowledge that they're guaranteed to hit someone who hates them. Oil price goes through the roof, leading to global economic chaos and, whoa, WW3.

3. Iran. By way of saying sayonara to eight splendid years in the White House, good old Cowboy George, he of the faltering syntax and unconvincing grin, drops a couple of bunker-busters into Tehran's nuclear power generation plant then withdraws to Texas to watch the fireworks. And what fireworks. Iranian missiles, Syrian warplanes,

Hizbollah suicidists, Palestinian stone-throwing urchins, the lot, all of them biffing stuff at Israel because the States are too big and too far away. All of which not only sends the oil price through the roof and leads to, whoa, WW3, but also gives a good shove to global warming.

4. Global warming. Fires eat Southern Europe and California. Sand eats North Africa. The sea eats Holland, the Galapagos and numerous Pacific islands. Burnt, drenched and hungry human beings try to migrate to the cool bits of the globe where it's still possible to grow cereals. The cool bits immediately mobilise and surround their territories with troops and razor wire. Armaments industry shares go through the roof, ancient tribal enmities surface like bubbles in boiling water and, whoa, WW3.

5. Water. After eight successive blistering summers, Europe, Australia and the mid-west of the States run out of water. Mass emigration. Real estate prices in New Zealand, Canada and Tierra del Fuego go through the roof. New Zealand, Canada and Tierra del Fuego form the Wetlands Alliance and develop an armaments industry which is immediately bombed by the White House in alliance with Canberra, Brussels and, because they've always loved a stoush, Beijing. New Zealand, Canada and Tierra del Fuego are annexed by the superpowers who then squabble over the details of who gets what. Whoa, WW3.

6. China. Despite confident Western assertions that China would become the first industrial superpower not to harbour imperial ambitions, China invades somewhere, probably Taiwan. Taiwan appeals to the international community but the international community looks the other way because it relies on China for cheap underwear and washing machines. Greatly encouraged, China starts buying satellite maps of Japan with the more accessible beaches marked in red. Real estate prices anywhere a long

way from Japan go through the roof. New Zealand, Canada and Tierra del Fuego cop it again.

7. Cricket. A bit improbable this one, but you never know. An Australian umpire accuses Islamic Pakistan of ball-tampering. A militant Islamic group of cricket fanatics bombs Lord's. The England and Wales Cricket Board demands reparations from Pakistan who reply by bombing the Oval. Whoa, WW3, only without China and the States, who don't play cricket but who hover like vultures waiting for the dust to settle on the territorial carrion before embarking on, whoa, WW4.

8. Things muddle along somehow as usual.

My money's on 8, just, but you never know. I'll keep smoking.

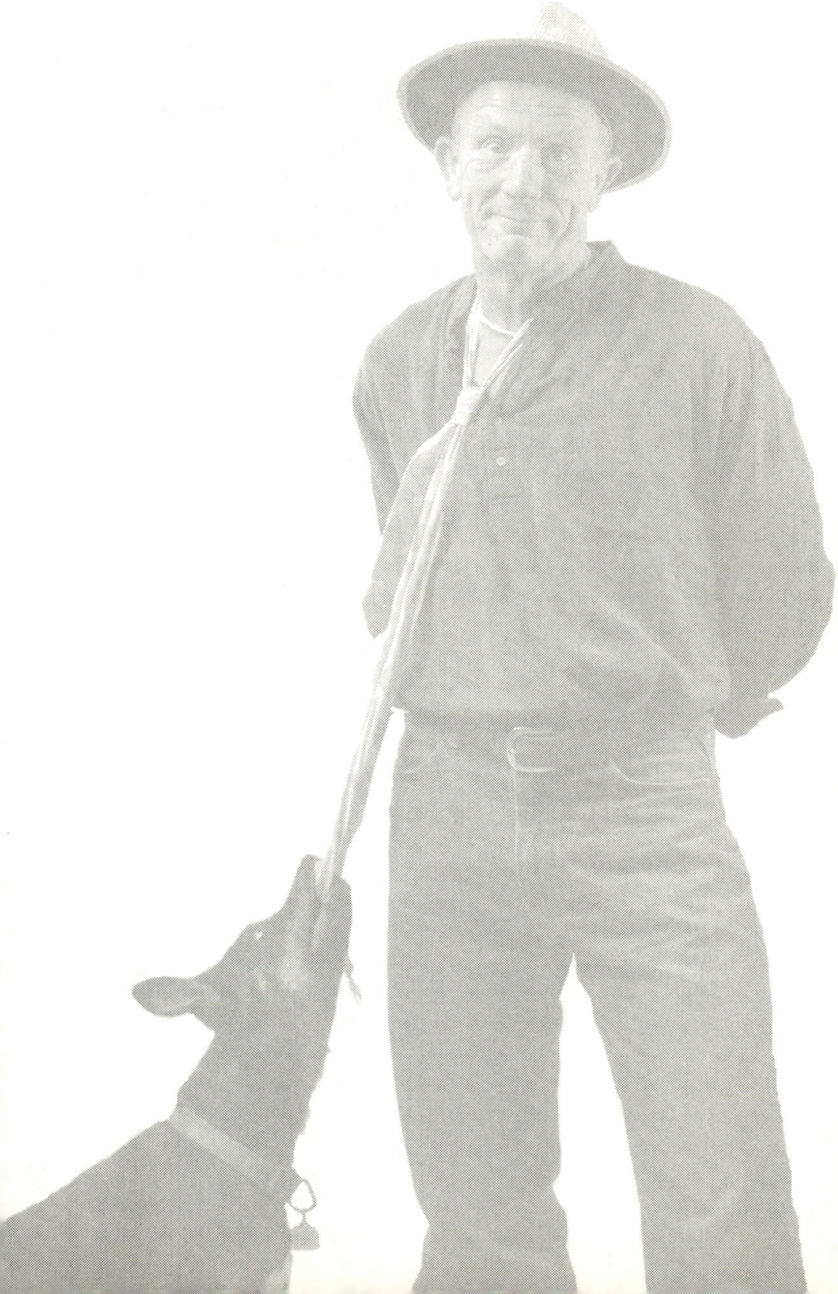